国际雅思真题题源系列

IELTS

国际雅思阅读
真题题源（第2册）

刘创
RODNEY H. SMITH（英）
AUSTEN PETER（美） 编著
KELVIN LESTER（澳）
JIM ZHANG（中）

科学出版社
北京

图书在版编目(CIP)数据

国际雅思阅读真题题源（第2册）/刘创等编著．—北京：科学出版社，2005
（国际雅思真题题源系列）
ISBN 7-03-015631-5

Ⅰ．国… Ⅱ．刘… Ⅲ．英语－阅读教学－高等学校－入学考试，国外－习题 Ⅳ．H319.4-44

中国版本图书馆CIP数据核字（2005）第055758号

责任编辑：郝建华 胡升华／责任校对：李奕萱
责任印制：钱玉芬／封面设计：孙希前

科学出版社 出版
北京东黄城根北街16号
邮政编码：100717
http://www.sciencep.com

中国科学院印刷厂 印刷
科学出版社发行 各地新华书店经销

*

2005年7月第 一 版 开本：787×1092 1/16
2005年7月第一次印刷 印张：18 1/4
印数：1—10 000 字数：430 000

定 价：36.00元
（如有印装质量问题，我社负责调换〈科印〉）

前　言

近年来，留学出国的热潮一浪高过一浪，一批批莘莘学子以及各行业的优秀人才怀着对未来美好生活的憧憬，为了实现人生理想而踏上人生的又一次旅程——为通过“雅思”考试（IELTS）而努力拼搏。

“雅思”（IELTS）考试是“国际英语语言测试系统”（International English Language Testing System）的简称，是由英国剑桥大学考试委员会（The University of Cambridge Local Examination Syndicate— UCLES）、澳大利亚教育国际开发署（IDP Education Australia）及英国文化委员会（The British Council）共同开发的国际英语水平测试。与传统的英语考试相比，雅思更为重视英语语言的实际运用水平，侧重于考查考生在英语国家的生存能力，是目前最权威、最科学、最实用、最全面的考核考生英语综合能力的测试。随着认可雅思的国家日益增多，加之雅思的适用面广、考试次数较多，因而它深受广大出国留学人员的喜爱，并成为他们走出国门时首选的语言考试。此外，还有越来越多的人把参加雅思考试当作证实自己英语水平的手段，这也使得近年来报考的人数激增。

笔者从事雅思考试培训 5 年来，一直在一线执教雅思培训课程，受训人次逾 5 万。还曾多次应邀到清华大学、北京大学、北京理工大学、北京师范大学、中国人民大学、中国农业科学研究院、中央音乐学院、北京广播学院等高等院校、专业研究院所进行雅思专场演讲，并数次接受北京电视台、搜狐教育频道等多家重要媒体的专门采访。作为一名雅思教师，笔者深感有义务、有责任解决广大雅思考试在学习、考试过程中遇到的困难，并且一直在探索能帮助广大考生在相对较短的时间内顺利通过雅思考试、快速提高雅思成绩的方法。为此，笔者在 5 年雅思培训及潜心研究历年雅思真题的基础上，根据历年阅读版本号，汇聚了大量考生心得编著了这本《国际雅思阅读真题题源》。本书凝聚了笔者多年来的雅思阅读培训、学习心得，浓缩再现了真题的精华。

本书有以下鲜明特点：

真题版本号最全，真实性强

（1）本书编入的内容均以历年阅读真题为基础，以真题机经版本回顾为依据，再现原汁原味的国外原版材料，覆盖 V8 ~ V67 及实验版本阅读真实考试内容。

（2）以雅思考试的原文为背景进行编写，信息均出自《国家地理杂志》等国外 20 多家杂志及媒体网站。

增加科普性知识背景

雅思阅读文章大约 1500 ~ 2000 字，共 3 篇文章。试题来源于世界范围内所发生的真实事件。许多考生因对知识背景不熟、对科普性常识缺乏了解而不能顺利通过。本书按版本号整理分类为生态环境、动物、医疗、教育、语言、发展史、交通管理和海底世界等内容，以便广大考生在短时期内获取真实考题的信息，丰富考生的科普知识。

扩充真题词汇量

雅思阅读考试涉及范围较广，涉及的词汇量较大，因而考试中许多考生备受挫折。本书根据雅思阅读考试规律，精心挑选了雅思真题词汇，使广大考生不再因词汇量缺乏而苦恼。

大幅提高成绩

笔者用真题及剑桥解题技巧，对212名学生进行了小型测试。学生们考后发现真题考试文章几乎都是培训课堂讲过的，例如海底火山、医疗保健、日本塔、蝴蝶农场、钢化玻璃和老龄职工等，而且他们的成绩比同水平学生高1～1.5分。学生们顺利地通过雅思考试后，纷纷发e-mail告知笔者。班上的学生赞道："破解雅思阅读，指日可待。"

鸣谢：

本书在编著过程中，得到学生们的大力支持。感谢在清华大学参加雅思培训的广大师生，没有他们的期待及建议，我也不会努力到深夜。

感谢北京雅思学校的全体学生，没有他们老围着我要真题，我也没有挑战的勇气和信心。

感谢支持我、关心我的同事、朋友及合作者，以及父母的关怀和支持。

由于水平及时间所限，书中难免有不足之处，望广大考生谅解。

美好的人生就此开始，愿所有考生心想事成，梦想成真，能飞到大洋的彼岸。在此祝你们成功。

刘　创

2005年3月

写给老师和考生的话

目前，去英联邦国家留学和移民的人越来越多，雅思考试大军也随之不断壮大，综观历年的雅思阅读考试情况，预计2005～2006年雅思阅读的难度将有所增加。作为一名长期奋战在雅思培训一线的教师，我和所有的雅思教师一样有着共同的心愿——提高雅思考生的阅读水平。经常为雅思阅读考试的备课而废寝忘食，常常为大批的考生找不到合适的雅思阅读材料而发愁，我萌发了为中国广大考生编写一套雅思阅读实战辅导丛书的想法。经过和英国、美国、澳大利亚雅思考官的沟通与交流，对资料的收集与整理，最终完成了《国际雅思阅读真题题源》丛书。

本书以大量的雅思考生回忆为背景，根据历年雅思阅读真题走势，追溯历年雅思阅读真题题源，全面总结了历年雅思阅读的文章，分十大类别进行排列，为广大雅思考生及教师提供了真实的信息来源。文章的选材和剑桥雅思系列有异曲同工之处，便于广大考生复习备考及教师教学参考之用，大幅度提高雅思考生的阅读实战能力。选题具真实性、规范性、知识性、趣味性等鲜明的原版风格，最大范围突出了真题的题源。

根据雅思阅读考试的未来走势，文章的涉猎范围将更加广泛。雅思考试G类的阅读中前两部分通常是实用性强的功能性短文，如菜单、产品说明、通知、住宿安排和广告等，非常贴近西方的实际生活，但对我们国内绝大多数考生而言会很陌生。A类阅读主要是关于历史中的重要人物、事件和发明，以及科学现象、学科最新动向、地理现象以及社会发展、经济状况等。其中大部分文章选自国外人文类、经济类和科学类的知名报纸、杂志或各政府、组织的研究报告，例如：*New Scientist*、*Financial Times*、*The Economist*、*Popular Science*、*National Geographic* 等。雅思阅读考试对单词量要求加大，长句子增多，句式复杂，如倒装或插入语；定位越来越难，同义词替换现象多。因而，时间更加紧迫，许多考生不能在规定的1小时内完成所有的题目。

为此，笔者建议广大考生及教师采取必要的策略，着重从以下三个方面进行准备：

第一点：应在阅读作者所编写的文章时，突出理解、记忆真题单词，雅思阅读考查对文中词义的理解能力。若想达到7分的成绩，6000单词是必要的。也就是说以真题为背景的词汇记忆。

第二点：提高英语阅读的速度。这不是一日之功，通常需要相当长一段时间的学习及训练。但是，加强对中英文的对比训练、掌握必要的测试技巧和摈弃一些不正确的方法，都会有助于考生们阅读文章时加快速度。IELTS考试的阅读部分，无论是A类还是G类都是同时测试考生的阅读速度和理解的精确度的，考生们既不能为了在1小时的时间内答完考题而单一求快，也不能为了答题的准确性高而放弃回答一些问题。如快速阅读就是用扫描文章的方法对其结构有大致的了解，并把握其主旨。同时，在重点句子和词汇上做出标记。这种方法对阅读考试帮助极大，平时可多加练习。考生们应摈弃逐词阅读的不正确的习惯，逐词阅读不但速度太慢，而且容易引起误解。应学会词汇组合阅读。

第三点：在句子理解方面，考生切记不要根据自己已有经验片面理解。IELTS 阅读中有的题目考的是对于文章中某一句子的理解，要参考上下文客观地看问题。考生应对一些复合句，尤其是双重否定句、比较句、指代句等有较深了解。特别在遇到复杂句时，应静心思考，从把握句子主干——主谓结构着手来分析解剖句子结构。切记不能自己主观臆断，一定要以原文为本，所有答案均要回原文定位。这需要考生在平时做大量的练习，熟悉雅思阅读文章的框架风格，适应长句、复杂句的阅读，这一点也最能考察考生基本功是否扎实。最后要掌握每种题型的出题要点和规律，特别是数量较多的判断题。

总之，作者真诚地希望每一位雅思考生能顺利取得雅思阅读高分，追求人生的最大梦想，实现自我的人生价值。作为一名雅思培训教师，我的梦想深深地植根于你们的雅思梦想之中。

刘　创

国际雅思考试历年真题版本一览表

版本号	SECTION 1	SECTION 2	SECTION 3
V08 （补充）	语言学校招生广告		飞行器的发展
V14 （补充）	职业介绍培训中心	远程教育	工作环境和工人健康
V16 （补充）	骑自行车募捐活动	培训课程介绍和招生	3 种美国青少年的性格
V17 （补充）	绘画课程	双语教育	8 种课程的简介
V18 （补充）	3 个旅游项目的广告	学生俱乐部	培训动物说话
V19 （补充）	旅馆预订	分类广告	缉毒犬
V20 （补充）	澳洲旅游入境表填写	航空公司招聘口语测试	大学招生介绍
V22 （补充）	工作场所吸烟	俄罗斯考古	翅膀的进化和飞机
V23 （补充）	如何提交阅读速度	太空生命探索	生物学防治病虫害
V24 （基本）	面试技巧	澳洲医疗与中医	眼镜蛇毒液
V25 （基本）	Rhythm 对生物的影响	运动与英国青少年健康	小孩与成人语言能力比较
V26 （基本）	染料与颜料	美国电影发展史	音乐语言教学书籍介绍
V27 （基本）	两种房屋构造和功能	小学生的智商研究	语言改革问题
V28 （基本）	人造丝的制造	大学教学方法的改进	全球气候变暖
V29 （基本）	公司的管理	减少闪电危害的方法	南非黄金的开采
V30 （基本）	交传口译和同声翻译	大雾使伦敦人致命	噪声对人的影响
V31 （基本）	移民史	电信技术发展史	非洲某国的交通改善
V32 （基本）	旅游业与经济	外语对商业的影响	盲人以符号传递情感
V33 （基本）	中国和日本的塔	英国校园暴力	母亲受教育程度与孩子的关系
V34 （基本）	火山爆发	工作职务与空间	天才
V35 （基本）	桥梁检测	厄尔尼诺现象	欧洲森林的保护
V36 （基本）	孩子对热带雨林的认识	地图发展史	摩斯电码
V37 （基本）		科学研究中的欺诈	
V38 （基本）	职业妇女工作家庭冲突	各国的古代钱币介绍	海滩侵蚀与海沙流失
V39 （基本）	老龄职工对公司的作用	未来汽车的发展	创业与革新的不安
V40 （基本）	计时器的发展史	47 个城市的交通调查	数字发展史
V41 （基本）	公共交通工具的发展史	纸币发展史	人类运动的体能极限
V42 （基本）	城市公交改革	电压对人体的心理实验	人类视觉暂留实验
V43 （基本）	煤气使用常识	弹性工作时间和旅行社	澳洲皮肤癌研究
V56 （基本）	研究热带鱼林的蝴蝶	信息技术与运输业	冒险心理研究

国际雅思考试历年真题版本一览表

（续表）

版本号	SECTION 1	SECTION 2	SECTION 3
V63 （基本）	海底热资源	市场营销方式的变化	语言学研究
V65 （基本）	蝴蝶农场		海底探测船
V66 （基本）		阿拉斯加的鲑鱼的保育	
V67 （基本）	医生与药品推销	英国绿色农业	动物的思考与直觉
新版本	阿斯旺水坝	医疗保健	不同年代的医疗
新版本	强化玻璃	蚂蚁智慧	澳洲树袋熊
新版本	小班授课的优越性	地震	鸟类成长
新版本	加拿大气候问题	海豚与鲸鱼	鲸的听觉视觉味觉
新版本	体育运动	气候对纽因特人的影响	人类与动植物绝种
新版本	潮流消费	法国城堡	风力与金字塔
新版本	动物的/形体语言能力	海啸预警	基因
新版本	日本数学教育	摩天大楼	萤火虫研究
新版本	拉丁语对英语的影响	学生体罚	鸟的方向感

国际雅思考试历年真题版本分类一览表

（括号中的“N”指近年新增加的版本）

一、	动物类 10 篇	(V24); (N);	(N); (N);	(N); (V19);	(N); (N)	(V22);	(N);
二、	语言类 9 篇	(N); (V18);	(V27); (V20);	(V25); (N)	(V32);	(V67);	(V63);
三、	人类重大发展史 14 篇	(V22); (V41); (N);	(V34); (V38); (N31)	(V31); (V40);	(V36); (N);	(V08); (V26);	(V40); (36);
四、	交通运输类 6 篇	(V40);	(V39);	(V31);	(V41);	(V42);	(V56)
五、	教育类 18 篇	(V16); (V27); (V08);	(N); (V28); (V14);	(V17); (N); (V17);	(V17); (V33); (V18);	(V23); (V37); (V20);	(V33); (V26); (N)
六、	公司管理类 5 篇	(V29);	(V39);	(V38);	(V39);	(V34)	
七、	建筑结构类 8 篇	(N); (V27);	(N); (V35)	(N);	(V33);	(V65);	(N);
八、	医疗健康类 15 篇	(V16); (V25); (V67);	(V30); (V24); (V56);	(V43); (V42); (V14)	(N); (V42);	(V22); (N);	(N); (V41);
九、	自然环境类 15 篇	(V29); (V35); (V35);	(V63); (V35); (V36);	(N); (V34); (N)	(V30); (N);	(V38); (V25);	(V28); (A);
十、	农业、工业、商业类 22 篇	(V16); (V26); (V32); (V18);	(V67); (V23); (N); (V20);	(V32); (V23); (V63); (V19);	(V30); (V28); (V43); (V19)	(V24); (V65); (V29);	(V43); (V66); (V14);
总计：122 篇							

目 录

第一章 雅思阅读概论

1. 雅思阅读考试内容

IELTS是International English Language Testing System的缩写，在国内被译为"雅思"。雅思考试是由英国剑桥大学考试委员会、英国文化委员会和澳大利亚教育国际开发署共同研发而成。主要是为出国学生和移民人士而准备的国际语言资格考试。雅思阅读考试分为A类（即学术类）和G类（即普通类）。

雅思A类阅读测试的主要对象是欲赴国外获取学位的英语非母语的人士，主要考查学生在英语为背景的英联邦国家、北欧及美国等一些国家的学习能力。文章主要选自《国家地理杂志》、《经济周刊》等西方主流报纸及刊物。雅思阅读考试内容包括：动物类、人类重大发展史、国际交通运输、教育类、语言类、公司管理类、建筑构造类、医疗类、自然环境类、农工商业类和综合科技类。题材一般为议论文及说明文。

雅思G类即普通类，测试的主要对象是移民及出国工作的人员，主要考查他们在英语为母语的社会里的生存能力。文章主要来源于西方主流的报纸及刊物。内容包括广告、说明书、小册子介绍等。

2. 雅思阅读由几部分组成,题型是什么

雅思阅读试卷无论是A类还是G类共3篇文章，时间为60分钟，A类每篇约为1000 ~ 2000字。G类第一部分为3篇短文(如广告)，第二部分为中等难度的文章(如大学简介)，第三部分为长文章，字数约为1500字。考试题目为40题，每部分为12~15题之间，有时会有38、39、41、42题。雅思考试题型多样化，题型共分8种。

(1) list of headings 找小标题

(2) true \ false \ not given 是非题

(3) summary 摘要填空

(4) short answer questions 简答题

(5) multiple choice 选择题

(6) matching 匹配题(从属、因果、作者及观点)

(7) sentence completion 完成句子

(8) diagram \ flowchart \ table completion 图表题

3. 雅思阅读的分数怎么评判

学术类阅读分数段：

正确题目	分数
13 ~ 15	4
16 ~ 17	4.5
18 ~ 20	5
21 ~ 22	5.5
23 ~ 25	6
26 ~ 27	6.5
28 ~ 30	7
31 ~ 32	7.5
33 ~ 35	8
36 ~ 38	8.5
39 ~ 40	9

移民类阅读分数段：

正确题目	分数
15 ~ 17	4
18 ~ 19	4.5
20 ~ 22	5
23 ~ 24	5.5
25 ~ 27	6
28 ~ 29	6.5
30 ~ 32	7
33 ~ 34	7.5
35 ~ 37	8
38 ~ 39	8.5
40	9

4. 雅思阅读的真题版本及机经是什么

机经这个词最早出现是在GRE考试的机考中，原意为机考的经验。由于GRE机考的试题重复，所以很多人靠背以前考过的朋友总结的经验得了高分。我们这里用机经这个词并不是说雅思考试也有机考，雅思的机考现在国内是没有的，我们的机经泛指一切有关考试的总结和试题的回忆。

首先，机经是用来帮助我们了解雅思试题的形式和内容的。应该承认，机经的使用具有很大的局限性，任何人都不可以把机经当作考试复习的全部。由于它是各位考生回忆的，所以难免会有偏差，没有人可以对机经的准确负完全的责任。大家可以以手中有的雅思资料作为复习重点，同时兼顾一下机经中提到的口语题目、作文题目以及听力场景，以便熟悉真正考试的情况。

对于没考过雅思的朋友，“版本”这个词可能的确很陌生。雅思考试的每一科每一张卷子都有一个号码，就是“Version XX”，每一个号码只对应一套试题。这个号码是世界通行的，会写在你的成绩单上面。我们在论坛上讨论的“版本”就是这个试卷上的号码，实际上就是试题。特别提醒一下，论坛上一般把Version简写成V，所以大家看到V37、V41的时候不要奇怪。

5. 雅思考试的出题规律及阅读法则是什么

雅思阅读题的出题规律及注意要点：

a. 首尾现象: 50% 左右的题目分布在首尾句及首尾段落;
b. 顺序现象: 即每种题目基本上根据文章的顺序排列;
c. 改写现象: 即出题基本上是文章的改写, 而不是原文;
d. 名词现象: 即雅思出题基本是以名词为考点;
e. 数字现象: 即会有四则运算(short answer) ;
f. 下定义现象: 即破折号、同位语、定语从句;
g. 举例现象: (fox example、for instance、such as)这些句子前面是重点;
h. 连词现象: 即因果、转折、相似及递进、比较、最高级等连词会有题目;
i. 特殊符号、字体现象: 括号、引号、黑体、斜体、生词;
j. 图表现象: 即图表方面会出题。

由此可见雅思的出题规律, 因而考生可以按以下的步骤迅速扫读全文。

STEP 1: 分析文章后的题目

拿到一篇阅读文章, 考生应该首先细读题目要求, 确定哪些是关于文章结构的题目, 哪些是关于文章细节的题目, 同时找出题目中的中心词。

STEP 2: 带着问题扫描文章

扫描标题

考生拿到一篇雅思学术类阅读文章, 首先应该看一下文章的标题, 而迄今为止, 雅思学术类阅读理解考试中大致出现过下列三种题日类型: 第 种是正规标题, 可用来判断文章大意、类型、进而得知文章结构; 第二种是主标题加副标题, 副标题有时承担揭示文章结构的重任; 第三种是无标题, 这种考试形式自1999 年开始在中国考区出现, 一般文章较长而且难, 但仍然可以在文章第一段发现揭示文章主题的主旨句。考生应注意: 描述性标题应该予以忽略; 如果文章分几个SECTION论述, 则SECTION的标题也应该加以注意。

扫描全文的分段情况及其他信息

考生应注意数字、百分比、分数、时间或货币符号出现较多的段落; 引号、大写专有名词、括号及破折号出现较多的段落; 斜体字、黑体字、下画线出现较多的段落。

扫描每个段落的首末句, 把握文章主题

主题句提示文章每段的主题含意, 进而合成整个文章的大意。因此, 一定要找出主题句, 从而找出这一段的主题。主题句通常是一段文章的首句(当然并非永远如此), 寻找主题句的方法可按下列顺序: 首句 → 第二句→中间句→ 末句。

注意: 如果首句是描述性语句则应该予以忽略。

通过段落首末句判断段落主题的关键是找准中心词(key word)。中心词最可能是表示主要概念的名词, 一般是句子的主语和宾语; 表明状态的动词; 表示程度高低、范围大小、肯定或否定的副词; 中心词会在题目及原文中以同义词形式大量出现。

扫描连接上下文的连词

扫描文章文章中是否有图表或示意图

这些图表一般包含了一些有关回答问题的信息，因此可以先对这些图表做一扫描，了解其内容从而加快答题速度，不然的话，就可能陷在文章中四处找寻答案而乱无头绪。但应注意，一般照片、地图、漫画可以予以忽略。

STEP 3：找中心词

以问题为中心，通过上述扫描工作，找出文章中对应的中心词，从而定位正确答案。

6. 雅思阅读技巧重要吗

任何一个科目的考试都应有应试技巧，雅思阅读考试尤为重要。作者长期在雅思一线教授了大量的学生，许多学生因为没有雅思的阅读技巧，不能在60分钟内完成考题，以至于考试分数过低；对各种题型不熟悉，不能理解题目与考题的关系，因而不能取得高分，错失了出国深造的机会。所以作者认为雅思阅读技巧是非常重要的。

7. 雅思高分阅读必备五要素

（1）词汇

掌握四六级基本词汇 +3000 左右高频词，通过上下文推断词义，利用同义或反义理解词汇，利用定义或释义，利用举例或暗示，利用构词法。

学生应掌握雅思词汇高频词，请见本系列丛书中的《国际雅思真题题源词汇大全》。

（2）语法、句型

1) 应注意结构复杂的简单句、并列句、复合句、被动句、倒装句、插入语等结构。

2) 看四六级语法书。

（3）扩大知识面

1) 阅读和真题有关的文章。

2) 多上网查阅有关国外的英文网站。

3) 尽可能的多读议论文及说明文。

（4）熟悉雅思阅读题型掌握解题技巧

1) 可适当地选择参加雅思培训。

2) 可选择国外原版雅思书籍(剑桥雅思系列）。

3) 结合作者的系列教程有针对地复习，必定事半功倍。

(5) 有针对性的大量练习

1) 每天坚持1小时的精读、泛读资料。

2) 根据雅思教师的要求每星期做1~2套雅思试题。

3) 每天阅读两篇真题题源文章。

雅思阅读真题十大分类（五～八类）

五、教育类(18篇)

（V17真题题源）

1. This university has the following curriculums that are open to international students

八种课程简介

1. Management (code: 582X). Corporate Governance and Leadership. Cr. 3. *Prereq*: 501 *or permission of instructor*. Shrader. Examination of top managers and corporate boards of directors in terms of roles, responsibilities, and tasks. Examination of corporate governance structure and functioning. Topics include CEO tenure and compensation, board monitoring and composition, board responsibility and accountability, board structure and performance, CEO and board roles in strategic management, shareholder and stakeholder representation, corporate social responsibility, ethics and corporate governance, international governance, and executive leadership style.

2. Botany (code: 567X). Empirical Population Genetics. (Same as Gen 567X and Zool 567X). Cr. 3. *Prereq: Bot/Biol* 303; *Stat* 401; *a course in calculus*; permission of instructor. Principles underlying population genetics and its application to research. Emphasis will be placed on mechanisms of evolution; null models of evolutionary change; genetic marker systems; fixation indices; effective population size; models of genetic structure; inbreeding and relatedness; genealogy reconstruction; estimation of gene flow; population bottlenecks and admixture; phylogeography; and the use of the bootstrap and Monte Carlo methods in population genetics.

3. Transportation and Logistics (code: 487X). Strategic Supply Chain Management. (Same as POM 487X). Cr. 3. *Prereq: POM/TRLOG* 485X *and TRLOG* 463; *POM* 422 *or TRLOG* 460. Crum. This is the capstone course in supply chain management. The course focuses on the analysis and design of interorganizational supply chain systems, including product, information, and financial flows and processes; and management of the various supply chain processes and activities with an emphasis on the areas of inventory, transportation, production operations, distribution facilities, and supply chain information systems. The course will integrate and apply the theories, concepts, and methods covered in the prerequisite courses through the use of readings, case studies, projects, and industry speakers. Nonmajor graduate credit.

4. Anthropology (code: 465X). Conflict, Civil Society and Development. (Dual-listed with 565X; same as Soc 465X) Cr. 3. *Prereq: 6 credits of Anthropology and/or Sociology and senior classification*. Theories of ethnic or regional conflict and conflict management or resolution practices; outcomes of intergroup peacemaking negotiations; approaches to cultural transformation in civil society; and development issues of access and control, governance, engagement strategies, processes and implementation. Nonmajor graduate credit.

5. Architecture (code: 505X). Architectural Design I. Cr. 5. *Prereq: Admission to the M. Arch program.* Coreq: 595X; 541X. An introduction to comprehensive architectural design projects (individual and collaborative) with coordinated studies in design media, history, theory, culture, science and technology. The studio projects establish a framework for designing buildings as aspects of dynamic circumstances such as environmental forces, construction methods, economic and political regulations, social relationships, and cultural values. **Course content and assignments coordinated with 541X and 595X.**

6. Architecture (code: 596X). Cultural Inquiry II. Cr. 5. Prereq: 595X; 505X; 541X. *Coreq:* 506; 542X. Cardinal-Pett. A continuation of 595X. Contemporary issues that implicate architecture construct an armature for learning about the history of architecture, the profession, technology, and the relationships among architecture, nature, and culture. The contemporary issues create occasions for reference to selected key buildings, vernacular types, seminal essays and excerpts from important publications. Course content is global in scope and addresses pre-historical times through present day. Course content and assignments coordinated with 506 and 542X.

7. Art: Integrated Studio (code: 227X). Intro to Digital Photography. Cr. 3. *Prereq: Must be a student in the department of Art & Design.* Digital photography as a medium of design expression and communication. The course will include camera operation, scanning, image manipulation, color management and printing. Must have access to own 35mm SLR film camera, or 4 megapixel (minimum resolution) digital camera. **Cameras must have manual override.**

8. Construction Engineering (code: 481). Bidding Construction Projects II. Cr. 1. *Prereq: Permission of the instructor.* Team development of construction process designs and cost estimates for transportation construction projects under closely simulated conditions. Public contracting agency officials compare student bids directly with professional bids. With instructor assistance, students independently arrange site visits to examine project sites, consult with construction industry mentors, obtain subcontractor and supplier quotations, and submit bids. Students with previous experience attempt projects with larger scope or lead students with less experience. Offered in the following specialties:

A. Bridges and Structures
B. Grading
C. Portland Cement Concrete Paving
D. Asphalt Cement Concrete Paving
E. Building
F. Mechanical
G. Electrical
H. Mechanical & Electrical
I. Miscellaneous

Further information will be accommodated upon request for the said courses.

(THE END)

必备词汇

corporate governance 公司管理，公司治理
boards of directors 董事会
tenure / 'tenjuə / 任期
shareholder / stakeholder / 'ʃɛəhəuldə / / 'steikhəuldə(r) / 股东
leadership style 领导风格
empirical / em'pirikəl / 经验的
mechanisms of evolution 进化机理
inbreed / 'in'bri:d / 同系繁殖，近亲交配
genealogy / ˌdʒi:ni'ælədʒi / 家谱，宗谱
bottleneck / 'bɔtlˌnek / 瓶颈
logistics / lə'dʒistiks / 物流，后勤
supply chain 供应链
nonmajor graduate credit 非专业毕业学分
peacemaking negotiations 调停谈判
architectural / ˌɑ:ki'tektʃərəl /建筑学的
megapixel / 'megə'piksəl / 兆像素
image manipulation 图像操作
resolution / ˌrezə'lju:ʃən / 分辨率
concrete paving 混凝土路面
miscellaneous / misi'leinjəs, -niəs / 杂项，其他

重点剖析

— Course content and assignments coordinated with 541X and 595X. 课程内容和作业与541X和595X同步进行。

— Cameras must have manual override. 相机必须有手动调节功能。

— Further information will be accommodated upon request for the said courses. 如对上述课程还有疑问，我们将会提供相关信息。

（V08 真题题源）

2. Admissions

语言学校招生广告

Undergraduate Admissions

The functions of the Undergraduate Admissions Office include administering programs for prospective students, such as campus tours, open houses, area receptions, high school and community college visits. Students, parents, high school and community college counselors are consulted on a continual basis regarding all aspects of admissions and general information on the academic, social, and living components of the University.

Campus Tours

Tours of campus are available to all interested individuals and are an excellent way to view first hand the facilities offered at the University. Campus tours are conducted by trained student volunteers and last approximately 45 minutes. Appointments are not necessary.

Tours leave from the information booth on the second floor of the Administration

Building at 11:00 a.m. and 2:00 p.m., Monday-Friday, except holidays. Group tours or special requests may be scheduled by calling Undergraduate Admissions at (407) 823-5592.

Application For Admission

All interested applicants must complete the state university system application for admission, and include a 20 dollar (US$), non-refundable application fee. Applicants should also request official transcripts from each educational institution attended to be forwarded directly to the Undergraduate Admissions Office. Students should apply *several months in advance* of an anticipated start date.

Applications for admission will be accepted up to one year prior to the start of the term desired. The priority application deadlines are July 15 for the Fall semester, November 15 for the Spring semester, and April 15 for the Summer term. The priority deadline for most financial assistance and scholarships is March 1. Information and an application for university housing are sent at the time of acceptance into the University. Requests for housing are subsequently reviewed by date of the receipt of the housing application.

Documentation Required For Admission

All supporting admissions documents must be received directly from the issuing institution or testing agency to be considered official. All final supporting documents (official transcripts and test scores) must be received by Undergraduate Admissions no later than 20 days after the first day of classes. **Those students who have not submitted completed records by the deadline will be placed on administrative hold. Students with incomplete records will not be permitted to register for a future term until all transcripts and other required documentation have been received. Students whose records are not satisfactory may be placed on academic probation, admission status changed to non-degree or transient, and may, in some cases, be withdrawn from the University.**

Reactivation

Students who have submitted an application to UCF and did not attend, may reactivate the original application within one year of the term for which they first applied. To update the application, students should request and complete a reactivation form by the published deadline. This form is available in the Undergraduate Admissions

Office or by calling (407) 823-3000.

Limited Access Programs

Admission to the University does not guarantee admission to a limited access program, and some majors at the University limit the number of students who may enroll. Limited access status is justified when student demand exceeds available resources, such as faculty, instructional facilities, or equipment, or when specific accrediting requirements apply. Criteria for admissions are selective to include: indicators of ability and indicators of performance, creativity, or talent to complete required work within the program. For admission to limited access programs, community college transfer students with Associate of Arts degrees from Florida public community colleges are given equal consideration with UCF students. Admission to such programs are governed by A-10.24 (8), the Articulation Agreement, and by 6C-6.01, FAC, of the Board of Regents rules.

Orientation

All undergraduate degree-seeking students are required to attend orientation prior to enrollment. Information on orientation is mailed to all students once accepted to the University.

Admission Categories

Students may make application to the University in one of the following categories:

A. Freshman (first-time-in-college)

B. Dual Enrollment (includes early admission and dual enrollment, on- or off-campus)

C. Transfer

D. Second Bachelor's Degree

E. International (non-U.S. citizens who possess a valid visa)

F. Transient (one term enrollment only, not from a Florida public university)

G. Non-Degree Seeking

IMPORTANT: Furnishing false or fraudulent statements or information in connection with an application for admission or residence affidavit may result in disciplinary action, denial of admission, and invalidation of credits or degrees earned.

Freshman Applicants

Any first-time-in-college (FTIC) student who meets the minimum admission requirements is encouraged to submit an application. The University will do everything possible to accept all qualified applicants who apply by the priority deadline date. **If the number of qualified applicants exceeds the number the University is permitted to enroll, admission will be on a selective basis. An applicant's total high school record including grades, test scores, educational objective, and pattern of courses completed, counselor recommendations, and personal achievements and honors will be considered in the selection process. An application pool will be maintained when the number of applicants exceeds the number of qualified students to whom admission may be offered. Based on the number of cancellations received, selections will be made from the applicant pool.**

The University reaffirms its Equal Educational Opportunity (EEO) commitments and seeks to increase the enrollment of minority students.

Entrance Examination Scores

All applicants for admission must submit test scores from the Scholastic Aptitude Test (SAT) or from the American College Test (ACT). In addition, any student whose native language is not English must submit a Test of English as a Foreign Language (TOEFL) score.

Applicant Eligibility

Admission into the University is limited by space availability. The degree of competition for space depends on the number and qualifications of those who apply for admission. To increase the chance of admission, high school students should present credentials which are stronger than the minimum requirements for consideration as listed above. If the number of qualified applicants exceeds the number that the University is able to enroll, a waiting list will be established.

(THE END)

prospective / prəs'pektiv / 未来的
reception / ri'sepʃən / 接待
admission / əd'miʃən / 招生，录取
appointment / ə'pɔintmənt / 预约

volunteer /vɔlən'tiə(r)/ 志愿者
non-refundable 不退还
transcript / 'trænskript / 成绩单
anticipated 预期的
scholarship / 'skɔləʃip / 奖学金
probation / prə'beiʃən / 试用，试读
reactivation / riˌækti'veiʃən / 重新激活
update / ʌp'deit / 更新
enroll / in'rəul/ 登记，注册
credential / kri'denʃəl / 证明文件
major / 'meidʒə / 专业
accredit 认证
orientation / ˌɔ(ː)rien'teiʃən / 迎新情况介绍（班）
freshman 新生，大学一年级学生
entrance examination score 入学考试分数
eligibility 资格，合格
availability / əˌveilə'biliti / 可用性，有效性

重点剖析

— Tours of campus are available to all interested individuals and are an excellent way to view first hand about the facilities offered at the University. Campus tours are conducted by trained student volunteers and last approximately 45 minutes. Appointments are not necessary. 所有有兴趣的个人都可以参加校园游览，这是一手了解大学各种设施的最好方法。校园游览由经过培训的学生志愿者组织进行，游览一次约需45分钟。无需预约。

— All interested applicants must complete the state university system application for admission, and include a 20 dollar (US$), non-refundable application fee. Applicants should also request official transcripts from each educational institution attended to be forwarded directly to the Undergraduate Admissions Office. Students should apply several months in advance of an anticipated start date. 所有感兴趣的申请人必须填写大学系统招生申请表，并交纳20美元申请费，此费用不退还。申请人还应向参加过的教育机构索取正式成绩单，直接寄给大学生招生办。学生们应在预计开学日期前几个月提交申请。

— Applications for admission will be accepted up to one year prior to the start of the term desired. The priority application deadlines are July 15 for the Fall semester, November 15 for the Spring semester, and April 15 for the Summer term. The priority deadline for most financial assistance and scholarships is March 1. 录取申请将在开学前一年开始接收。秋季学期的优先申请截止日期是7月15日，春季学期是11月15日，夏季学期是4月15日。大多数资金补助和奖学金的优先申请截止日期是3月1日。

— Those students who have not submitted completed records by the deadline will be placed on administrative hold. Students with incomplete records will not be permitted to register for a future term until all transcripts and other required documentation have been received. Students whose records are not satisfactory may be placed on academic probation, admission status changed to non-degree or transient, and may, in some cases, be withdrawn from the University. 在截止日期前没有提交全部记录的学生将被延期考虑。记录不完整的学生不能注册后来的学期，直到我们收到所有的成绩单和其他所需的文件。记录不令人满意的学生可能被允许试读，录取状态被改变为非学位或临时状态，某些情况下还可能被劝退。

— Admission to the University does not guarantee admission to a limited access program, and some majors at the University limit the number of students who may enroll. Limited access status is justified when student demand exceeds available resources, such as faculty, instructional facilities, or equipment, or when specific accrediting requirements apply. 被录取到本大学并不担保被录取入有限的准入课程，本大学的一些专业限制学生注册的人数。当学生的需求超过现有的师资力量、教学设施或设备或包含有专门的认证要求，有限准入状态是合理的。

— If the number of qualified applicants exceeds the number the University is permitted to enroll, admission will be on a selective basis. An applicant's total high school record including grades, test scores, educational objective, and pattern of courses completed, counselor recommendations, and personal achievements and honors will be considered in the selection process. An application pool will be maintained when the number of applicants exceeds the number of qualified students to whom admission may be offered. Based on the number of cancellations received, selections will be made from the applicant pool. 如果合格申请人数超过了本大学允许招收的人数，则进行择优录取。录取时，申请者的全部高中纪录，如评价等级、考试分数、教育目标和已修课程结构、以及教师推荐信和个人成果及荣誉，都在考查之列。当申请人数超出要招收的合格学生的人数时，我们将保留一份申请名单。我们将根据收到的取消就学者的人数，从申请名单中进行挑选。

— Admission into the University is limited by space availability. The degree of competition for space depends on the number and qualifications of those who apply for admission. To increase the chance of admission, high school students should present credentials which are stronger than the minimum requirements for consideration as listed above. 能否被录取入本大学受到剩余名额的限制。名额竞争的激烈程度取决于申请录取者的人数和资格。为增加被录取的机会，高中学生应提交证明自己能力超过上述考查项目最低要求的文件。

（V17真题题源）

3. English Learner Educational Services at Mcdaniel College

双 语 教 育

The English Learner Educational Services classes are designed to meet the Maryland requirements for certification in English for Speakers of Other Languages (ESOL). **This is a credit count program which means students may enroll as a non-degree seeking student and only take the classes they need.** If you are currently employed as a teacher in Maryland, your county human resources department will tell you specifically which classes you need to take to become certified in ESOL.

If you are interested in earning a Master's degree, the English Learner Educational Services courses count toward McDaniel's MS in Curriculum and Instruction. **The courses provide important background for educators who would like to know more about meeting the needs of English language learners, but do not wish to pursue full certification.**

To enroll in the English Learner Educational Services courses, you need to apply to Graduate and Professional studies as a non-degree student. The application and registration forms are available online at http://www.mcdaniel.edu Select 'Graduate and

Professional Studies'. The $40 application fee is waived with a letter of recommendation from a McDaniel alum. Attach a copy of your undergrad transcript or your teaching certificate to prove that you already have a Bachelor's degree.

English Learner Educational Services Courses

- EDU 522 Foundations in English Learner Education (Includes ESOL Teaching Methods) (Fall 2003)
- EDU 523 Literacy Development in Multilingual Communities: Reading (Fall 2003, Summer 2004)
- EDU 524 Literacy Development in Multilingual Communities: Writing (Spring 2004, Summer 2004)
- EDU 525 Assessment of English Learners (Spring 2004)
- EDU 566-1 Linguistics for ESOL Teachers (Summer 2003)
- EDU 566-2 American English Grammar for ESOL Teachers (Summer 2003)
- EDU 566-01 First Language Acquisition (Fall 2003)
- EDU 001 Second Language Acquisition (Spring 2004)

Registration

Forms and Catalogs

If you have been accepted into a McDaniel College graduate program, then you should receive in the mail a registration form, a class schedule, and a course catalog.

How to Register

Complete the entire registration form, filling in all information. Return the completed registration form to the McDaniel College Registrar's Office via:

- **Online:** Online Registration Form
- **Fax:** Obtain registration form from Web site or enclosed in schedule. Complete and fax to 410-857-2752.
- **Mail:** Obtain registration form from Web site or enclosed in schedule. Complete and mail to
  Registrar's Office
  Elderdice Hall
  McDaniel College

2 College Hill
Westminster, MD 21157-4390

- In-person: Visit the Registrar's Office, Elderdice Hall

Dates to Register

No forms will be processed before the starting dates listed below.

Fall term: July 1
Spring term: December 1
Summer session: April

How to Pay

Tuition and Fees may be paid by check or money order made out to McDaniel College. Tuition during the Fall and Spring semesters may be paid according to a Tuition Contract Payment Plan approved by the Bursar's Office. Request Payment Plan information at the bottom of your registration form, or print out a copy of the contract now.

Course Availability

Early registration can prevent the cancellation of a course due to insufficient enrollment or can guarantee a place in a course that may be closed due to overenrollment. To ensure your place in a course, please register early.

Courses with insufficient enrollment will be canceled one week before their starting date. If you have registered for a course that is canceled, then you will be notified by the McDaniel College Registrar's Office.

Late Entry

After the first day of classes, a course may be entered only if space is available and with the approval of the instructor. After you have registered, you may only add or drop a course by using the Add/Drop Form. This form may be obtained from the Registrar's Office or the Graduate Office. You may drop off the completed form at the Registrar's Office from 8:30am to 4:30 pm weekdays or, after hours, put the form through the mail slot in the door of the Registrar's Office.

NOTE: Adds and Drops will not be accepted over the phone.

If you are adding a class on or after the first day it meets, you will be charged

a $35.00 late fee.

Withdrawal

It is assumed that a student will not withdraw from the College during a term. In the event that such a withdrawal is necessary, the student will complete an official withdrawal form obtained from the Registrar's Office, or submit a written request to the Registrar. Failure to attend classes or to pay a billing statement by the due date does not constitute an official withdrawal. **The grade of "W" will be recorded if the withdrawal occurs before the midpoint of the course. Withdrawal after that date will result in an "F" grade.**

(THE END)

必备词汇

ESOL /'esəl/ 英语作为外国语
pursue / pə'sjuː / 从事，追求
alum / ə'lʌm / 校友，毕业生
curriculum / kə'rikjuləm / 课程
withdraw / wið'drɔː / 退学
waive / weiv / 放弃，免除
registration / ˌredʒis'treiʃən / 注册，登记
enrollment / in'rəulmənt / 招生，注册
cancellation / kænsə'leiʃən / 取消
instructor / in'strʌktə / 讲师，教师

重点剖析

— This is a credit count program which means students may enroll as a non-degree seeking student and only take the classes they need. 这是一个学分制的课程项目，这就意味着不以拿学位为目的学生可以来注册，只上自己需要的课程。

— The courses provide important background for educators who would like to know more about meeting the needs of English language learners, but do not wish to pursue full certification. 这些课程为那些希望更多了解英语学习都有什么要求、但不想得到完全认证的教育人士提供了重要的背景知识。

— The $40 application fee is waived with a letter of recommendation from a McDaniel alum. Attach a copy of your undergrad uate transcript or your teaching certificate to prove that you already have a Bachelor's degree. 如果持有McDaniel毕业生写的推荐信，我们将免收40元申请费。附上一份你的大学成绩单或教学证书，证明你拥有学士学位。

— Early registration can prevent the cancellation of a course due to insufficient enrollment or can guarantee a place in a course that may be closed due to overenrollment. To ensure your place in a course, please register early. 提前注册可以避免由于报名人数不足而取消课程，或者由于报名人数过多导致报不上名。为了确保能参加课程，请及早登记。

— If you are adding a class on or after the first day it meets, you will be charged a $ 35.00 late fee. 如果在开课后你要增加一门课程，我们将收取35元迟到费。

— The grade of "W" will be recorded if the withdrawal occurs before the midpoint of the course. Withdrawal after that date will result in an "F" grade。在课业进程前一半中退出，将会记"W"。在后一半中退出，将会记"F"。

(V33真题题源)

4. Bullying at School: Tackling the Problem

校 园 暴 力

The research community in the UK and elsewhere has come to realise over the past 20 years that it needs to examine what is understood to be bullying behaviour and in particular the complexity of the interaction between bully and bullied by looking at its nature, extent, frequency and intensity.

There are many definitions of bullying. Roland in 1988 defined it as **"long standing violence, physical or psychological, conducted by an individual or a group and directed against an individual who is not able to defend himself in the actual situation"**

Besag defined bullying in 1990 as, "the repeated attack—physical, psychological, social or verbal—by those in a position of power, which is formally or situationally defined, on those who are powerless to resist, with the intention of causing distress for their own gain or gratification." She acknowledges that no definition can satisfactorily encompass all the aspects of a highly complex behaviour such as this and that it is in the interpretation of the behaviour by victim and bully that the power lies.

Bullying has existed in schools for as long as schools have existed though it has not been measured in a systematic way until recently. We can now conclude from the research done over the past 17 years that at least 10% of children in schools are probably at any one time involved in bullying to a marked degree either as bully or victim. Research in Scandinavia by Olweus in 1978 showed that approximately 10% were victims and 8% bullies. He also found that many people seemed to regard it as an essential part of growing up, toughening up children, especially boys for adult life.

Perhaps this is why the education community has been so long in acknowledging it as a problem. In 1990 Rigby and Slee suggest that there are features, like the competitive ethos, in the school environment that harden the attitudes of children towards victims. School student victims are reluctant to tell parents or teachers for fear of making it worse and some assume an attitude of blaming themselves.

The effects of bullying are far reaching. Apart from the physical dangers they are exposed to, victims may lose their self-esteem and experience emotional and social difficulties as shown by Olweus in 1978. Some victims begin to think that they deserve to be bullied as shown by Roland in 1980.

O'Moore and Hillery in 1991 found that children who were victims of bullying had low self-esteem and seeing themselves in a more negative light than students who had not been bullied. They also found that bullies had low self-esteem in relation to intellectual and school status. Tattum and Tattum in 1992 found that such low self-perceptions are damaging and persist into adulthood. They also showed how bullying affects the other children who witness it, with less aggressive pupils being drawn in or feeling intimidated.

The bullies are also at risk. **Lane in 1989 showed that they develop anti-social attitude patterns which can endure into adult life.** Olweus found that 8 year-old bullies are five times as likely to obtain a criminal record by the age of 30 than 8 year-old who are not bullies.

These findings are confirmed by a 22 year longitudinal study in the USA by Eron and others in 1987. They found that young bullies have a 1 in 4 chance of having a criminal record by age 30, whilst other children have a 1 in 20 chance. By the age of 30 they found that those who had been bullies as children were more likely to have children who were bullies and to have convictions for violent crimes.

Kidscape conducted in 1998 a retrospective survey of over 1000 adults to find out if bullying in school affects people in later life. It showed that bullying not only affects self esteem in adulthood but also the ability to make friends, succeed in education and in work and social relationships.

46% of those who were bullied committed suicide compared to 7% who were not.

There tends to be a belief that because bullying is by nature a secretive activity, there is little that teachers can do about it. In fact a number of studies reflect the underestimation by teachers and parents of bullying when compared with self and peer reports by students. For example Ziegler and Rosenstein-Manner in a Canadian study 14% of parents were aware of their children being bullied compared to 20% of children reporting being bullied. 14% of teachers said there was no bullying in their classes in one week compared to 6% children.

Until recently in the United Kingdom neither the government nor the heads of schools have paid much attention to the occurrence and the effects of bullying. In 1987 the literature on disruptive behaviour was extensive but there was very little written on bullying in the UK.

In that year the Council of Europe had a conference about bullying in Norway where there had been a national anti-bullying campaign since 1983 after the suicide of three adolescent boys who had been victimised. In the five years that followed there was significant progress on raising awareness of the problem in the UK.

Over the past eight years there has been a raising of awareness and interest in bullying in schools amongst researchers, the media and teachers. Various approaches have been made both in research and in prevention activities with regard to bullying. In 1988 the first book on bullying was published here. Other initiatives emerged, like the Calouste Gulbenkian Foundation joining with British Telecom to fund a national anti-bullying campaign in the UK to send copies of Bullying: a Child's View (La Fontaine,1991) and Governors and Bullying (ACE1990) to all schools.

All research shows that bullying is a considerable problem during the school years. In the UK there have been deaths of several victims of bullying and the government has gradually accepted that bullying is serious and widespread. In the Elton Report on Discipline in Schools published in 1989, it was recommended that teachers be alert to bullying and to take action. In 1991 the DES commissioned research from Sheffield University aimed at developing strategies to combat bullying.

Boulton and Underwood's research in the UK with secondary school students (8-13) showed that 92% of schoolgirls and 75% of school boys reported that they had never been bullied. 21% of students reported they had been bullied and 17% reported bullying others. Boulton and Underwood also found out by a peer-nomination method that over half of the bullying is done by boys and one tenth by girls. 37 % of victims are girls and 30 % boys. They conducted the research over a four points in time which showed that the bullying behaviour was not a phase that school students grew out of. Boulton and Smith looked at the consequences of bullying and found that victims scored lower than nonvictims on social acceptance, athletic competence and global self-worth. They found evidence that bullying proceeds low self esteem for most children.

Ahmed, Whitney and Smith as part of the 1991 research based at Sheffield University used questionnaires adapted from Olweus't self- reporting inventories both before and after intervention strategies in 24 schools in Sheffield with a total of 4,135 students. The interventions comprised of: whole school anti-bullying policies and a variety of optional interventions such as use of videos, drama, literature, quality circles, assertiveness training, no blame approaches, peer counseling and playground work.

The research found that 27% of junior/middle school students (5-13) reported being bullied occasionally and 10% reported being bullied once or several times a week. In secondary schools (13-18) 10% were bullied occasionally and 4% at least once a week. After intervention, bullying was reduced from 20% to 13% of students being pushed or kicked, from 9% to 5% being threatened and from 10% to 6% being teased. Follow up research in Sheffield includes Whitney and Smith (1993) which exposed age and gender differences in the incidence of bullying. They found that bullying is worst during the early years at secondary school and that boys are more involved than girls and in different ways.

The survey revealed that three quarters of all secondary school students have been bullies and a similar number victims at least once in a year. Only 14% have been neither bully nor victim and a hard core of 7% suffer physical bullying frequently. 20% are affected by frequent verbal abuse and 7% have their property damaged. Students suffer physical harm in the playground, teasing in corridors, and even classrooms are places of misery unless staff have good management skills. Glover and Cartwright show that pro-active management of bullying in schools can bring about an improvement despite these disturbing figures.

How to address the bullying at school? **The first step is for whole school communities to admit there is a problem and to desire change, to publish a kind of written document. School policy in detail is also needed to tell teachers how to and what to do in dealing with bullying. Teachers should encourage the potential victims to be confident to avoid being bullied. Special teachers should be trained to identify the bullying and playing fighting.** Families and the larger community need to be involved and those schools who showed the most success integrated their anti-bullying work with social activities and the subject curriculum. **In Norway, research proved that two years after such campaign, the bullying was halved.**

(THE END)

必备词汇

bully / ˈbuli / 欺负

violence / ˈvaiələns / 暴力

encompass / inˈkʌmpəs / 包含，包括

victim / ˈviktim / 受害者，被欺负者

ethos / ˈiːθɔs / 思潮，风气

reluctant / riˈlʌktənt / 不情愿

self-esteem 自信

adulthood / ˈædʌltˌhud / 成人期

anti-social behaviour 反社会行为

suicide / ˈsjuisaid / 自杀

peer / piə / 同学，同龄人

campaign / kæmˈpein / 行动，活动

questionnaires 调查问卷

junior school / ˈdʒuːnjə skuːl / 小学

secondary school / ˈsekəndəri skuːl / 高中

halve 减少了一半

重点剖析

— Long standing violence, physical or psychological, conducted by an individual or a group and directed against an individual who is not able to defend himself in the actual situation. Roland（1988）认为，欺负行为是指个体或群体长期对一个在现实情境中无自卫能力的个体进行生理、心理上的伤害。

— Lane in 1989 showed that they develop anti-social attitude patterns which can endure into adult life. Lane（1989）的研究表明，受欺负儿童的反社会态度能够延续至成年期。

— 46% of those who were bullied committed suicide compared to 7% who were not. 受欺负的学生中，46%的人曾有过自杀行为，而没有受过欺负的学生中只有7%的曾有过自杀行为。

— The first step is for whole school communities to admit there is a problem and to desire change, to publish a kind of written document. School policy in detail is also needed to tell teachers how to and what to do in dealing with bullying. Teachers should encourage the potential victims to be confident to avoid being bullied. Special teachers should be trained to identify the bullying and playing fighting. 首先，校方要承认存在校园暴力现象并亟待解决，要出版书面文件说明这一问题。学校要制定政策培训老师如何应对。老师要鼓励有可能受欺负的孩子，使他们有自信以避免被欺负。还要培训专业教师识别什么是欺负行为并采取适当措施制止。

— In Norway, research proved that two years after such campaign, the bullying was halved. 在挪威，研究证实经过开展这一运动，校园欺负行为减少了一半。

（V27 真题题源）

5. Intelligence and Giftedness

小学生的智商研究

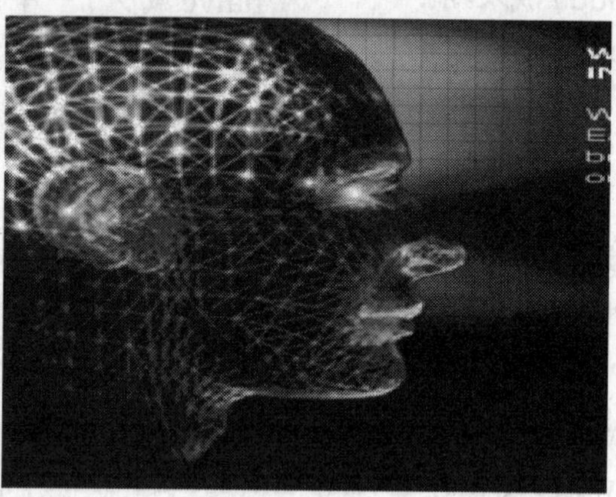

In 1904 the French Minister of Education, facing limited resources for schooling, sought a way to separate the unable from the merely lazy. Alfred Binet got the job of devising selection principles and his brilliant solution put a stamp on the study of intelligence and was the forerunner of intelligence tests still used today. He developed a thirty-problem test in 1905, which tapped several abilities related to intellect, such as judgment and reasoning. The test determined a given child's 'mental age'. The test previously established a norm for children of a given physical age. (For example, five-year-old on average get ten items correct).

Therefore, a child with a mental age of five should score 10, which would mean that he or she was functioning pretty much as others of that age. The child's mental age was then compared to his physical age.

A large disparity in the wrong direction (e.g., a child of nine with a mental age of four) might suggest inability rather than laziness and mean he or she was earmarked for special schooling. Binet, however, denied that the test was measuring intelligence. Its purpose was simply diagnostic, for selection only. This message was however

lost, and caused many problems and misunderstanding later.

Although Binet's test was popular, it was a bit inconvenient to deal with a variety of physical and mental ages. So in 1912 Wilhelm Stern suggested simplifying this by reducing the two to a single number. He divided the mental age by the physical age, and multiplied the result by 100. **An average child, irrespective of age, would score 100. A number much lower than 100 would suggest the need for help, and one much higher would suggest a child well ahead of his peer.**

This measurement is what is now termed the IQ (for intelligence quotient) score and it has evolved to be used to show how a person, adult or child, performed in relation to others. (The term IQ was coined by Lewism Terman, professor of psychology and education of Stanford University, in 1916. he had constructed an enormously influential revision of Binet's test, called the Stanford-Binet test, versions of which are still given extensively.)

The field studying intelligence and developing tests eventually coalesced into a sub-field of psychology called psychometrics (psycho for 'mind' and metrics for 'measurements'). The practical side of psychometrics (the development and use of tests) became widespread quite early. By 1917, when Einstein published his grand theory of relativity, mass-scale testing was already in use.

Germany's unrestricted submarine warfare (which led to the sinking of the Lusitania in 1915) provoked the United States to finally enter the first World War in the same year. The military had to build up an army very quickly. It had two million inductees to sort out. Who would become officers and who would become enlisted men?

Psychometricians developed two intelligence tests that helped sort all these people out, at least to some extent. This was the first major use of testing to decide who lived and who died, as officers were a lot safer on the battlefield. The tests themselves were given under horrendously bad conditions, and the examiners seemed to lack commonsense. A lot of recruits simply had no idea what to do and in several sessions most inductees scored zero! The examiners also came up with the quite astounding conclusion from the testing that the average American adult's intelligence was equal to that of a thirteen-year-old!

Nevertheless, the ability for various authorities to classify people on scientifically justifiable premises was too convenient and significant to be dismissed lightly. So with all good astounding intentions and often over enthusiasm, society's affinity for psychological testing proliferated.

Back in Europe, Sir Cyril Burt, professor of psychology at University College London from 1931 to 1950, was a prominent figure for his contribution to the field. He was a firm advocate of intelligence testing and his ideas fitted in well with English cultural ideas of elitism. A government committee in 1943 used some of Burt's ideas in devising a rather primitive typology on children's intellectual behavior. **All were tested at age eleven. The top 15 or 20 per cent went to grammar schools with good teachers and a fast pace of work to prepare for the few university places available. A lot of very bright working-class children, who otherwise would never have, made it to grammar schools and universities.**

The system for the rest was however disastrous. These children attended lesser secondary or technical schools and faced the prospect of eventual education oblivion. They felt like dumb failures, having been officially branded as such be science, and their motivation to study naturally plummeted. It was not until 1974 that the public education system was finally reformed. (Nowadays it is believed that Burt has fabricated a lot of his data; having an obsession that intelligence is largely genetic, he apparently made up twin studies, which supported this idea, at the same time inventing two coworkers who were supposed to have gathered the results.)

Intelligence testing enforced political and social prejudice. Their results were used to argue that Jews ought to be kept out of the United States because they were so intelligently inferior that they would pollute the racial mix; and blacks ought not to be allowed to breed at all. And so abuse and test bias controversies continued to plaque psychometrics.

Measurement is fundamental to science and technology. Science often advances in leaps and bounds when measurement devices improve. Psychometrics has long tried to develop ways to gauge psychological qualities such as intelligence and more specific abilities, anxiety, extroversion, emotional stability, compatibility, with marriage partner, and so on. Their scores are often given enormous weight. A single IQ measurement can take on a life of its own if teachers and parents see it as definitive. It became a major issue in the 70s, when court cases were launched to stop anyone from making important decisions based on IQ test scores. The main criticism was and still is that current tests don't really measure intelligence. **Whether intelligence can be measured at all is still controversial. Some say it cannot. Others say that IQ tests are psychology's greatest accomplishments.**

(THE END)

必备词汇

schooling / 'skuːliŋ / 学校教育
mental age 智力年龄，心理年龄
physical age 生理年龄
intellect / 'intilekt / 智力
reasoning / 'riːzəniŋ / 推理
previously / 'priːvjuːsli / 以前，先前
disparity / dis'pæriti / 不同，差别
diagnostic / ˌdaiəg'nɔstik / 诊断的
inconvenient / ˌinkən'viːnjənt / 不方便的
a variety of 各种
simplify / 'simplifai / 简单化
intelligence quotient (IQ) 智商
eventually / i'ventjuəli / 最后，终于
sub-field / sʌb/ / fiːld / 分支，子学科
coalesce / ˌkəuə'les / 合并
psychometrics / ˌsaikə'metriks / 心理测量学
relativity / ˌrelə'tiviti / 相对论
submarine / 'sʌbməriːn, sʌbmə'riːn / 潜水艇
warfare / 'wɔːfɛə / 战争
provoke / prə'vəuk / 激怒，驱使
inductee / ˌindʌk'tiː/ 就任者，应召入伍的士兵
sort out 挑选
enlist / in'list / 征募，征召
commonsense / ˌkɔmən'sens / 常识
astounding / ə'staundiŋ / 令人惊骇的
justifiable / 'dʒʌstifaiəbl / 有理由的，有道理的
premise / 'premis / 前提
affinity / ə'finiti / 吸引力，亲和力
proliferate / prəu'lifəreit / 扩散
prominent figure 著名人物
advocate / 'ædvəkit / 提倡者，鼓吹者
elitism / ei'liːtizm, i'liːtizm / 杰出人物统治论
typology / tai'pɔlədʒi / 类型学，体型学
disastrous / di'zɑːstrəs / 灾难性的
oblivion / ə'bliviən / 遗忘，湮没
plummet / 'plʌmit / 垂直落下
fabricate / 'fæbrikeit / 伪造，捏造
obsession / əb'seʃən / 迷住，困扰
prejudice / 'predʒudis / 偏见
bias / 'baiəs / 偏见
controversy / 'kɔntrəvəːsi / 论战，辩论
plaque / plɑːk / 测试
fundamental / ˌfʌndə'mentl / 基础的，基本的
gauge / geidʒ / 测量，衡量
extroversion / ˌekstrəu'vəːʃən / 外向
emotional stability 情绪稳定性
compatibility / kəmˌpæti'biliti / 相容性

重点剖析

— In 1904 the French Minister of Education, facing limited resources for schooling, sought a way to separate the unable from the merely lazy. Alfred Binet got the job of devising selection principles and his brilliant solution put a stamp on the study of intelligence and was the forerunner of intelligence tests still used today. He developed a thirty-problem test in 1905, which tapped several abilities related to intellect, such as judgment and reasoning. The test determined a given child's 'mental age'. The test previously established a norm for children of a given physical age. (For example, five-year-old on average get ten items correct). 由于学校教育资源有限，法国教育部在1904年开始寻求把弱智儿童和懒于思考的儿童加以区分的方法。比奈负责设定筛选原则，他提出的解决方案非常出色，在智力研究领域写下了浓重的一笔，成为现在广泛采用的智力测验的先驱。他于1905年设计出了一个30题的智力测验量表，用来测验与智力有关的几大能力，如判断和推理能力。该测验能测出儿童的"智龄"，并提前确定了某个生理年龄的儿童应该达到的标准。（如，5岁儿童平均能答对10道题。）

— Therefore, a child with a mental age of five should score 10, which would mean that he or she was functioning pretty much as others of that age. The child's mental age was then compared to his physical age. 因此，如果智龄为5岁的儿童其测验成绩为10分，说明该儿童的智力发展与同龄儿童一致。然后，将其智龄与生理年龄相比。

— A large disparity in the wrong direction (e.g., a child of nine with a mental age of four) might suggest inability rather than laziness and mean he or she was earmarked for special schooling. Binet, however, denied that the test was measuring intelligence. Its purpose was simply diagnostic, for selection only. This message was however lost, and caused many problems and misunderstanding later. 如果二者差异较大（如9岁儿童的智龄只有4岁），则可能意味着该儿童智力发展欠佳，而不是懒于思考。也就是说，该儿童需要接受特殊教育。不过，比奈否认该测验是用来测智力的。它的目的仅为了诊断和筛选。但这一点几乎不为人知，因此后来导致了许多问题、引起了许多误解。

— An average child, irrespective of age, would score 100. A number much lower than 100 would suggest the need for help, and one much higher would suggest a child well ahead of his peer. 一个普通的孩子，不管年龄多大，能得100分。大大低于100分将意味着他需要帮助，分数高得多将可能表示他的智力强过同龄人。

— This measurement is what is now termed the IQ (for intelligence quotient) score and it has evolved to be used to show how a person, adult or child, performed in relation to others. 这种测验目前称为IQ（智商）分数，它已经发展到用来表明个人（成人或孩子）与其他人相比表现如何。

— Psychometricians developed two intelligence tests that helped sort all these people out, at least to some extent. This was the first major use of testing to decide who lived and who died, as officers were a lot safer on the battlefield. 心理测量学家们设计

了两套智力测验，至少在某种程度上可以协助进行人员挑选。这是智力测验第一次被用来确定谁生谁死，因为军官在战场上更为安全一些。

— All were tested at age eleven. The top 15 or 20 per cent went to grammar schools with good teachers and a fast pace of work to prepare for the few university places available. A lot of very bright working-class children, who otherwise would never have, made it to grammar schools and universities. 所有人都在11岁接受测试。得分居前15%或20%的孩子进入语法学校，那儿的师资强，课程安排紧，是为进入名额很有限的大学做准备的。许多很出色的工人家庭的孩子，以前从没有机会、但如今可以进入语法学校和大学了。

— The system for the rest was however disastrous. These children attended lesser secondary or technical schools and faced the prospect of eventual education oblivion. They felt like dumb failures, having been officially branded as such be science, and their motivation to study naturally plummeted. 然而，这一系统对其他孩子来说是灾难性的。这些孩子由于上的是较差的中学和技工学校，最终面临着被教育淘汰的命运。他们面对失败无话可说，因为这个甄选系统被标榜为科学的，所以他们的学习动力一落千丈。

— Whether intelligence can be measured at all is still controversial. Some say it cannot. Others say that IQ tests are psychology's greatest accomplishments. 智力到底能不能被测出来，这仍旧是个有争论的话题。有些人说不能，但另外有人却认为智商测验是心理学的最大成就。

（V14真题题源）

6. Distance Learning

远 程 教 育

Distance Learning courses offer students more convenience than traditional courses. Students are not required to come to campus as often for a Distance Learning course since much of the course work can be done in the student's home. Students have flexibility in selecting the time they will complete their weekly lessons. **Students also have the freedom to determine which day and time during a particular week they will attend orientation, seminars, and take their exams.**

In exchange for convenience, Distance Learning courses require students to have maturity, self-motivation, and self-discipline. All assignments are carefully explained in the written course materials, but the student must supply the motivation and discipline to complete each week's work. It is the student's responsibility to complete assignments and tests during the scheduled time period. Students in remote areas who wish to test at a site other than Tarrant County College must obtain approval from the Director of Distance Learning at Tarrant County College before enrolling in a course. Approval must be obtained and all arrangements for testing completed at least three weeks prior to the beginning of the semester.

Each course requires a commitment of time equal to that required by an on-campus course. Students who are employed, or who plan to seek employment, should carefully consider the amount of college work they attempt in relation to the number of hours they are employed each week. **The College reserves the right to limit the course load carried by any student.**

Upon successful completion of a course, a student will receive full college credit. The courses and the credit hours are equivalent to those offered on campus. All courses apply toward associate degree requirements; many fulfill certificate program requirements and/or requirements for bachelor degrees. Students should consult their TCC catalog for additional information.

Registration And Materials

Students should have completed the registration process when they have entered their courses on the Internet, at the TCC Connect station, or by telephone registration, and then paid their tuition. After completing registration, students should purchase any textbooks, study guides, and/or other supplies that are required for their course from a bookstore. ITV students will purchase their course booklet (syllabus), for a nominal fee, at a TCC campus bookstore, or they may download their course booklet from the Distance Learning Web site for free. Required textbooks and materials for all Distance Learning classes are listed under the orientation schedules at the back of this booklet. To ensure that the proper books are obtained, students should refer to this booklet when purchasing their materials.

Students who are unable to find the textbooks or supplies needed for a Distance Learning course should notify the Center for Distance Learning immediately at (817) 515-4532. **When calling, please have the following information: course title and synonym, textbook, and author.**

Orientation Requirements

There is an orientation session for each Distance Learning course. Specific orientation requirements vary according to the mode of instruction as described in the sections containing the orientation schedules. It is the student's responsibility to arrange his/her work/school schedule to see that orientation requirements are met. Students will meet their instructor at the on-campus session and review the course booklet/syllabus detailing course requirements. Children are not allowed at orientations.

Weekly Lessons

ITV students will be required to watch approximately two 30-minute programs per week for each course; this viewing schedule may vary depending on the course. Additional information regarding video lessons and broadcasts is given later in this booklet. **Internet students are required to sign on to TCC's Distance Learning Web site frequently to complete lessons and requirements. In addition to completing the weekly lessons, students must allocate sufficient time to complete readings and/or other assignments which may be required for the course.**

Seminars

Many Distance Learning courses, particularly those offered through ITV, offer periodic seminars during the semester. Seminars are additional meetings conducted by course instructors to discuss relevant topics, assignments, and/or to review for tests. Additional information regarding seminars is included in the course syllabus/booklet.

Examinations

Most Distance Learning courses have two to four examinations covering information contained in the weekly lessons, textbooks, and study guide. ITV exams are usually objective in nature, although some may involve essay questions; ITV English courses require on-campus compositions during scheduled testing weeks. Internet exams vary in format depending on the course. Specific information concerning exams will be given at orientation and in the course syllabus/booklet.

Receipts

A computerized Scantron form will be filled out for most Distance Learning activities, and a receipt will be given to the student to verify completion of the activity. Students should keep all test and seminar receipts, as well as any graded papers and/or assignments, until verification of the final semester grade. At that time, students should confirm that the grade received is correct. Students should contact the Center for Distance Learning if they believe an error has been made in computing their grade. **In the event a grade is challenged, the student must provide a complete set of original receipts and/or assignments showing proof of completion of all required activities.**

Current Mailing Address

Newsletters containing pertinent course information may be mailed out during the semester. There may also be times when an instructor or the Center for Distance Learning must contact a student. All students must maintain a current mailing address with the Center for Distance Learning and the Office of the Registrar. Address changes are not accepted over the telephone.

Inclement Weather

In the event of inclement weather, students should listen to their radio or television, or check the TCCD Web site for information concerning TCC closings. If regular classes are meeting, so will Distance Learning orientations, seminars, and testing sessions. If classes are cancelled, these meetings will also be cancelled. In addition, ITV cablecasts may not be broadcast when TCC is closed.

No Children On Campus

Children are not permitted at orientation sessions, seminars, in the library viewing areas, in computer or science labs, or in the Testing Centers. Children are **not** to be left unattended on college property at any time.

Orientations

Many Distance Learning courses are offered via both the Internet and Instructional Television. It is critical, therefore, that students attend the correct Orientation session. As students check the Orientation schedules, they should make certain to look in the correct section, Internet or Instructional Television, for the course in which they are enrolled. Students must check their course schedule and compare the synonym for the course on their schedule to the synonym listed on the Orientation schedule. **A header or footer on each page of the Orientation schedules indicates whether the courses listed are Internet courses or Instructional Television courses.**

(THE END)

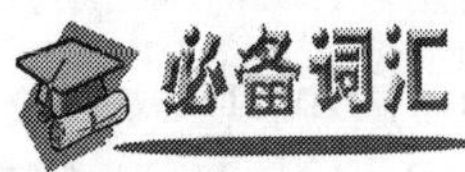

distance learning 远程教育

flexibility /ˌfleksəˈbiliti/ 灵活性

freedom / 'fri:dəm / 自由
maturity / mə'tjuəriti / 成熟
self-motivation / self ˌməuti'veiʃ ən / 自我激励
self-discipline / self 'disiplin / 自律
assignment / ə'sainmənt / 作业
commitment / kə'mitmənt / 承诺
credit / 'kredit / 学分
tuition / tju:'iʃ ən / 学费
booklet / 'buklit / 小册子
syllabus / 'siləbəs / 课程大纲
composition / kɔmpə'ziʃ ən / 作文
papers 考卷
unattended / 'ʌnə'tendid / 没人照顾的

重点剖析

— Students also have the freedom to determine which day and time during a particular week they will attend orientation, seminars, and take their exams. 学生们还可以自由决定在一周中哪一天的什么时间参加迎新介绍会、研讨会和考试。

— In exchange for convenience, Distance Learning courses require students to have maturity, self-motivation, and self-discipline. All assignments are carefully explained in the written course materials, but the student must supply the motivation and discipline to complete each week's work. It is the student's responsibility to complete assignments and tests during the scheduled time period. 享受便捷条件的同时，远程教育课程要求学生们要成熟、自我激励、自律。所有的作业在书面课程材料中得到详细解释，但学生们必须激励约束自己完成每周的作业。学生们有责任在规定的时间段内完成作业和测验。

— The College reserves the right to limit the course load carried by any student. 学院保留限制学生课程负担的权利。

— When calling, please have the following information: course title and synonym, textbook, and author. 来电话时，请提供下列信息：课程名称和代号、教科书和作者。

— Internet students are required to sign on to TCC's Distance Learning Web site frequently to complete lessons and requirements. In addition to completing the weekly lessons, students must allocate sufficient time to complete readings and/or other assignments which may be required for the course. 网校学生们要求经常登录TCC的远程教育站点，完成课程和要求。除了完成每周的课程外，学生们必须分配出足够的时间完成课程要求的阅读和其他作业。

— ITV exams are usually objective in nature, although some may involve essay questions; ITV English courses require on-campus compositions during scheduled testing weeks. Internet exams vary in format depending on the course. ITV考试一般都考查客观题，虽然有些也可能涉及评论问题；ITV 英语课程需要在规定的测验周内写校园作文。通过互联网的考试形式根据课程内容而有所变化。

— In the event a grade is challenged, the student must provide a complete set of original receipts and/or assignments showing proof of completion of all required activities. 如果对评分有疑问，学生们必须提供一套完整的原始收据和作业，证明已完成了所有必需的活动。

— In the event of inclement weather, students should listen to their radio or television, or check the TCCD Web site for information concerning TCC closings. 如果遇到坏天气，学生们应听广播或看电视，或查看 TCCD 的网站了解有关 TCC 结束的信息。

— A header or footer on each page of the Orientation schedules indicates whether the courses listed are Internet courses or Instructional Television courses. 入学时间表每页的页眉和页脚上都标记着列出的课程是互联网课程还是辅导性电视课程。

（V31 真题题源）

7. Fraud in Scientific Research

科学研究中的欺诈

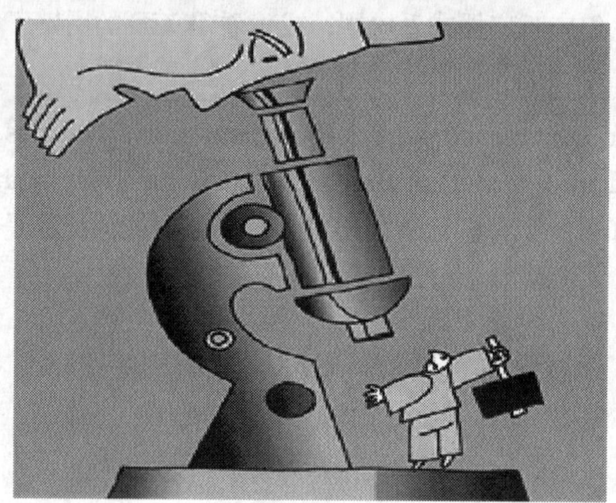

Introduction

In recent years the National Science Foundation (NSF), and various scientific organizations such as the National Academy of Sciences (NAS) have spent considerable time and effort in trying to agree on a definition of scientific misconduct. A good definition is needed in developing and implementing policies and regulations concerning appropriate conduct in research, particularly when federal funding is involved. This is an important area of concern because, although serious scientific misconduct itself may be infrequent, the consequences of even a few instances can be widespread.

Those cases that reach the public's attention can cause considerable distrust among both scientists and the public, however infrequent their occurrence. **Like lying in general, we may wonder which scientific reports are tainted by misconduct, even though we may be convinced that relatively few are. Furthermore, scientists depend on each other's work in advancing their own. Building one's work on the incorrect or unsubstantiated data of others infects one's own research; and the chain of con-**

sequences can be quite lengthy, as well as very serious. This is as true of honest or careless mistakes as it is of the intentional distortion of data, which is what *scientific misconduct* is usually restricted to. Finally, of course, the public depends on the reliable expertise of scientists in virtually every area of health, safety, and welfare.

Although exactly what the definition of *scientific* misconduct should include is a matter of some controversy, all proposed definitions include the fabrication and falsification of data and plagiarism. As an instance of fraud, the fabrication of data is a particularly blatant form of misconduct. It lacks the subtlety of questions about interpreting data that pivot around whether the data have been *fudged, or manipulated.* Fabricating data is making it up, or faking it. Thus, it is a clear instance of a lie, a deliberate attempt to deceive others.

Two well-known cases illustrate this, both of which feature ambitious, and apparently successful, young researchers.

Background

Dr. John Darsee was regarded a brilliant student and medical researcher at the University of Notre Dame (1966~970), Indiana University (1970~974), Emory University (1974~979), and Harvard University (1979~981). He was regarded by faculty at all four institutions as a potential "all-star" with a great research future ahead of him. At Harvard he reportedly often worked more than 90 hours a week as a Research Fellow in the Cardiac Research Laboratory headed by Dr. Eugene Braunwald. In less than two years at Harvard he was first author of seven publications in very good scientific journals. His special area of research concerned the testing of heart drugs on dogs.

The Darsee case

All of this came to a sudden halt in May 1981, when three colleagues in the Cardiac Research Laboratory observed Darsee labeling data recordings 24 *seconds*, 72 *hours*, one week, and two weeks. In reality, only minutes had transpired. Confronted by his mentor Braunwald, Darsee admitted the fabrication; but he insisted that this was the only time he had done this, and that he had been under intense pressure to complete the study quickly. Shocked, Braunwald and Darsee's immediate supervisor, Dr. Robert Kroner, spent the next several months checking other research conducted by Darsee in their lab. Darsee's research fellowships were terminated, and an offer of a faculty position was withdrawn. However, he was allowed to continue his research projects at Harvard for the next several months (during which time Braunwald and Kroner observed his work very closely).

Hopeful that this was an isolated incident, Braunwald and Kroner were shocked again in October. A comparison of results from four different laboratories in a National Heart, Lung and Blood Institute (NHLBI) Models Study revealed an implausibly low degree of invariability in data provided by Darsee. In short, his data looked "too good." Since these data had been submitted in April, there was strong suspicion that Darsee had been fabricating or falsifying data for some time. Subsequent investigations seemed to indicate questionable research practices dating back as far as his undergraduate days.

What were the consequences of John Darsee's misconduct? Darsee, we have seen, lost his research position at Harvard, and his offer of a faculty position was withdrawn. The National Institutes of Health (NIH) barred him from NIH funding or serving on NIH committees for ten years. He left research and went into training as a critical care specialist. However, the cost to others was equally, if not more, severe. Harvard-affiliated Brigham and Women's Hospital became the first institution NIH ever required to return funds ($122,371) because of research involving fraudulent data. Braunwald and his colleagues had to spend several months investigating Darsee's research, rather than simply continuing the work of the Cardiac Research Laboratory. Furthermore, they were severely criticized for carrying on their own investigation without informing NIH of their concerns until several months later. The morale and productivity of the laboratory was damaged. A cloud of suspicion hung over all the work with which Darsee was associated. **Not only was Darsee's own research discredited, but insofar as it formed an integral part of collaborative research, a cloud was thrown over published research bearing the names of authors whose work was linked with Darsee's.**

The months of outside investigation also took others away from their main tasks and placed them under extreme pressure. Statistician David DeMets played a key role in the NIH investigation. Fifteen years later, he recalls the relief his team experienced when their work was completed.

For the author and the junior statistician, there was relief that the episode was finally over and we could get on with our careers, without the pressures of a highly visible misconduct investigation. It was clear early on that we had no room for error, that any mistakes would destroy the case for improbable data and severely damage our careers. Even without mistakes, being able to convince lay reviewers such as a jury using statistical arguments could still be defeating. Playing the role of the prosecuting statisticians was very demanding of our technical skills but also of our own integrity and ethical standards. Nothing could have adequately prepared us for what we experienced.

The most creative minds will not thrive in such an environment and the most promising young people might actually be deterred from embarking on a scientific career in an atmosphere of suspicion. **Second only to absolute truth, science requires an atmosphere of openness, trust, and collegiality.** Given this, it seems that William F. May is right in urging the need for a closer examination of character and virtue in professional life. He says that an important test of character and virtue is what we do when no one is watching. The Darsee case and Brauwald's reflections seem to confirm this. If this is right, then it is important that attention be paid to these matters before college, by which time one's character is rather well set.

The Bruening case

In December 1983, Dr. Robert Sprague wrote an eight page letter, with 44 pages of appendices, to the National Institute of Mental Health (NIMH) documenting the fraudulent research of Dr. Stephen Breuning. Breuning fabricated data concerning the effects psychotropic medication have on mentally retarded patients. Despite Breuning's admission of fabricating data only three months after Sprague sent his letter, the case was not finally resolved until July 1989. (Sprague credits media attention with speeding things along!) During that five and one-half year interval, Sprague himself was a target of investigation (in fact, he was the first target of investigation), he had his own research endeavors severely curtailed, he was subjected to threats of lawsuits, and he had to testify before a United States House of Representatives Committee.

Writing nine years after the closing of the Bruening case, Sprague obviously has vivid memories of the painful experiences he endured and of the potential harms to participants in Bruening's studies. However, he closes the account of his own experiences by reminding us of other victims of Bruening's misconduct—namely, psychologists and other researchers who collaborated with Bruening, but without being aware that he had fabricated data.

Dr. Alan Poling, one of those psychologists, writes about the consequences of Bruening's misconduct for his collaborators in research. Strikingly, Poling points out that between 1979 and 1983, Bruening was a contributor to 34% of all published research on the psychopharmacology of mentally retarded people. For those not involved in the research, initial doubts may, however unfairly, be cast on all these publications. For those involved in the research, efforts need to be made in each case to determine to what extent, if any, the validity of the research was affected by Bruening's role in the study. Even though Bruening was the only researcher to fabricate data, his role could contaminate an entire study. **In fact, however, not all of Bruening's research did involve fabrication. Yet, convincing others of this is a time-consuming, demanding task.** Finally, those who cited Bruening's publications in their own work may also suffer "guilt by association." As Poling points out, this is especially unfair in those instances where Bruening collaborations with others involved no fraud at all.

(THE END)

必备词汇

misconduct / mis'kɔndʌkt / 不法行为，不端行为
infrequent / in'friːkwənt / 罕见的，很少发生的
instance / 'instəns / 实例，情况
consequence / 'kɔnsikwəns / 结果
widespread / 'waidspred, -'spred / 普遍的
distrust / dis'trʌst / 不信任
taint / teint; tent / 污染，感染
distortion / dis'tɔːʃən / 扭曲，曲解
controversy / 'kɔntrəvəːsi / 论争，论战
fabrication / ˌfæbri'keiʃən / 伪造
falsification / ˌfɔːlsifi'keiʃən / 串改，伪造，歪曲
plagiarism / 'pleidʒərizəm / 剽窃
fraud / frɔːd / 欺诈
blatant / 'bleitənt / 俗丽的，炫耀的
deliberate / di'libəreit / 深思熟虑的，故意的
deceive / di'siːv / 欺骗
brilliant / 'briljənt / 有才华的
halt / hɔːlt / 停止，中断
transpire / træns'paiə / 泄露
mentor / 'mentɔː / 导师
fellowship / 'feləuʃip / 奖学金
terminate / 'təːmineit / 停止，终止
observe / əb'zəːv / 观察
suspicion / səs'piʃən / 怀疑，猜疑
undergraduate / ˌʌndə'grædjuit / 大学生
invariability 不变性
ban / bæn / 禁止
morale / mɔ'rɑːl / 士气
discredited 不足信的，不名誉的
relief / ri'liːf / （痛苦的）减轻，安慰
episode / 'episəud / 事件，情节
curtail / kəː'teil / 缩减，剥夺
lawsuit / 'lɔːsuːt, 'lɔːsjuːt / 诉讼
testify / 'testifai / 作证
contaminate / kən'tæmineit / 污染，玷污

重点剖析

— Like lying in general, we may wonder *which* scientific reports are tainted by misconduct, even though we may be convinced that relatively few are. Furthermore, scientists depend on each other's work in advancing their own. Building one's work on the incorrect or unsubstantiated data of others infects one's own research; and the chain of consequences can be quite lengthy, as well as very serious. This is as true of honest or careless mistakes as it is of the intentional distortion of data, which is what *scientific misconduct* is usually restricted to. 就像日常生活中可能怀疑某人撒谎一样，我们可能会怀疑某些科学报告中包含有不实成分，尽管我们深信这种情况极为少见。而且，为了推进自己的研究，科学家们需要彼此依赖对方的成果。把自己的研究建立在别人错误的、站不住脚的数据上，这会影响自己的研究；由此导致的一系列后果很大也很严重。故意歪曲数据资料，就如同有意或无意犯错误，这就是所谓的科学不端行为。

— Hopeful that this was an isolated incident, Braunwald and Kroner were shocked again in October. A comparison of results from four different laboratories in a National Heart, Lung and Blood Institute (NHLBI) Models Study revealed an implausibly low degree of invariability in data provided by Darsee. 本来希望这是一件孤立的事件，但 Braunwald 和 Kroner 在十月份又受了一次震惊。从国家心肺血液学会(NHLBI)模型研究的四个不同实验室查找的结果对比发现，Darsee提供的数据的一致性非常低。

— Not only was Darsee's own research discredited, but insofar as it formed an integral part of collaborative research, a cloud was thrown over published research bearing the names of authors whose work was linked with Darsee's. 不仅Darsee本人的研究让人不相信，而且因为这是联合研究的一个组成部分，刊有和Darsee有关的已发表的研究成果也同样让人怀疑。

— Second only to absolute truth, science requires an atmosphere of openness, trust, and collegiality. 科学需要公开、信任、协作的气氛。这一点很重要，仅次于对绝对真理的追求。

— Writing nine years after the closing of the Bruening case, Sprague obviously has vivid memories of the painful experiences he endured and of the potential harms to participants in Bruening's studies. 在Bruening的案子结束后9年，Sprague写了文章，他对自己经受的痛苦和对Bruening研究的参与者遭受的潜在伤害经历记忆犹新。

— In fact, however, not all of Bruening's research did involve fabrication. Yet, convincing others of this is a time-consuming, demanding task. 然而，实际上不是所有的Bruening的研究都有伪造。但是，说服别人相信这一点是耗时耗力的工作。

（New Version 真题题源）

8. Mathematic Education of Japan

日本的数学教育

Generally speaking, people emphasize that elementary school children should be taught just basic mathematic fundamentals and knowledge, such as basic calculation or understanding the names and the properties of simple diagrams. In such lessons, teachers teach mathematics lessons in a way that children do not think deeply about mathematical matters, that is, children just learn the procedures of calculation, the properties of diagrams, etc. **I am sure that children should learn basic and fundamental skills and knowledge, however, such lessons do not promote interest and appreciation of mathematical learning. I think that children do need to think for themselves and act for themselves through mathematics lessons in addition to mathematic fundamentals.**

Then, how can we foster children's abilities to think and express themselves mathematically? I will present my fundamental ideas and an actual record of lessons.

Add Advanced Learning in Mathematics Curriculum or Develop the Curriculum

Curriculum standards show explicitly minimum essentials that children have to learn in school. **Japanese textbooks are written based on the curriculum standards and it has no extension because of limitation. It is a teacher's responsibility to lead his/her lesson to develop children's thinking beyond the restrictions of the textbook.** Furthermore, we need to plan advanced learning in our mathematics curriculum within limited teaching hours. This means that we should intersperse the curriculum standards with expanded content.

Changing from "Knowledge Pouring-type Lessons" to "Knowledge Creating-type Lessons"

Next, we teachers need to change our views of elementary mathematics lessons. We should try to change from traditional "Knowledge Pouring-type Lessons" to "Knowledge Creating-type Lessons." **Knowledge pouring-type lesson means a traditional and conventional style where teachers give children ready-made mathematics knowledge and concepts in a one-sided way. On the contrary, knowledge creating-type lesson means that children create mathematics knowledge and concepts themselves.** This change is needed for children as well as for teachers. It is important that children feel that learning mathematics is to create new mathematics thinking, while talking about mathematical matters together.

The Way of Thinking about "Knowledge Creating-type Lessons"

The necessary condition to approve "Knowledge Creating-type Lessons" is the thought that elementary mathematics lessons consist of children's constructive activities (the view of constructive learning). Constructive learning is done through children's collaborative and interactive learning about each thought. Therefore, teachers do not explicitly teach children their knowledge and skill but children grasp a problem themselves, pursue, and solve the problem. Thus, they create new knowledge themselves through the learning of problem solving. (But, I do not agree to what is called "New-New Math", overemphasizing constructive learning without basic drills.)

Until now it has been said that such learning is only for advanced children; however, this method could be used to deepen mathematical understanding in low-level children also. The situation where the class includes various types of children all thinking together in mathematics lessons makes it possible to practice knowledge creating-type lessons. That is, in normal classrooms of mixed abilities, we can make use of children's thoughts, developing their learning and creating new knowledge. Because of this we do not need to group children specially.

The Role of Teacher is to Draw Out Children's Thoughts

What is the way to be able to make use of low-level children's thoughts as I stated in the above chapter? It means that children's simple and natural questions and thoughts could be important elements of mathematics lessons. **That is, children's expressions, words, attitudes, and responses could be elements that are integrated into mathematics lessons. Sometimes, children's murmuring and mistakes can be important cues.** The teacher needs the ability to draw out children's expressions and to teach children how to express their thoughts. The teacher has to draw out children's thoughts, listen to them, and let children discuss them together, and by doing so expanding their thoughts. In other words, a teacher would act as a chair presiding over a lesson or as the coordinator of it.

When in a Lesson Children's Mathematical Thinking and Expression Abilities Should be Advanced

Although we might say we can do it in every lesson stage, it is first clear that we can encourage children when they ask questions. Children discover new problems when facing various mathematical teaching materials that the teacher presents in a lesson. When discovering new problems, they have to think about it in many ways and express their thoughts.

Next, their abilities can be developed at the stage where they pursue their problem cooperatively. Then, they have to think out and express their thoughts and solutions. Moreover, to analyze the expression presented also can become a matter to think about together. Therefore, it is important that we teachers lead children to discover other new problems after they solve the previous problem. That is, knowledge creating-type lessons show continuous problem solving from problem to problem. Such lessons make it possible to draw out and encourage children's thinking and expression. The point is that we let children think about and discuss mathematical matters, which can be a method to foster children's mathematical thinking and expression abilities.

Recently, it has been said loudly that we should reform our mathematics education. But frankly speaking, we cannot say it has been very fruitful. Various proposals have been made about how to teach mathematics lessons, however, I have not heard mathematics classroom in school has been actually reformed. **The reason why lesson reform has been less successful may be that teachers have not considered much of**

children's thoughts and feelings in mathematics lessons until now. Therefore, we need to accept and consider children's thinking and expression much more. In other words, we need to reform our lessons into continuous problem solving lessons that foster children's mathematical thinking and expression abilities. Through continuous practising lessons that make children think and express themselves mathematically, children acquire basic skills and knowledge. It is not too much to say that basic mathematic fundamentals can be acquired through advanced learning and developing curriculum standards. Moreover, teachers also need to develop new teaching materials in order to create lessons fostering children's mathematical thinking and expression abilities. It is important that teachers study the subject of mathematics themselves and teach children mathematics creatively.

(THE END)

必备词汇

generally speaking 一般而言
emphasize / ˈemfəsaiz / 强调
elementary school 小学
appreciation / əˌpriːʃiˈeiʃən / 欣赏
foster / ˈfɔstə / 培养
curriculum / kəˈrikjuləm / 课程
explicitly 明确地，明白地
essential / iˈsenʃəl / 要点，实质
textbook / ˈtekstbuk / 教科书，课本
intersperse / ˌintə(ː)ˈspəːs / 散布，点缀
consist of 由……组成
collaborative / kəˈlæbəreitiv / 协作的
interactive / ˌintərˈæktiv / 交互式的
grasp / grɑːsp / 掌握，领会，抓住
overemphasize / ˈəuvəˈemfəsaiz / 过分强调
murmuring 抱怨（的），喃喃声音（的）
cue / kjuː / 暗示，提示
chair / tʃɛə / 主席
preside over 主持
coordinator / kəuˈɔːdineitə / 协调员
pursue / pəˈsjuː / 从事，追求，追踪
frankly speaking 坦白地说
fruitful / ˈfruːtful / 有成效的

重点剖析

— I am sure that children should learn basic and fundamental skills and knowledge, however, such lessons do not promote interest and appreciation of mathematical learning. I think that children do need to think for themselves and act for themselves through mathematics lessons in addition to mathematic fundamentals. 我认为孩子们应该学习基本的技能和知识，但是这样的课程不会促进他们对数学学习的兴趣和欣赏。我觉得孩子们除了掌握数学基础外，确实需要通过数学课程来自行

思考，自行行动。

— Japanese textbooks are written based on the curriculum standards and it has no extension because of limitation. It is a teacher's responsibility to lead his/her lesson to develop children's thinking beyond the restrictions of the textbook. 日本的课本是根据课程标准编写，由于有限制而不含有引申的内容。教师有责任使自己的课能促进孩子的思维发展，以超越课本的限制。

— Knowledge pouring-type lesson means a traditional and conventional style where teachers give children ready-made mathematics knowledge and concepts in a one-sided way. On the contrary, knowledge creating-type lesson means that children create mathematics knowledge and concepts themselves. 知识灌输型课程意味着传统的模式，教师以一边倒的方式把备好的数学知识和概念传授给孩子们。相反，知识创造型课程意味着孩子们自我创造数学知识和概念。

— Until now it has been said that such learning is only for advanced children; however, this method could be used to deepen mathematical understanding in low-level children also. 直到今天，这样的学习还被认为仅为高年级学生准备的。然而，这一方法也可以用来让低年级学生深化对数学的理解。

— That is, children's expressions, words, attitudes, and responses could be elements that are integrated into mathematics lessons. Sometimes, children's murmuring and mistakes can be important cues. 也就是说，孩子们的表情、话语、态度和反应可以作为合成到数学课程中的要素。有时，孩子们的喃喃抱怨声和犯下的错误可以作为重要的提示。

— The reason why lesson reform has been less successful may be that teachers have not considered much of children's thoughts and feelings in mathematics lessons until now. 课程改革很少成功的原因可能是，教师们直到今天还没有在数学课程中太多地考虑孩子们的思想和感受。

(V33真题题源)

9. Educational Level of Mothers in Relation to Children

母亲受教育程度与孩子的关系

Maternal education has been deemed by some the single best predictor of children's later intellectual functioning because of its ability to consistently predict children's cognitive and academic outcomes across different measures and populations. Duncan and Brooks-Gunn coordinated analyses among 12 groups of researchers working with different developmental datasets. Eight of the datasets included measures of both maternal education and children's academic or cognitive outcomes at various points in childhood and adolescence. Analyses conducted with all of these datasets indicated that maternal education was positively and significantly associated with children's cognitive and educational outcomes. For example, Smith, Brooks-Gunn and Klebanov conducted analyses with two samples of young children from different datasets. **They found that maternal education was positively associated with measures of children's intelligence at 2-, 3-, and 5- years of age in the Infant Health and Development Study sample, and children's verbal ability at 3- and 4- years of age, as well as math and reading achievement at 5- and 8-years of age in a sample drawn from the National Longitudinal Survey of Youth.**

Maternal education is associated not only with children's academic achievement,

but also their academic difficulties such as grade retention and special education placement. Both grade retention and special education placement in elementary school are an indication of severe academic problems. **Holloman, Dobbins and Scott found that maternal education was negatively associated with special education placement by 10 years of age, particularly for a learning disability. Children of mothers with less than a high school diploma were twice as likely to be in special education as children of mothers with a high school diploma. Byrd and Weitzman found that children of mothers who did not graduate from high school were 1.4 times more likely to repeat kindergarten or first grade compared to children of mothers who had graduated from high school.** Despite being used as tools for remediation, grade retention and special education placement do not seem to improve, and may even harm, a student's subsequent educational achievement.

Unfortunately, most work in this area cannot attribute the maternal education-child development correlation to mothers' education per se, as opposed to genetic differences or other characteristics that differentiate individuals who acquire different levels of schooling. We know of no studies that link experimental increases in maternal schooling and children's development. Two noteworthy non-experimental studies, both using data from the National Longitudinal Study of Youth (NLSY), take advantage of the fact that young mothers often acquire more formal schooling after the birth of a child, or between the births of first and subsequent children. To estimate whether children's achievement and behavior improved after their mothers returned to school, Kaestner and Corman associated the increases in maternal schooling to children's individual differences in scores on the Peabody Individual Achievement Tests (PIATs) when children were ages 5 and 7 years old.

They found no effect of increased maternal education on children's achievement scores. To estimate whether achievement and behavior differences between earlier- and later-born siblings is related to increases in mother's formal schooling, Rosenzweig and Wolpin associated increases in mother's educational attainment to differences in siblings' scores on achievement tests. **In contrast to the Kaestner and Corman, they found that an additional year of maternal schooling had a modestly positive and marginally significant effect on children's PIAT scores for children ages 5- to 9- years old. Interestingly, they found that mothers' enrollment in school during a child's first three years had a significant and large positive effect on children's scores on the Peabody Picture Vocabulary Test (PPVT), a measure of children's receptive vocabulary, for children ages 3- to 9-years old, but no effect on children's PIAT scores.**

Why might children with more highly educated mothers show higher levels of cognitive development and academic achievement as well as fewer academic problems? Higher levels of maternal education have been associated with higher quality home learning environments and mother-child interactions as well as greater maternal participation in children's schooling. The association between maternal education and teaching strategies may be of particular importance for the early school success of young children. Laosa demonstrated that a mother's educational attainment correlates with her teaching style with her preschool-age children. Specifically, a higher level of education was related to a mother's greater use of verbal reinforcement, inquiry, modeling strategies and reading to children. Although Laosa and others' work provides a theoretical explanation of the effect of maternal education on children's school outcomes, it cannot rule out alternative explanations of the maternal education-child development correlation. Consequently, all told, the spare and inconsistent nature of the evidence makes it impossible to reach conclusions regarding the role of parental education per se in promoting the academic and cognitive development of children.

Although many studies report correlations between maternal education and children's cognitive development, the instrumental variable approach we use provides a more convincing estimation of the causal effect of a mother's education on her children's academic problems and school readiness. We find evidence that increases maternal education improves children's academic outcomes. Experimental comparisons of the control and HCD program groups in each site did not yield significant program impacts on children's academic school readiness, but by pooling data across sites in an instrumental variable analysis we find that an additional month of maternal education is positively associated with children's academic problems and school readiness.

As expected our experimental findings confirmed earlier reports that assignment to the Human Capital Development (HCD) treatment of the JOBS program significantly increased mothers' participation in educational activities. The relative strength of the program impacts varied by the type of educational activity, and the program treatment stream, and we use the variability in these experimentally induced differences in educational activities to estimate IV models.

Current welfare-to-work strategies have eschewed the human capital approach in favor of the work first approach. However, the emphasis on moving mothers into the work force, may also limit their opportunities to improve their basic skills through education. Because maternal education benefits children, policymakers should continue to consider ways and develop ways to improve mothers' education. Our analysis of educational participation among mothers' who were assigned to the NEWWS education treatment stream suggests that increasing a mother's education may be more difficult than previously considered. Consequently, policymakers should consider a variety of ways to increase maternal education in combination with employment, but also through other programs and policies.

(THE END)

必备词汇

maternal / mə'tə:nl / 母亲的
deem / di:m / 认为，相信
predictor / pri'diktə / 预言者，预报器
intellectual functioning 智力机能
cognitive / 'kɔgnitiv / 认知的
dataset / 'deitə,set / 数据集
childhood / 'tʃaildhud / 儿童期
adolescence / ,ædəu'lesəns / 青春期，青少年期
grade retention 留级
special education placement 特殊教育编班
learning disability 学习障碍
remediation / ,ri,midi'eiʃən / 补习
sibling / 'sibliŋ / 兄弟，姐妹
attainment / ə'teinmənt / 造诣，才能
in contrast to 与……相比
correlate with 和……相关
preschool-age children 学龄前儿童
reinforcement / ,ri:in'fɔ:smənt / 加强，强化
strategy / 'strætidʒi / 策略
per se 自身，本身
promote / prə'məut / 促进
convincing / kən'vinsiŋ / 令人信服的
instrumental variable approach 工具变量方法
readiness / 'redinis / 准备就绪
variability / ,vɛəriə'biliti / 可变性
eschew / is'tʃu: / 避开，远避

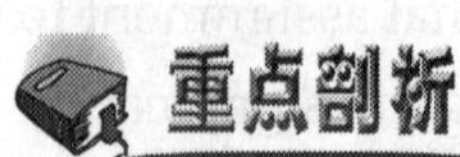

重点剖析

— Maternal education has been deemed by some the single best predictor of children's later intellectual functioning because of its ability to consistently predict children's cognitive and academic outcomes across different measures and populations. 用不同测量方法在不同人群中所进行的研究一致表明，母亲的受教育程度可以预测儿童的认知能力和学习成就，因此有人认为它是儿童将来智力表现好坏唯一最好的预测源。

— They found that maternal education was positively associated with measures of children's intelligence at 2-, 3-, and 5- years of age in the Infant Health and Development Study sample, and children's verbal ability at 3- and 4-years of age, as well as math and reading achievement at 5- and 8-years of age in a sample drawn from the National Longitudinal Survey of Youth. 他们发现，在"幼儿健康和发展研究"样本中，母亲的受教育程度和孩子2、3和5岁时的智力表现呈正相关。在从"国家青少年纵向调查研究"抽取的样本中发现，孩子在3、4岁时的表达能力、在5岁和8岁时的数学成绩和阅读成绩也和母亲的受教育程度呈正相关关系。

— Maternal education is associated not only with children's academic achievement, but also their academic difficulties such as grade retention and special education placement. 母亲的受教育程度不仅和孩子的学业成绩有关，而且和他们的学业困难如留级和特殊教育编班也有关系。

— Holloman, Dobbins and Scott found that maternal education was negatively associated with special education placement by 10 years of age, particularly for a learning disability. Children of mothers with less than a high school diploma were twice as likely to be in special education as children of mothers with a high school diploma. Byrd and Weitzman found that children of mothers who did not graduate from high school were 1.4 times more likely to repeat kindergarten or first grade compared to children of mothers who had graduated from high school. Holloman. Dobbins 和 Scott 发现，母亲的受教育程度与孩子10岁前被编入特殊教育班呈负相关。孩子被编入特殊教育班，主要是因为他们有学习障碍。受教育程度低于高中的母亲，她们的孩子进入特教班的几率是持有高中文凭的母亲们的孩子的两倍。Byrd 和Weitzman发现，受教育程度低于高中的母亲，她们的孩了在幼儿园或 一年级复读的可能性1.4倍于那些读过高中的母亲的孩子们。

— In contrast to the Kaestner and Corman, they found that an additional year of maternal schooling had a modestly positive and marginally significant effect on children's PIAT scores for children ages 5- to 9- years old. Interestingly, they found that mothers' enrollment in school during a child's first three years had a significant and large positive effect on children's scores on the Peabody Picture Vocabulary Test (PPVT), a measure of children's receptive vocabulary, for children ages 3- to 9-years old, but no effect on children's PIAT scores. 与Kaestner 和 Corman 的研究相比，他们（Rosenzweig和Wolpin）发现母亲多上一年学对孩子5~9岁在Peabody个体成就测验（PIAT）上的得分有中等程度的积极影响，且这一效用达到了边缘显著水平。他们另一个有意思的研究结果是，母亲在孩子3岁前参加学校教育，会对孩子在Peabody图片词汇测验（PPVI，用来测试儿童对词汇的理解能力）上的得分有显著正效用，但对孩子3~9岁时的PIAT得分无影响。

— Why might children with more highly educated mothers show higher levels of cognitive development and academic achievement as well as fewer academic problems?

Higher levels of maternal education have been associated with higher quality home learning environments and mother-child interactions as well as greater maternal participation in children's schooling. 因为母亲的受教育水平越高，其家庭学习环境可能就更优越，母子沟通得就越好，母亲就会更多地参与到孩子的学习中。

(V17真题题源)

10. Painting Courses

绘 画 课 程

Drawing & painting

WNYOCN Levels 1, 2 and 3

WNYOCN Visual Analysis Drawing and Painting Levels 1, 2 and 3 and Drawing and Painting Levels 1, 2 and 3

The WNYOCN PT Art & Design course in this information guide is studied as part of a larger unitized programme offered in the pathways set out at the beginning of this cluster leaflet. **Through study of appropriate subjects and levels, this can enable you to consider further education and training in Art, Craft & Design Levels 2 & 3. Please Note: Should you wish to be considered for this course/programme you may be required to speak to a tutor prior to enrolling onto this course of study.** Should you require any further advice or guidance please contact Student Services.

How long does the course last and what is the main pattern of attendance?

One morning per week for 36 weeks over 3 terms.

Programme Content

The aim of the course is to provide students with the knowledge required to develop an individual approach to various themes of study. The early part of the course is tightly structured and directed giving way to a greater emphasis to the students' individual approach.

Themes to be covered will be broad and flexible:-

- Methods and materials in Art & Design ? Abstract and figurative compositions
- Still life · Art appreciation - Gallery visits
- The human figure · Display and presentation
- Individual objects · Self directed study, e.g. a sketch book
- Landscapes

Course consists of:

- Class contact time and tutorial input and instruction, tutor set assignments, individual tuition within a workshop/studio setting.
- Self-directed study - sketchbook/notebook, assignment research.

What qualifications or experience do I need to be accepted on the course?

Level 1

Students who do not meet the normal entry requirements can gain entry on to this course if they have appropriate commitment, experience or a mixture of work experience and qualifications.
Students gaining entry to this course will have some basic level of achievement eg. Entry level, grades E to F GCSE, ASDAN, NOCN.
All applicants will be able to demonstrate some progress in Maths and English.

Level 2

Students who do not have the normal entry qualifications can gain entry to this course if they have appropriate experience or a mixture of work experience and qualifications.

Normally students gaining entry to this course will hold as a minimum: either 3 GCSE D grades; or equivalent levels of qualifications including GNVQ Foundation, NVQ 1, other level 1 equivalent qualifications eg. ASDAN, NOCN, GNVQ Part 1 (Foundation). All applicants will be able to demonstrate some progress in Maths and English.

Level 3

Students who do not have the normal entry qualifications can gain entry to this course if they have appropriate experience or a mixture of work experience and qualifications. Normally students gaining entry to this course will hold as a minimum: either 4 GCSE grades at C or above; or equivalent levels of qualifications including GNVQ Intermediate, First Diploma / Certificate; NVQ 2, other Level 2 equivalent qualifications e.g. ASDAN, NOCN, GNVQ Part 1 (Intermediate).
All applicants will be able to demonstrate some progress in Maths and English.

What will the course cost?

Please see the course guide for up-to-date details of course fees, concessions, methods of payment and enrolment details. In addition to this there may be some additional costs for books, materials, residentials. Please ask at enrolment.

How will I be assessed and how often?

Assessment is by a mark/checklist at the end of each term, group appraisals, tutorials and discussions, self assessment, advice and guidance on a one to one basis.

On completion of the course where do most students move on to?

It is hoped that students will progress from one level to another enabling students to build a portfolio of work either to apply to a range of BTEC courses or other WNYOCN courses that will be offered or on to HNC Fine Art courses.

Achievement and Retention figures

For those students who completed the course at Levels 1, 2 & 3 the achievement was 100%, retention was 87%.

What qualifications will I get at the end?

4 credits.

Accommodation:

Course participants can book their accommodation at our campus or may attend as

a non-resident on a daily basis. Non-painters are also welcome to stay in the campus. The campus retains the atmosphere and character of the old family home built at the turn of the last century by John's great grandfather, Thomas Madigan. During the past 30 years John and Chris O'Neill have devoted much of their attention to upgrading the facilities for the comfort of their guests. The private car park, adjacent to the studio at the rear of the house provides secure guest parking.

SuppliesandEquipment:

A supply of art materials is available for sale each morning in the studio at 9:45 a.m. **Stools and easels may be hired at a reasonable charge and should be pre-booked to ensure availability. The studio also provides a welcome retreat for indoor work and is accessible from early morning until late evening.** Tea and coffee making facilities and art magazines are also provided for your enjoyment.

(THE END)

必备词汇

flexible / 'fleksəbl / 灵活的
assignment / ə'sainmənt / 作业
sketchbook 写生簿
entry requirement 入学要求
equivalent level 相当的水平
concession / kən'seʃ ən / 折扣
residentials / ˌrezi'denʃəri / 住宿
welcome retreat 研讨会
assessment / ə'sesmənt / 评估
intermediate / ˌintə'miːdjət / 中级
mark / mɑːk / 分数
check list 清单
credit / 'kredit / 学分
studio / 'stjuːdiəu / 画室
stool / stuːl / 长凳
easel / 'iːzl / 画架

重点剖析

— Through study of appropriate subjects and levels, this can enable you to consider further education and training in Art, Craft & Design. 通过学习合适的科目和等级，可使你进一步考虑在艺术、工艺和设计方面的培训和教育。

— Should you wish to be considered for this course/programme you may be required to speak to a tutor prior to enrolling onto this course of study. 如果你想参加本课程，需要在注册前向一名指导教师咨询。

— Please see the course guide for up-to-date details of course fees, concessions, methods of payment and enrolment details. In addition to this there may be some additional costs for books, materials, residentials. Please ask at enrolment. 请查询课程指南了解课程学费、折扣、支付方法和注册详情等最新信息。除了这些费用外，书本、教材、住宿还要额外收费。请在注册时咨询。

— Assessment is by a mark/checklist at the end of each term, group appraisals, tutorials and discussions, self assessment, advice and guidance on a one to one basis. 根据每学期期末的分数/清单、小组评估、指导和讨论、自我评估、建议和指导来进行评定，对各个学生分别进行。

— For those students who completed the course at Levels 1, 2 & 3 the achievement was 100%, retention was 87%. 完成1、2、3级课程的学生，通过率为100%，升学率为87%。

— Course participants can book their accommodation at our campus or may attend as a non-resident on a daily basis. 课程参加者可以预定我们校园内的住宿，也可以以走读生身份参加。

— Stools and easels may be hired at a reasonable charge and should be pre-booked to ensure availability. The studio also provides a welcome retreat for indoor work and is accessible from early morning until late evening. 可以租用长凳和画架，收费合理，但应提前预订确保有空闲设备提供。画室还给室内作品提供研讨会，从一早到较晚都可以。

（V23真题题源）

11. How to Improve Your Reading Speed

如何提高阅读速度

We all have a capacity for reading much faster than we typically do. Our reading speed changes as we go through life. When we are in high school, we go through about two hundred words a minute. We get to college and, because we have to read faster due to more time constraints and a much greater amount to read, we read faster. Most people in college average about 400 words per minute. Then we get out of college, and now we don't have to read so fast. There are no longer time constraints, and we can read slow and easy. We find ourselves dropping back down to about 200 words per minute.

Think of reading like you do a muscle, the more you read, the better you get at it, the faster you're going to read. And we have a great capacity for reading faster. We aren't even scraping the surface of how fast we can read. You see, we have 1,000,000,000,000 brain cells. In fact, the inner connections, the synapses, in our mind are virtually infinite. It has been estimated by a Russian scientist that the number of synapses we have would be one followed by 10 million kilometers of zeros. **Our physical capacity for reading**

is beyond our comprehension. Our visual unit has the capability to take in a full page of text in 1/20 of a second. If we could turn the pages fast enough, our brain could process it faster than our eyes can see it. If we could turn those pages fast enough, our eyes have the capacity to read a standard book in six to twenty-five seconds depending on the length of the book. We could take in the entire Encyclopedia Britannica in one hour. So reading 700-1,000 words a minute is easily within our reach.

The key to improving our speed is to SIGHT READ, and that's what we are going to show you how to do. We are going to start being pure sight readers. Obstacles get in our way, however. What do we mean by obstacles? Well, these are things that impede us from reading faster.

REGRESSIONS are the most wasteful. **Regressions are going back over words. You can call it backskipping if you want.** You go back over words you previously read. People do it for two reasons. Initially we read it to clarify the meaning of what we're reading. We want to be sure of the words we read as we go along. In our early years in school, when we were first taught—incorrectly—to "read slowly and carefully," it became easy to go back over words.

Well, this not only slows you down, it causes you comprehension problems. For instance, let's say you have a sentence, "The man jumped over the log". Well, if you back-skip, you read that passage like this: "The man jumped", "the man . . . jumped. . . over the log", "jumped over the log". So, what your brain is processing, "The man jumped", "the man jumped", "jumped over the log". Our brain is used to processing our flaws, so the brain thinks, OK, I know what this clown is saying, "The man jumped over the log". But this takes time to sort out. And it's confusing. Think how much easier it would be if you simply took the sentence in one sight", The man jumped over the log. "There's no confusion there. Then you move on to the next phrase. **Regressing or back-skipping is the most harmful thing we do to slow our reading speed.**

Our second obstacle is that we have BAD HABITS that we pick up. Bad habits manifest themselves in a number of ways. For one, you've got people who have MOTOR habits as they read. These are the people who are tapping a pencil when they read, tapping a foot when they read, moving a book, flicking their hand, etc. If they're sitting next to you, they drive you nuts. But they are the people who have to be moving while they read.

Some may even move their lips. If they do that, they're a kind of edging over into another bad habit where we find AUDITORY readers. This is the bad habit that we have that is the hardest to drop. Auditory reading is difficult to beat because we are used to reading and hearing the words in our minds. Some people even go so far as to mumble the words. You can see their lips moving sometimes, or you can even hear a guttural growl as they go through the words.

The other obstacle are the FIXATIONS. Fixations are the actual stops or pauses between eye-spans when the eye is moving to its next fixation point. **We can't see while the eye moves so you do need the fixation points to see. The problem is, most people fixate word by word by word. They stop their eyes on each separate word. The fixations slow you down because you are stopping on each word.**

The problem that comes up here is this that, like the other obstacles, it impedes concentration and comprehension as well. The paradox with reading slowly is that it really hurts your concentration.

Research has shown a close relation between speed and understanding. **In checking progress charts of thousands of individuals taking reading training, it's been found that in the vast majority of cases, that an increase in speed reading rate has also been paralleled by an increase in comprehension. The plodding word-by-word analyzation actually reduces comprehension.**

In this day and age, our brains are used to constant stimulation. Television, radio, even people talking to you, provide constant stimulation. So when we are reading along slowly and carefully, it's kind of like watching a movie and we encounter a slow motion scene. The slow motion scene is a kind of interesting at first because the movie has been moving along at a rapid clip and now we have a change of pace. We've got the slow motion scene of the guy getting shot or the couple running across to each other across a field, and the mind initially says, "Oh, this is cool. This is something different." After a while we get a little impatient and we're ready for the guy who got shot to hit the ground, or the couple who are running across the field to finally get to each other. We start thinking about other things...we've lost our focus on the movie.

The brain does the same thing when we read. The brain is getting all the stimulation it normally gets, then we hit this patch where you're reading slowly. And boom, the brain says, "I don't like this. I think I'm going to start thinking about something else." And the reader starts thinking about the date they had Saturday night or the date they hope to have Saturday night. And therefore, you've got another impediment to comprehending the reading correctly.

OK, what do we do? Well, there are several things we are going to do to increase reading speed. First of all. we are going to increase the EYE SPAN. Eye span is the number of words that you take in as you look at the words. In other words, if my eye span is just one word, I am going to move from word to word to word. If my eye span is two words, I am going to move along twice as fast. If my eye span is three words, three times as fast. If I am moving along in phrases, I'm flying along pretty good.

That's where you increase the rate of eye span. You also want to learn to work in THOUGHT UNITS. Thought units help you move faster. This is where you group the words according to context. For instance, let's say you have, "He said something." It's easy to put that in a phrase, then you move to the next phrase. If I had this sentence, "It's safe to say that almost anyone can double his speed of reading while maintaining equal or higher comprehension." If I want to read that in phrases, "It's safe to say that almost anyone...can double his speed...of reading while maintaining...equal or even higher comprehension." You move much faster that way.

So, we are going to increase the number of words we see and we are going to group them according to context. One of the key things that we are also going to work on is RETURN EYE SWEEP. When you get to the end of the sentence or the end of the line on the written page, if your eye meanders back to the other side, you have a chance to pick up words. If you're picking up words and you're sight reading, that can be confusing. So you want to dramatically, quickly, forcefully, go from the end of one line to the beginning of the next one. **Using a fingertip or pen as a pointer is a great way to quickly and directly to the next line.**

The other thing that helps us increase our speed is CONFIGUATION. As you read faster and faster, you've got to learn to rely on your increased recognition of how words are configured, how they look, as you do it. In other words, "material" looks different than "response". "Recognition" looks different than "perceptual". The words have visual configurations. As you learn to read faster and faster you learn to pick up on the configurations and, as you do better and better, your skills at this improve with practice.

A good place to practice this is magazines or newspapers. They have narrow columns that almost make a perfect thought unit. You can almost go straight down the column, taking that finger and putting it in the middle of the column and moving it straight down the page. **You will be stunned how soon you will be able to improve and comprehend what you are reading that way.** You find that it's quick. It's easy reading.

(THE END)

必备词汇

capacity / kə'pæsiti / 能力，容量
constraint 限制
scrape / skreip / 刮，擦
virtually / 'vɜːtjuəli / 事实上
infinite / 'infinit / 无限的
inner connection 内在联系
synapse / si'næps / 神经键
estimate / 'estimeit / 估计
sight read 扫读
obstacle / 'ɔbstəkl / 障碍，阻碍
impede / im'piːd / 阻止
regression / ri'greʃən / 退回，倒退
back-skip 回读
clarify / 'klærifai / 澄清
flaw / flɔː / 缺点，缺陷
sort out 分类，拣选
confusing 混乱的
manifest / 'mænifest / 表现，证明
tap / tæp / 轻拍，轻扣
flick / flik / 弹，拍
mumble / 'mʌmbl / 喃喃自语
guttural growl 喉咙发音
fixation / fik'seiʃən / 注视，凝视
paradox / 'pærədɔks / 似是而非的论点
plodding / 'plɔdiŋ / 单调的
stimulation / ˌstimju'leiʃən / 刺激，激励
focus / 'fəukəs / 注意力
eye span 视力跨度
thought unit 思考单位
context / 'kɔntekst / 上下文
meander / mi'ændə / 蜿蜒，弯曲
rely on 依靠
perceptual / pə'septjuəl / 有知觉的
stun / stʌn / 使晕倒，使惊奇

重点剖析

— We all have a capacity for reading much faster than we typically do. Our reading speed changes as we go through life. When we are in high school, we go through about two hundred words a minute. We get to college and, because we have to read faster due to more time constraints and a much greater amount to read, we read faster. 我们每个人都有能力比通常阅读得更快。我们的阅读速度随年龄而不断变化。上高中时，一分钟可以读大约200单词。上大学后，由于有更多的时间限制有更多的资料需要阅读，这就需要我们读得更快一些，所以我们就读得快了。

— Think of reading like you do a muscle, the more you read, the better you get at it, the faster you're going to read. 把阅读想作是肌肉运动，你练习得越多，就会读得越快。

— Our physical capacity for reading is beyond our comprehension. Our visual unit has the capability to take in a full page of text in 1/20 of a second. If we could turn the pages fast enough, our brain could process it faster than our eyes can see it. If we could turn those pages fast enough, our eyes have the capacity to read a standard book in six to twenty-five seconds depending on the length of the book. We could take in the entire Encyclopedia Britannica in one hour. So reading 700~1,000 words a minute is easily within our reach. 我们进行阅读的生理机能快得不可思议。我们的视觉单元能在二十分之一秒内读完一整页文章。如果翻书的速度足够快，则我们的大脑处理得将比眼睛看得要更快。根据书的厚度，如果我们翻书足够快，则眼睛能在6~25秒内读完一本标准厚度的书。1小时内，我们可以读完整整一本《大不列颠百科全书》。所以1分钟阅读700~1000单词简直是小菜一碟。

— Regressions are going back over words. You can call it back-skipping if you want. 退回指返回去读单词。又叫回读。

— Regressing or back-skipping is the most harmful thing we do to slow our reading speed. 退回或回读是阅读中最有害的东西，因为这将放慢阅读速度。

— Our second obstacle is that we have BAD HABITS that we pick up. 阅读的第二障碍是我们养成的一些坏习惯。

— Some may even move their lips. If they do that, they're a kind of edging over into another bad habit where we find AUDITORY readers. This is the bad habit that we have that is the hardest to drop. 有些人甚至阅读时嘴唇在动。这样做，他们就有了另一个坏习惯，这个坏习惯存在于有声阅读者中。这个坏习惯是我们最难丢掉的。

— We can't see while the eye moves so you do need the fixation points to see. The problem is, most people fixate word by word by word. They stop their eyes on each separate word. The fixations slow you down because you are stopping on each word. 眼睛移动时我们看不见东西，所以你确实需要凝视一下要看的内容。但问题是，大多数人是一个字一个字地注视着。他们把目光停留在每一个单词上。凝视使阅读速度放慢了，因为你在每个字上面都要停留。

— In checking progress charts of thousands of individuals taking reading training, it's been found that in the vast majority of cases, that an increase in speed reading rate has also been paralleled by an increase in comprehension. 在考察几万名参加阅读训练的人的进展曲线时，调查人员发现大部分阅读速度提高的人其理解能力也同步增强。

— So, we are going to increase the number of words we see and we are going to group them according to context. 所以，我们要增加看到的字数，并根据上下文来分类。

— Using a fingertip or pen as a pointer is a great way to quickly and directly to the next line. 用指尖或铅笔作为指示器来快速直接地移动到下一行是一个不错的方法。

— You will be stunned how soon you will be able to improve and comprehend what you are reading that way. 用这些方法来阅读，你会惊奇地发现，很快你将会提高阅读速度，理解能力也增强了！

（V28真题题源）

12. Reform of University Teaching

大学教学方法改革

Good university teaching is important. It improves the quality of students' learning, enables them to develop the skills of lifelong learning, and enhances the capacity of graduates to contribute to the well-being of the society in which they live. In the last few years higher education has expanded to include a wider range of students; at the same time, there is an unprecedented emphasis on the quality of provision. This is an opportune time to address the question of how to encourage and reward good teaching.

There is a widespread perception among academics that universities do not properly recognise good teaching. Many staffs feel that their colleagues overlook the effort that they put into teaching; most of the rewards, they say, including promotion, seem to go to those who perform well in research. Most academics would agree that universities regard research as a high status activity. Good research work, it seems, can be reliably identified and is suitably rewarded. In contrast, it is widely believed that good teaching is both harder to identify and less likely to lead to rewards.

What might be needed to change the perception that teaching and research are not accorded equal recognition in today's universities? The answer will depend in part on academic staff themselves seeing convincing evidence that good teaching can be identified reliably and consistently rewarded. It will also depend on providing university decision-makers with methods which they might use to acknowledge and advance good teaching. The purpose of this project was to examine existing policies and practices for recognising teaching, and to suggest processes that might make it easier for universities to identify good teaching, support good teaching, and reward good teaching. In the longer term the project's recommendations may encourage a movement towards an academic culture in Australian universities where both teaching and research are valued and recognised as equally important academic functions.

Whatever the pressures towards pre-eminence of research in the modern university, there is an unquestionably room for greater valuing of academics as teachers, for elevating the importance accorded to teaching, and for demonstrating that an academic's professional commitment to his or her students' learning is recognised and appropriately rewarded. Greater valuing of teaching might make for more fruitful interaction between research and teaching. The benefits of greater valuing of teaching would flow to students, to graduates, to employers, and to institutions, as well as to the academics themselves.

In recent years there has been a growing movement to revitalise the status of teaching as an important university function, and a central aspect of the academic profession. **Appointments and promotions have been said for many years to be too dependent on research in UK and Australian universities. Students and employers have continued to criticise the quality of undergraduate teaching. Funding for Australian universities has been increasingly linked to performance and innovation in teaching; institutions have introduced more opportunities for academic staff development in teaching and have increasingly provided incentives to perform highly in teaching such as teaching awards.**

Good teaching may take a variety of forms. The following list includes those qualities that researchers generally agree are essential to good teaching at all levels of education:

* Good teachers are also good learners; for example, they learn through their own reading, by participating in a variety of professional development activities, by listening to their students, by sharing ideas with their colleagues, and by reflecting on classroom interactions and students' achievements. Good teaching is therefore dynamic, reflective and constantly evolving.
* Good teachers display enthusiasm for their subject, and a desire to share it with

their students.

* Good teachers recognise the importance of context, and adapt their teaching accordingly; they know how to modify their teaching strategies according to the particular students, subject matter, and learning environment.
* **Good teachers encourage deep learning approaches, rather than surface approaches, and are concerned with developing their students' critical thinking skills, problem-solving skills, and problem-approach behaviours.**
* Good teachers demonstrate an ability to transform and extend knowledge, rather than merely transmitting it; they draw on their knowledge of their subject, their knowledge of their learners, and their general pedagogical knowledge to transform the concepts of the discipline into terms that are understandable to their students. In other words, they display what Shulman has termed "pedagogical content knowledge".
* Good teachers set clear goals, use valid and appropriate assessment methods, and provide high quality feedback to their students.
* Good teachers show respect for their students; they are interested in both their professional and their personal growth, encourage their independence, and sustain high expectations of them.

Evidence suggests that, at many higher education institutions, the only primary data that are systematically collected to evaluate teaching are student evaluations. Gibbs noted that the compulsory use of student feedback questionnaires is increasing in the UK. In addition, it is estimated that student evaluations have been the object of more research studies than all of the other data used in the evaluation of all aspects of academic work. These studies have generally found student evaluations to be reliable, valid and relatively unbiased, and to be sources of helpful information to guide teachers' professional development.

(THE END)

必备词汇

unprecedented /ʌn'presidəntid/ 空前的
emphasis /'emfəsis/ 重视
a wider range of 各种各样的
opportune /'ɔpətjuːn, ˌɔpə't-/ 适宜的
overlook /ˌəuvə'luk/ 忽略
promotion /prə'məuʃən/ 晋升，提拔
in contrast 与……对比
revitalize /'riː'vaitəlaiz/ 振兴
undergraduate /ˌʌndə'grædjuit/ 大学生
innovation /ˌinəu'veiʃən/ 革新，创新

incentive / in'sentiv / 激励
pedagogical / pedə'gɔdʒikəl / 教学的
systematically /sistə'mætikəli/ 系统地
evaluation / i,vælju'eiʃən / 评估
questionnaire / ˌkwestiə'nɛə, -tʃə- / 问卷
reliable / ri'laiəbl / 可信赖的
unbiased / 'ʌn'baiəst / 无偏见的

重点剖析

— There is a widespread perception among academics that universities do not properly recognise good teaching. Many staffs feel that their colleagues overlook the effort that they put into teaching; most of the rewards, they say, including promotion, seem to go to those who perform well in research. 学术界有一个普遍的看法，就是大学没有正确地认可良好的教学。许多教师感到同事对他们投入教学的努力视而不见。他们说，大多数奖金包括晋升似乎是给了那些在科研上做得好的人员。

— Appointments and promotions have been said for many years to be too dependent on research in UK and Australian universities. Students and employers have continued to criticise the quality of undergraduate teaching. Funding for Australian universities has been increasingly linked to performance and innovation in teaching; institutions have introduced more opportunities for academic staff development in teaching and have increasingly provided incentives to perform highly in teaching such as teaching awards. 据说，在英国和澳大利亚的大学里，任职和晋升多年来太过依赖科研成果。学生和雇主一直在批评大学教学质量。对澳大利亚大学资金的拨付正不断和教学的成绩和革新挂钩 ；机构为教师的教学发展引入了更多的机会，不断向那些时教学高度负责的人员提供激励，如教学奖。

— Good teachers encourage deep learning approaches, rather than surface approaches, and are concerned with developing their students' critical thinking skills, problem-solving skills, and problem-approach behaviours. 好的老师鼓励深度学习，而不是肤浅的学习，关心发展学生的批判性思维技巧、问题解决技能及问题解决行为。

— These studies have generally found student evaluations to be reliable, valid and relatively unbiased, and to be sources of helpful information to guide teachers' professional development. 这些研究一致发现，学生的评估可靠、有效、相对来说没有偏见，是指导教师职业发展的有用信息来源。

（New version 真题题源）

13. Research Shows Students Who Begin School in Small Classes Have an Edge

小班授课的优越性

Students beginning school in small classes continue to benefit many years later and outscore other students in high school mathematics, according to new research co-authored by scholars at the University.

"Mathematics achievement is often characterized as a gatekeeper for college admission, a critical filter restricting choice of majors and a significant predictor of overall college success," said Larry Hedges, the Stella M. Rowley Professor in Sociology and one of the authors of the study. He added that mathematics achievement also is an important predictor of how much income people earn throughout their careers.

The differences are particularly striking for minority students, the researchers found. The study was based on a statewide experiment in Tennessee in which teachers and students had been randomly assigned to small (13-17 students) and regular-sized (22-26 students) classrooms from kindergarten through third grade. **Minority students who had been in small classes from kindergarten through thirdgrade received scores**

that were 7.26 points higher than students who were in regular-sized classes.

Among whites, the students in small classes from kindergarten through third grade scored 3.91 points higher on standardized mathematics tests than students who had been in a regular-sized class. Among boys overall, the small class advantage was 4.69 points, and among girls it was 6.22 points.

The results are reported in "The Long-Term Effects of Small Classes in the Early Grades: Lasting Benefits in Mathematics Achievement at Grade 9" published in the current issue of the *Journal of Experimental Education*. Barbara Nye, Executive Director of the Center of Excellence for Research and Policy on Basic Skills at Tennessee State University and Syros Konstantopoulos, a researcher at Chicago, are the additional authors of the study.

Other studies have pointed to benefits for students in small classes, but "The Long-Term Effects of Small Classes in the Early Grades: Lasting Benefits in Mathematics Achievement at Grade 9" is the first study to track the impact of early small class size on high school mathematics achievement, which is an important predictor of future success, Hedges said.

Nye said the results point to an important lasting effect of early intervention. Efforts to improve educational achievement in the early grades are often successful, but usually fail to provide lasting benefits for students, she pointed out.

"Unlike other early education interventions, these effects persisted for several years after the children returned to regular-sized classes. Our analyses suggest that class size effects persist for at least six years and remain large enough to be important for educational policy," she added.

The scholars also studied students who received less than the full four years of small classes. The study found that these students also benefited from the experience, although the gains were larger for students who had the full four years of small classes.

It was not clear from the data why minority students benefited more from the experience of small class sizes. Teachers were not surveyed on their teaching styles.

Hedges said the researchers think small class sizes are effective because they provide opportunities for more individualized instruction. "For example, with small classes, teachers can identify and remedy incipient problems among students at risk for low achievement," he said.

Nye added, "Small classes may make existing instruction more effective. For example, small classes may lead to fewer disruptions and more time on academic instruction or more effective whole-class instruction."

The small class size experiment was initiated in the early 1980s in Tennessee in an effort by state legislators to determine if class size has an impact on learning. The random assignment, which did not group students according to race, social background or ability, provides much more reliable information than do other studies of class size, the researchers said.

All state schools were invited to participate in the program, called Project STAR (Student-Teacher Achievement Ratio). The program enrolled 79 elementary schools in 42 school districts, and students were tested periodically throughout the study and thereafter.

(THE END)

必备词汇

outscore / aut'skɔː / 得分超过

co-author 合作者

gatekeeper / 'geit,kiːpə(r) / 守门人，看家宝

predictor / pri'diktə / 预测源

striking / 'straikiŋ / 显著的，惊人的

randomly 随机地

regular-sized classrooms 普通人数的班级

intervention / ˌintə(ː)'venʃən / 干预

persist / pə(ː)'sist / 持续

individualized 个性化的

disruption / dis'rʌpʃən / 中断，破坏

initiate / i'niʃieit / 开始，发起

legislator / 'ledʒisˌleitə / 立法者

impact / 'impækt / 冲击，影响

participate in 参加

periodically /ˌpiəri'ɔdikəli/ 周期性地，定期地

重点剖析

— Students beginning school in small classes continue to benefit many years later and outscore other students in high school mathematics, according to new research co-authored by scholars at the University. 根据本大学学者们的最新调查，上学时参加小班的学生在后来许多年的学习中继续受益，在高中数学考试中得分高于其他学生。

— The differences are particularly striking for minority students, the researchers found. 研究者发现，少数民族学生中的差异非常显著。

— Minority students who had been in small classes from kindergarten through third grade received scores that were 7.26 points higher than students who were in regular-sized classes. 参加小班的少数民族学生从幼儿园到三年级取得的分数比参加普通规模班的学生的分数高7.26分。

— Among whites, the students in small classes from kindergarten through third grade scored 3.91 points higher on standardized mathematics tests than students who had been in a regular-sized class. Among boys overall, the small class advantage was 4.69 points, and among girls it was 6.22 points. 在白人学生中，从幼儿园一直到三年级都在小班上学的学生在标准数学考试中得分比参加普通规模班的学生高出3.91分。参加小班的男学生的分数比参加普通规模班的男学生分数高出4.69分，小班的女学生的得分超过普通规模班女学生分数6.22分。

— Nye said the results point to an important lasting effect of early intervention. Efforts to improve educational achievement in the early grades are often successful, but usually fail to provide lasting benefits for students, she pointed out. Nye说道，研究结果说明早期干预具有重要而持续的影响。在低年级时提高学习成绩的努力一般是成功的，但这通常不能使学生受益持续。

— It was not clear from the data why minority students benefited more from the experience of small class sizes. Teachers were not surveyed on their teaching styles. 从数据中看不出为什么少数民族学生从小班教学中受益会更多。研究中没有关注老师们的教学风格。

— Hedges said the researchers think small class sizes are effective because they provide opportunities for more individualized instruction. Hedges说，研究人员认为小班是有效的，因为小班可以为学生提供更多得到个人指导的机会。

— The small class size experiment was initiated in the early 1980s in Tennessee in an effort by state legislators to determine if class size has an impact on learning. 小班教学实验在田纳西州开始于20世纪90年代初期，是州立法人员们为确定班级人数是否对学习有影响而进行的。

（V18 真题题源）

14. Student Clubs

学生俱乐部

（第1篇）

An important part of college life is the personal enrichment students gain outside the classroom through student activities. Getting involved in campus activities gives students many educational experiences, leadership opportunities and the chance to interact with other students and faculty/staff members in an informal setting.

Seven organizations serve all members of the campus community. More than thirty clubs offer students the opportunity to explore special interests. Many of these clubs are directly affiliated with fields of study and augment classroom experiences.

In addition, art exhibits, dance productions, dramatic presentations, musical productions, and performances by guest artists are sponsored throughout the year. The Community Band is open to all residents who are experienced instrumentalists.

Formation of Clubs

If you are looking for an activity or club and you don't see it here, Mercer welcomes the opportunity to start new clubs. **To charter a club, you need a membership list of**

at least 10 students, a faculty advisor and a constitution. Student Government Association (SGA) and Student Activities staff members will help prepare the constitution. Once these requirements are met, the SGA will vote to charter the club at its next scheduled meeting.

Student Clubs

AA Step

Gives members the opportunity to share their experience, strength and hope to solve their common problem and help each other recover from alcoholism.

Accounting Club

Leadership skills development and opportunities for networking are a benefit to students in accounting and management.

Allied Health Club

Students studying allied health receive added support in this organization which promotes high standards of scholarship, community service and professional integrity. **The Club is also a vehicle for interaction between students and faculty.**

Alpha Mu Gamma

Achievement and interest in the foreign languages provide the commonality for students who participate in Alpha Mu Gamma. Workshops, lectures, films, and cultural programs are among club sponsored activities.

Architecture (AIAS)

Networking with professional architects and practitioners give members of the Architecture Club an added dimension to their education. An appreciation and understanding of the objectives of the American Institute of Architects enhances student performance and helps clarify future goals.

Art Club

Exposure to special workshops, presentations, speakers and museum trips broaden student knowledge and appreciation of art.

Chess Club

Playing chess, a passion with students in the Chess Club, provides relaxation and relieves stress in their busy lives.

(West Windsor and James Kerney Campuses)

Cheer Dance Team

High spirited cheer dancers enliven the atmosphere at MCCC sports events and student pep rallies. Tryouts are held each fall to select members.

Christian Fellowship

Christian students and other interested members of the college community gather to promote fellowship opportunities, hold Bible study, prayer and discussions. Students of faith find added strength for the difficult lives many lead.

Club Excel

Provides an atmosphere where students can meet fellow students, receive and provide support, participate in community service projects and build awareness about person with disabilities on campus.

Computer Club

Talking about computers is best understood by others who like computers. Sharing the latest knowledge, interacting with faculty and providing educational programs are among Computer Club activities.

Criminal Justice

In a society where law enforcement is fraught with controversy, the Criminal Justice Club plans activities related to the criminal justice program. Law Enforcement agencies provide networking opportunities for students as well as information about careers.

EOF Club

The college experience is enriched by participating in the EOF Club. Workshops on parenting, conflict resolution, diversity as well social, cultural and educational activities offer a well-rounded experience to students in the Educational Opportunity Fund program.

Flight Club

Aspiring pilots find the excitement of competition, the association with leaders and executives of the industry and other flight related activities in the Flight Club. Participation leads to a better understanding of aviation.

Fuerza Latina (WW) / Hispanic Club (JKC)

The opportunity to experience Latin culture through social and cultural events is available in Fuerza Latino. Latino students hear speakers, dance Salsa, take trips and enjoy one another in the well-established organization.

Gay Straight Alliance

Students who lead different lifestyles can find a safe place to meet other gay and lesbian students, to support one another, listen to speakers and to educate others about gay, lesbian and bi-sexual lifestyles.

Graphic Design Club

Keeping up with the rapid changes in the field sometimes goes beyond the classroom. Students have the chance to see first hand new developments in graphic design.

Horticulture Club

This award-winning club beautifies the campus, participates in competitions and serves the community. Their projects relate to the Ornamental Horticulture program. Their activities bring learning to life.

Leadership Club

Developing leadership is a part of education. This club promotes personal effectiveness through leadership development using improvisational role plays, debates, round table discussions and extemporaneous speaking experiences.

(THE END)

Student Enrolment Conditions

(第2篇)

1. Data Protection

1.1 The University may use and process personal data or information regarding you whilst you are a student of the University and after you have left the University.

1.2 By accepting a place on the Programme and completing Enrolment, either via on-line or in paper form, you are consenting to the University processing your data including sensitive personal data, for the purposes and in the manner set out in this Condition 1. **Sensitive personal data includes information held by the University as to your physical or mental health or condition, your racial/ethnic origin, the commission or alleged commission of any offence by you and any proceedings for an offence committed or alleged to have been committed by you (including the outcome or sentence in such proceedings).**

1.3 The purposes for which the University may process your personal data (including sensitive personal data) include:

1.3.1 The administration of your enrolment on and participation on a Programme, including the administration of examinations, the issue of results and certificates in connection with the Programme and (where applicable) the provision to your employer or other sponsor of information about your attendance and performance on a Programme;

1.3.2 **The provision of University services and facilities to you and the protection of your health, safety and welfare whilst at the University (which in either case may involve the University disclosing your personal data to the University Union of Students, University student health service providers and other third parties);**

1.3.3 The issue and operation of the University's "Smart Card" in accordance with Condition 11.5;

1.3.4 The collection of fees;

1.3.5 Equal opportunities monitoring;

1.3.6 Alumni activities;

1.3.7 The provision of references about you; and

1.3.8 The provision of information to any government body or agency (including, without Limitation, the Higher Education Funding Council for England) and the emergency Services for legitimate purposes.

1.4 In some circumstances, it may be necessary for the University to transfer your personal data to a country outside the European Economic Area (for example, if you undertake a Programme in such a country, or that is your country of origin). Such a transfer will only be made for the purposes specified in Condition 1.3. However, you should be aware that countries outside the European Economic Area may not offer data protection law equivalent to that applicable in the United Kingdom, and by signing the Enrolment

Form you consent to the transfer of data in these circumstances and for those purposes.

1.5 **The University will issue you with a "Smart Card" which will serve as a means of identification and your means of access to University services and facilities, including libraries, computing facilities and car parks.** The University may process personal data collected as a result of your use of such card for the purposes set out in Condition 1.3. The University may also disclose personal data about Smart Card holders to third parties to facilitate the provision of further services and facilities and for research purposes. If you do not wish your personal data to be disclosed to third parties, you should notify the Registrar in writing.

1.6 In line with the practice of many universities, the University may make results of examinations available by means of notices displayed in and around the University's premises. If you would prefer that your examination results not be made available in this way, you should notify the Registrar in writing.

1.7 In some circumstances, the University may wish to use data in the form of photographs of classroom situations as part of general marketing materials i.e. in the University's annual report, prospectus or course materials. Personal data alongside photographs will only be used with explicit consent.

(THE END)

必备词汇

enrichment / in'ritʃmənt / 丰富
campus / 'kæmpəs / 校园
interact / ˌintər'ækt / 互相影响，互相作用
affiliated / ə'filieitid / 附属的，有关联的
augment / ɔː g'ment / 增加，增大
alcoholism / 'ælkəhɔlizəm / 酒精中毒
accounting / ə'kauntiŋ / 会计
architect / 'ɑːkitekt / 建筑师
appreciation / əˌpriːʃi'eiʃən / 欣赏
clarify / 'klærifai / 澄清，阐明
enliven / in'laivən / 使活跃
conflict resolution 冲突解决
diversity / dai'vəːsiti / 多样性
consent / kən'sent / 同意
attendance / ə'tendəns / 参加，出席
alumni 校友，毕业生
disclose / dis'kləuz / 透露，泄露
identification / aiˌdentifi'keiʃən / 身份
explicit / iks'plisit / 清楚的

重点剖析

— An important part of college life is the personal enrichment students gain outside the classroom through student activities. Getting involved in campus activities gives students many educational experiences, leadership opportunities and the chance to interact with other students and faculty/staff members in an informal setting. 大学生活的一个重要组成部分是学生们通过学生活动在课堂之外丰富自己的人生。参加校园活动给学生们提供了许多教育经验、领导机会和在非正式的环境下与其他学生和老师及学校员工交流的机会。

— In addition, art exhibits, dance productions, dramatic presentations, musical productions, and performances by guest artists are sponsored throughout the year. 此外，客座艺术家常年来校举行艺术展览、舞蹈制作、戏剧展示、音乐制作和表演。

— To charter a club, you need a membership list of at least 10 students, a faculty advisor and a constitution. 要成立一个俱乐部，你需要有一个至少10名学生组成的会员名单、一名教师顾问和一个章程。

— The Club is also a vehicle for interaction between students and faculty. 本俱乐部也是教师和学生沟通的载体。

— Sensitive personal data includes information held by the University as to your physical or mental health or condition, your racial/ethnic origin, the commission or alleged commission of any offence by you and any proceedings for an offence committed or alleged to have been committed by you (including the outcome or sentence in such proceedings). 大学拥有的敏感性个人资料含如下信息：你的身心健康或状态、你的种族起源、违法或被诉违法、就你所犯或被诉犯下的违法行为提起的诉讼（包括此等诉讼的结果或判决）。

— The provision of University services and facilities to you and the protection of your health, safety and welfare whilst at the University (which in either case may involve the University disclosing your personal data to the University Union of Students, University student health service providers and other third parties) 在大学期间，大学向你提供的服务和设施，保护你的健康、安全和福利（在这几种情况下本大学需要把你的个人信息透露给大学学生会、大学学生健康服务提供者和其他第三方）。

— The University will issue you with a "Smart Card" which will serve as a means of identification and your means of access to University services and facilities, including libraries, computing facilities and car parks. 大学会给你发放一张“灵通卡”，它能提供身份验证，使你得以享受到大学的各种服务和设施，包括图书馆、计算机和停车场。

(New version 真题题源)

15. Voluntary Corporal Punishment Reduces Suspension Rates

体 罚 学 生

Corporal punishment

Twenty-seven states prohibit corporal punishment in public schools, and many school districts or individual schools have chosen not to use it (Head, 3). Head cites seven major reasons against the use of corporal punishment: **"it is ineffective, it can lead to abuse, it can unintentionally cause serious physical damage, it trains a child to use violence, slapping or any other type of force used on the buttocks is a sexual violation, spanking lowers a child's IQ, and spanking creates fear from the child."** (4-5).

Jeff Charles (2000) examined much research on the effects of corporal punishment and its effect on school items. Charles reported that in the "top 10" paddling states no positive outcomes could be found. The "top 10" included: Arkansas, Tennessee, Mississippi, Alabama, Georgia, Texas, South Carolina, Louisiana, Kentucky, and Oklahoma. Seven of these states have below average graduation rates. The SAT scores and the crime statistics in these states showed no significant improvement when compared to states where corporal punishment is not allowed. Five of the states have higher teen pregnancy rates than the national average.

Other research shows that corporal punishment is ineffective, leads to sexual abuse, causes physical damage, trains a child to use violence, and can lower a child's IQ. Research also shows that paddlings are given more regularly to male students and to minority students.

Despite all of its negative outcomes, corporal punishment does have some advantages. One advantage is that the student perceives the event as unpleasant;

however, this advantage does have limitations. Another positive is that corporal punishment can be administered quickly and be over with quickly, and it is a very clear, specific and obvious consequence.

In-School-Suspension (ISS)

Many of the same limitations of corporal punishment can be found in ISS. Although early reports showed ISS had promise, later research raises suspicion about the validity of ISS. "**Close examination of in-school suspension programs may reveal that their effectiveness has not been as complete as expected or claimed**".

ISS does not improve attendance and has a high recidivism rate. Students who have served time in ISS often fail to graduate. **Opponents of ISS point out that studies show a disproportionate number of minority students and male students are assigned ISS.** Silvey showed no significant difference in the academic achievement of students before and after serving ISS.

Aside from all of the negative aspects of ISS, the bottom line is it does not appear to reduce disruptive behavior, at least not in students with behavior disorders. "There were no apparent effects of the in-school suspension interventions on classroom disruptive behavior, since there were no systematic differences in disruptive classroom behavior by in-school suspension phase. In fact, the rate of student disruptive behavior remained rather constant across the four in-school suspension interventions, indicating that no type of in-school suspension generalized to classroom behavior any more efficaciously than another".

Out-of-School-Suspension (OSS)

Although many educators still perceive OSS to be an effective disciplinary strategy, much research has found OSS to be ineffective and in many cases discriminatory. One negative aspect of ISS cited in the literature is its punitive nature. Punishment, such as suspension, expulsion, and probation, keep students away from the learning environment but offers no corrective action. **Typically, students who get suspended are usually weak academically and by missing instruction, they may fall further behind in their studies.** A disproportional number of minority students, male students, and special education students receive OSS.

Another disadvantage with OSS is students who receive OSS may be labeled "whereby teachers and staff interact differently towards these students who are notorious for disruptive behavior" (Adams, 1992). A third problem with OSS is many of the suspended students go unsupervised if they are not in school (Collins, 1985). As a response to the problems associated with OSS, many students who are suspended drop out of school.

Current Study

This study involved examining the discipline records at Gordon Central High School (GCHS), a school of 1,378 students, in Calhoun, Georgia, and issuing questionnaires to teachers and students to determine their opinions about the new policy of volunteer corporal punishment. The study examined the discipline records for the months of October, November, January and February. The administration did not use corporal punishment at all in October and November. Volunteer corporal punishment began in January.

During the months of study, the discipline office received 2,063 office referrals. **From these referrals, 880 resulted from truancy/skipping, tardiness or failure to accept formal detention. This total includes repeat offenders.** The total does not reflect all referrals from teachers for tardiness because many times teachers assign formal detention, and the reason for the detention is not stated on the referral sheet. The consequence for truancy/skipping, tardiness and refusing formal detention range in severity from detention to ISS or OSS.

In an effort to give administrators an alternative to ISS, to ease overcrowding in ISS and to give more instantaneous punishment, GCHS began a voluntary corporal punishment program whereby students can decide to take a paddling or receive the standard punishment of detention, or ISS. Indirectly, this new alternative method decreases the number of formal detentions because students who previously would have neglected to attend formal detention can opt for corporal punishment. Students receive one to three swats with a wooden paddle on their buttocks from assistant principal Jerry Burkett. Another adult, usually another administrator or a teacher, always witnesses the paddlings. Before the voluntary corporal punishment began in late January 2000, no GCHS student had been paddled in almost 10 years, according to assistant principal Gary Lemmons. The Gordon County Board of Education did not prohibit corporal punishment; the two middle schools continue to use it, but GCHS chose not to use this discipline.

The voluntary corporal punishment has established rules to follow. Any male 17 or older referred to the attendance or discipline office for a minor infraction is given the option of corporal punishment. If a male is under 17, parental permission must be gained. **Female students can also receive corporal punishment, but the guidelines are a little different. The parents of all female students opting for corporal punishment must be contacted for approval.**

Thus far administrators have issued 215 paddlings to 125 individual students, 14 of which were females. Gender bias is not an issue because students must volunteer to receive corporal punishment; males simply choose to take this forms of punishment more frequently. Of the 215 paddlings, over 38% were for tardiness and almost 23% were for truancy/skipping. Under the former system, these 141 referrals would have resulted in formal detention, ISS or OSS.

Paddlings	Reasons
Male: 111	Tardiness- 38%
Female: 14	Truancy/Skipping- 23%
Total Paddlings: 215	Results: 141 less discipline alternative

According to Lemmons, the new program is meeting its goals. The number of students receiving ISS decreased by 38 in February and March when corporal punishment was an option. In October and November when no corporal punishment was used, 187 students received ISS, but in February and March only 149 received ISS. **While this is not a large number, the reasons as to why students receive ISS show the new corporal punishment option is working.** In October and November, 40% of the ISS assignments were for truancy/skipping, or tardiness. By contrast in February and March, 32% of the ISS assignments were for the same offenses. In October and November on 109 occasions, students refused to accept formal detention. In February and March, 81 students refused to accept formal detention.

Discipline	Feb. & March	Oct. & Nov.
ISS	Decreased by 38	Increased by 187
ISS for Truancy/Skipping	32%	40%
Refusal of Discipline	81 students	109 students

Lemmons admits the new program has a few problems that still need to be worked out. "No one consequence works for all students, but this seems to be having a more positive impact on the ninth graders and to a smaller degree of success with the tenth graders." He admits the new strategy is not working as effectively with the juniors

and seniors. Many of the repeat offenders are in these two groups of students. A few of repeat offenders have been paddled five or more times, but for some they eventually learn their lesson.

(THE END)

必备词汇

corporal punishment 体罚
abuse / ə'bjuːz / 滥用，虐待
buttock / 'bʌtək / 臀部
spanking / 'spæŋkiŋ / 拍击，打屁股
suspension / səs'penʃən / 暂令停学
suspicion / səs'piʃən / 怀疑
attendance / ə'tendəns / 上课，出勤
drop out of school 退学
recidivism rate 累犯率
bottom line 底线
intervention / ˌintə(ː)'venʃən / 干预
expulsion / iks'pʌlʃən / 开除
probation / prə'beiʃən / 留校查看，试用，缓刑
referral / ri'fəːrəl / 被推举的人，候选人
minor infraction 轻微的违反
gender bias 性别歧视
volunteer / vɔlən'tiə(r) / 志愿者

重点剖析

— "It is ineffective, it can lead to abuse, it can unintentionally cause serious physical damage, it trains a child to use violence, slapping or any other type of force used on the buttocks is a sexual violation, spanking lowers a child's IQ, and spanking creates fear in the child". 体罚根本没用。体罚会导致虐待，还可能给孩子的身体造成意想不到的伤害，它还会教孩子使用暴力。打屁股或用其他方式接触孩子的臀部都可以称为性侵犯，打屁股还可能使孩子的智商下降，引发孩子的恐惧感。

— Despite all of its negative outcomes, corporal punishment does have some advantages. One advantage is that the student perceives the event as unpleasant; however, this advantage does have limitations. Another positive is corporal punishment can be administered quickly and be over with quickly, and it is a very clear, specific and obvious consequence. 尽管体罚能带来许多消极影响，但它也有一些好处。首先，体罚会让学生意识到他的所作所为令人不满，不过这个作用也有其不足之处。其次，体罚可以快速进行并很快结束，这种（对学生错误的）处理结果清楚明了。

— Close examination of in-school suspension programs may reveal that their effectiveness has not been as complete as expected or claimed. 对校内暂令停学计划密切考察后发现其作用不像预期的那样有效。

— Opponents of ISS point out that studies show a disproportionate number of minority students and male students are assigned ISS. 反对者指出，学校给少数民族学生和男生校内暂令停学这一处罚的比例太高。

— Typically, students who get suspended are usually weak academically and by missing instruction, they may fall further behind in their studies. 一般来讲，受到暂令停学惩罚的学生通常学业较差，由于惩罚导致的缺课，会使他们的学习更加落后于人。

— From these referrals, 880 resulted from truancy/skipping, tardiness or failure to accept formal detention. This total includes repeat offenders. 在这些记录当中，有880条是关于学生旷课，迟到或拒不接受放学后的留校处罚。（从记录中可以看出，）有的学生多次违反校纪。

— Female students can also receive corporal punishment, but the guidelines are a little different. The parents of all female students opting for corporal punishment must be contacted for approval. 女生也可以自愿选择体罚，但指导原则有些不同。我们必须预先征求所有愿意接受体罚的女生家长的同意。

— While this is not a large number, the reasons as to why students receive ISS show the new corporal punishment option is working. 虽然（实行自愿体罚前后）实施校内暂令停学惩罚的次数的差异并不是很大，但通过询问学生接受校内暂令停学惩罚的原因，可以知道（从1月开始实施的）新体罚方法起到了作用。

— Lemmons admits the new program has a few problems that still need to be worked out. "No one consequence works for all students, but this seems to be having a more positive impact on the ninth graders and to a smaller degree of success with the tenth graders." He admits the new strategy is not working as effectively with the juniors and seniors. Many of the repeat offenders are in these two groups of students. A few of repeat offenders have been paddled five or more times, but for some they eventually learn their lesson. Lemmons 承认，新方案还存在一些问题，需要想办法解决。"结果表明，方案不是对所有学生都有效。对九年级学生的作用更明显，其次是十年级。"他认为，新方案对中学三、四年级学生的作用不大，而许多多次违反校纪的学生就是这两个年级的。

(V26真题题源)

16. Accelerate Teaching

音乐语言教学法

Suggestopedia And SA

Lozanov, a Bulgarian psychotherapist and physician, developed Suggestopedia (SA) in the early sixties using yoga-like relaxation and concentration techniques designed to tap subconscious abilities and increase retention of relatively greater amounts of second language information. **Claiming to increase learning ability by more than ten times, Suggestopedia received much scepticism.** One scholar went as far as to call it a "package of pseudo-scientific gobbledygook". **Whether or not we agree that Lozanov's suggestopedic package is gobbledygook, all teachers should recognize the worth of many of his successful and spectacular teaching techniques.**

Lozanov's Suggestopedia assumes that the teacher is responsible for offering the class an abundance of potentially useful information while at the same time, removing

learning barriers and students' inhibitions. For this reason, suggestopedic courses use relatively large amounts of language input. Students naturally select data that is easy for them to learn and of real interest.

In presenting the language data, Suggestopedia follows three basic assumptions: 1) If there is joy, there is learning. 2) When both sides of the brain are used simultaneously, learning improves. and 3) Tapping each student's unique potential helps learning to flourish. These three assumptions are also the essence of the SA course. Lozanov also stresses six essential methods to encourage positive emotions that lead to faster learning. These are: authority, double-planeness, infantilization, intonation, rhythm, and pseudo-passivity and will be discussed later. **The SA course places an evengreater emphasis on the importance of emotion and well-being in language learning.**

Basic Assumptions

Joy

Learning is quicker, easier, and less stressful in an environment filled with pleasant, positive emotions. The ability to learn diminishes if a student feels stress related to fear of making an error or failure. There are students who learn out of fear, or even from the thrill of competition, but these students are able to learn faster in a stress-free environment. Competition obviously creates winners; it also creates losers. Students who shy away from competition and the often unbearable burden of stress, find the Suggestopedic environment ideal. The Suggestopedic classroom reduces competition and stresses cooperation. Students do not become disillusioned with difficult tasks, and confidence is constantly reinforced by the teacher and awareness of their own progress. Once this comfortable environment is created, even apathetic students who would rather be anywhere but in the classroom, tend to find themselves participating and enjoying themselves. In these respects, Suggestopedia and SA are alike.

Right and Left Brain

The human brain consists of two hemispheres that are responsible for different learning activities. **Though there are remarkable individual differences, we generally refer to dreaming, imagination, creativity, music, colour, rhythm, visualization, and the like, as right-brain activities, while the left-brain is sequential, analytical, rational, objective, and mathematical.** To illustrate, when language teachers emphasize the orderly rudiments of grammar (the logistics of language), the left brain is called to work. Human beings' inherent appreciation for art, music, and culture rests in the right brain.

This area is responsible for an individual's writing and speaking style, creativity, and expression. The teacher who successfully gives students a thoughtful, deeply integrated program that taps the strengths of both the left and right brains, accelerates learning.

Tapping Reserves

It would seem that one's reserves (memories, past experiences, dreams, etc.) are also related to the left-right separation of the mind. Tapping one's reserves, however, is not maximizing the mind's capacity to add information. Tapping reserves is drawing information from a deeper consciousness to supplement new information. In this way, new information, like new vocabulary or a new phrase, is not an isolated piece of information. It is related to prior experience and receives assistance in being internalized; it becomes an integrated part of the student's linguistic ability. **By matching the meanings of new language units to a vast storehouse of conscious and unconscious associations, the ability to learn, seemingly, increases.**

Elements for Creating Positive Emotions

Authority

People seem to learn better when they believe information is coming from an authoritative source. For this situation to exist, students and teachers need to believe completely in their program. A teacher bearing an air of confidence in speech, gesture, dress, and manner, instills a similar confidence in the students. As Lozanov notes, the air of the Suggestopedic teacher "inspires respect, trust and intentiveness, without fear, suppression, or social distance".

Rhythm and Music

There is no question that music and rhythm affect us emotionally, physically, and mentally. The pounding of a hammer early in the morning generally causes annoyance, while a sonata by Mozart generally instills well-being. **Suggestopedia teachers carefully select music that tends to open certain areas of the mind. Baroque music, especially that by Bach, Vivaldi, and Corelli, seems to work the best for SA. The constant, flowing rhythm of Baroque music stimulates the students, whereas some symphony** music, with its irregular movements, is apt to make students lose their concentration. Also, Baroque music helps the teacher to read more smoothly as the music seems to pause at the same time the teacher does. In fact, the music seems to be written especially for the SA text.

Tchaikovsky's Symphony No. 4, for example, or Beethoven No. 5 are too dramatic for concert readings. And because of the sudden changes in the loudness of the music, teachers would be forever adjusting the volume to allow their voices to be heard. It would be difficult for the students to feel relaxed with blaring trumpets drowning their concentration. In Corelli's music, like the Concerto Grossi, Opus 6, the quiet mood projects, immediately putting the students in a state of relaxation that helps their attention span to continue to the end of the reading.

Student Response

There is no greater voice supporting SA Course than the students themselves. This year's comments (in the form of an open letter to their tutors who are members of the Japanese staff acting as their educational advisors) are positive. Of the 68 students enrolled in this year's course, 91% make some comment that SA classes are enjoyable: "Very fun", "I'm really enjoying", "I love SA course", etc.

Forty-percent note that the workload is very heavy and made comments like: "Class time is long for me", "CP takes 2 or 3 hours", "It is a little hard for me", "If I idle, there's lots to do." But, at the same time, 81% felt that the amount of work is either beneficial or that they are improving their English ability: "I think I'm becoming hard-working person", "I'm better than before", "Each lesson I progress", and the like.

It is expected that students would enjoy music, and they did as 66% noted that they enjoyed listening to music and becoming better and understanding songs with a faster tempo: "I am getting fast music", "I like music", "I like specifically music".

Conclusion

The course offers a unique method of language acquisition that can be successful where other methods have failed. It offers a great opportunity for those who have been restricted by their learning environment or who have been frustrated by the seeming insurmountable challenge of learning English.

The SA course has undergone and continues to undergo changes that improve the course as a whole. Deviations from Suggestology based on directives from Yoshizumi have become so unique that a new name for the program is anticipated. Using the **three keys offered by Lozanov—joy, whole-brain, and reserves**—as a foundation, the SA course continues to be successful in not only teaching language, but also in teaching self-awareness and humanistic values that are also important for the students' success in the future.

(THE END)

必备词汇

physician / fi'ziʃən / 医师
psychotherapist 精神治疗医师
yoga-like relaxation and concentration techniques 类似瑜珈术那样的放松和集中技能
tap subconscious abilities 开发潜能
skepticism / 'skeptisizəm / 怀疑论，怀疑主义
barrier / 'bæriə / 障碍
inhibition / ˌinhi'biʃən / 压抑
pseudo-scientific gobbledygook 伪科学的官样文章
flourish / 'flʌriʃ / 活跃，繁荣
intonation / ˌintə'neiʃən / 声调
rhythm / 'riðəm, 'riθəm / 韵律
diminish / di'miniʃ / 下降，减小
stress / stres / 紧张
thrill / θril / 发抖
become disillusioned with 沉迷于……
in these respects 在这些方面
creativity / ˌkri:ei'tivəti / 创造
visualization / ˌvizjuəlai'zeiʃən / 视觉
rudiment / 'ru:dimənt / 入门，初步
appreciation / əˌpri:ʃi'eiʃən / 欣赏
accelerate / æk'seləreit / 加快
reserve / ri'zə:v / 潜能
internalized 使内化
authoritative source 权威来源
intentiveness 专心，专注
authoritative source 权威来源
instill 慢慢地灌输
annoyance / ə'nɔiəns / 烦恼
sonata / sə'nɑ:tə / 奏鸣曲
symphony music 交响乐
be apt to 倾向于
tutor / 'tju:tə / 教师，辅导员
tempo / 'tempəu / 速度，节拍
frustrated / frʌ'streitid, 'frʌ-/ 失败的，落空的
insurmountable challenge 不能克服的挑战
imagination / iˌmædʒi'neiʃən / 想像

重点剖析

— Claiming to increase learning ability by more than ten times, Suggestopedia received much scepticism. 虽然他声称暗示感应教学法可以让学习能力提高10倍，但该方法仍然受到很多质疑。

— Whether or not we agree that Lozanov's suggestopedic package is gobbledygook, all teachers should recognize the worth of many of his successful and spectacular teaching techniques. 无论我们是不是认同罗扎诺夫有关暗示感应教学法的论述是官样文章的说法，所有的老师都应该认识到他的方法中许多成功、奇妙的教学技术的价值。

— Lozanov's Suggestopedia assumes that the teacher is responsible for offering the class an abundance of potentially useful information while at the same time, removing learning barriers and students' inhibitions. 罗扎诺夫的暗示感应教学法认为老师有责任向学生提供丰富的潜在有用信息，同时消除学生的学习障碍和压抑心理。

— The SA course places an even greater emphasis on the importance of emotion and well-being in language learning. 暗示法课程极为强调情绪和健康语言学习中的重要性。

— Learning is quicker, easier, and less stressful in an environment filled with pleasant, positive emotions. The ability to learn diminishes if a student feels stress related to fear of making an error or failure. 在充满欢乐的情境中、带着积极的情绪，学习变得更快、更容易、也更轻松。

— Though there are remarkable individual differences, we generally refer to dreaming, imagination, creativity, music, colour, rhythm, visualization, and the like, as right-brain activities, while the left-brain is sequential, analytical, rational, objective, and mathematical. 虽然个体差异很大，但一般认为右脑负责做梦、想像、创造、音乐、色彩、韵律、视觉等，左脑负责顺序、分析、推理、客观和数学计算。

— By matching the meanings of new language units to a vast storehouse of conscious and unconscious associations, the ability to learn, seemingly, increases. 通过把新语言单位的涵义与众多有意记忆、无意记忆的内容建立联结，就能够明显地提高个体的学习能力。

— There is no question that music and rhythm affect us emotionally, physically, and mentally. 毫无疑问，音乐和韵律能影响我们的情绪、体能和精神。

— Suggestopedia teachers carefully select music that tends to open certain areas of the mind. 暗示法的老师们精心挑选可以触发大脑某些区域的音乐。

— Baroque music, especially that by Bach, Vivaldi, and Corelli, seems to work the best for SA. The constant, flowing rhythm of Baroque music stimulates the students, whereas some symphony music, with its irregular movements, is apt to make students lose their concentration. 巴洛克风格的音乐，特别是巴赫、维吾尔第、科莱利等人的音乐尤为适合在暗示法中使用。它们行云流水般的旋律刺激学生去联想。而某些交响乐由于节奏不规律，容易让学生走神。

— three keys offered by Lozanov—joy, whole-brain, and reserves. Lozanov提出的语言学习三要素指的是——心情愉悦、左右脑并用、激发潜能。

(V16真题题源)

17. The Program

培训课程介绍和招生

The Iowa Intensive English Program (IIEP) provides intensive English instruction and a cultural, social, and academic orientation to the United States. Instruction emphasizes spoken and written English crucial to college and university work in the U.S. The basic language skills of grammar, writing, reading, listening, comprehension, pronunciation, and conversation are taught each day in all levels (beginning, intermediate, and advanced). Students receive 20 hours of instruction per week in addition to individual work in the language laboratory. Because class size is small (12-15), each student receives personal supervision and encouragement. A wide variety of methods and materials is used to provide a high quality language learning opportunity.

Eligibility

All applicants must have been graduated from an upper secondary school or its equivalent. The applicant must also have a source of funds sufficient to pay for all expenses while in the IIEP. Scholarships and financial aid are not available. The beginning level of IIEP presumes some formal exposure to language instruction. The IIEP welcomes students preparing to enter universities or technical schools at either the undergraduate or graduate levels as well as business and professional persons and other adults who wish to improve their English skills.

English Ability Testing

Upon registering in the IIEP, students are given a placement exam to determine their proficiency in English. Assignments to levels of instruction are based upon the results of these examinations. Students are required to attend all classes in which they are placed. The TOEFL is administered at the end of the program. The IIEP does not regard TOEFL scores as the goal of language instruction. Therefore, the curriculum of the IIEP concentrates on the students' total language development, the only way to achieve good results on the TOEFL.

Length of Study

Students starting intensive English studies at the beginning level will normally acquire sufficient proficiency to begin academic work after three terms in the IIEP. Intermediate students usually require two terms, and advanced students normally require one term. The duration of intensive English study required for an individual student varies depending on personal motivation, level of proficiency, and aptitude.

Certificates

At the end of the program, the IIEP issues a Certificate of Completion to students who have attended class regularly and have received passing grades. Students receive official grades for each of their courses. These grades are recorded on an official University of Iowa transcript.

Admission to The University of Iowa

Students should be aware that admission to the IIEP does not constitute admission to The University of Iowa. Admission to the University requires separate application and qualifications based on high school and university transcripts, personal recommendations, and English proficiency.

Conditional Admission

Applicants who are otherwise academically admissible but submit TOEFL scores between 450 and 530 (paper based) or 133 and 197 (computer based) may be granted conditional admission to the College of Liberal Arts and Sciences. To change their admission status from conditional to regular (a prerequisite for beginning study in a degree program), students must attain a minimum TOEFL score of 530 (paper based) or 197 (computer based). As space permits, conditionally admitted students may enroll in the IIEP for up to one year. Students without TOEFL scores and those with scores below 450 (paper based)/133 (computer based) may also enroll in the IIEP; however, IIEP enrollment without conditional admission to the College of Liberal Arts and Sciences does not imply or guarantee admission to an academic program at The University of Iowa.

Admission Procedure

All applicants must submit the following items:

1. A $50 application fee.
2. An Application for Admission - All items on the application form must be completed.
3. A copy of the passport page that contains your picture and the exact spelling of your name. If you do not have a passport yet, please be sure your full name on the application is spelled exactly as you expect it to appear on your passport.
4. **A $100 Reservation Deposit - This deposit is applied toward the tuition due for the first term of study; it is NONREFUNDABLE, although it can be transferred to a later term if a student is delayed in coming to the IIEP.**
5. A $35 express mailing fee.

(THE END)

The University Library

- The University Library has about 1 million printed volumes and 10 kilometres of archives in its main building and Modern Records Centre. There are also small research-only collections in the Biological Sciences and Mathematics Departments.
- There are 14000m^2 of usable floor area in the University Libraries with 1,600 reader places and over 40,000 linear metres of shelving.
- The Library has over 25,000 registered users and employs around 150 (c.90 full time equivalent) staff, including 20 academic-related librarians.
- Expenditure for 2001/2002 on materials, information systems, document delivery and binding will be £1.95m. Expenditure on Library staff is below the national average.
- Over 26,500 items are accessioned each year, adding 1.1 km of stock (700 metres of printed materials, 400 of archives). Over 5000 printed periodical titles (including statistical serials) are currently received, and around 6000 electronic journals.
- There are 5 public Floors.
  The Entrance Floor, Floor 1, has general services. Each of the upper Floors contains specific subject areas:
  Floor 2 Sciences, Floor 3 Arts, Floor 4 Education, Law, Statistics and Official

Publications, and Floor 5 Social Sciences and the Corporate Information Library. The Student Reserve Collection (SRC), a short-loan collection of heavy-use material, is in the Floor 2 Extension.

- Special areas in the Library are a 200-seat Silent Reading Room, a soundproof Group Study Room (allowing groupwork without disturbing other users), a Postgraduate Reading Room, and the Wolfson Room, a postgraduate-only PC cluster. All Floors have study seating.
- **A controlled entry policy operates, with turnstiles triggered by the University/ Library Card, in order to give priority for use of facilities to members of the University.**
- Around 1 million people enter the Library each year, with 4000-6000 coming through the turnstile during a typical term weekday. At peak times (during the exam term) over 1000 users can be in the Library.
- Organisational Structure

User support

The primary structure comprises: Information Services, providing the Subject Support and Enquiry services Reader Services, providing circulation, document delivery and shelving Technical Services, which includes Acquisitions, Cataloguing and Processing, and Collection Management Modern Records Centre Systems Team

Library Management Group

The Librarian, Deputy Librarian, Archivist, and the Heads of Information, Reader and Technical Services form the Management Group. Each Division also holds its own meetings, reporting to/from the Management Group. In addition, working groups involving all levels of staff are formed as required to carry out projects.

Services and Facilities

For most of the year (during parts of the vacations as well as the University terms) the Library is open 7 days a week (Monday to Friday 8.30a.m.-midnight), for 95.5 hours per week. This is increased to 105.5 hours during the exam period. For some vacations reduced hours operate. To help Library users there are guides, plans and signing covering the whole building. Detailed guides are produced for Subject Floors, for specific subject areas and for specific groups of users such as part-time and international students. There are also guides to the Library catalogue and individual databases. The main Enquiry Desk is on Floor 1, staffed Monday to Friday 9a.m.—7.30p.m. and for limited periods at weekends. There are additional enquiry services supporting the Corporate Information Library and the Education, Law, Official Publications and Statistics collections on Floor 4. There are photocopiers on Floor 1 and in SRC. Double-sided and transparency copying are available (plus copying from microform materials). Photocopying staff are on duty:

8.30 a.m.— 5.00 p.m. Monday to Thursday
8.30 a.m.— 4.00 p.m. Friday

The cost of a standard A4 copy is 6p. Over 3.5 million self-service copies are made each year.

(THE END)

必备词汇

intensive / in'tensiv / 加强的，集中的
orientation / ˌɔ(ː)rien'teiʃən / 方向，导向
crucial / 'kruːʃiəl, 'kruːʃəl / 至关重要的
emphasize / 'emfəsaiz/ 强调
beginning, intermediate, and advanced 初、中、高级
eligibility 合格性
applicant / 'æplikənt / 申请人
equivalent / i'kwivələnt / 同等的，相当的
scholarship / 'skɔləʃip / 奖学金
presume / pri'zjuːm / 假定，认为
undergraduate / ˌʌndə'grædjuit / 大学本科
placement exam 定位考试，分班考试
proficiency / prə'fiʃənsi / 熟练，精通
curriculum / kə'rikjuləm / 课程
concentrate on 集中于，专注于
motivation / ˌməuti'veiʃən / 动力，动能
aptitude / 'æptitjuːd / 能力
Certificate of Completion 结业证书
transcript / 'trænskript / 成绩单
be aware 明白，了解
admission / əd'miʃən / 录取，进入
prerequisite / 'priː'rekwizit / 前提
attain / ə'tein / 获得
minimum / 'miniməm / 最少，最低
imply / im'plai / 按时，意味
guarantee / ˌgærən'tiː / 确保，担保
volume / 'vɔljuːm; (*US*) -jəm / 卷，册
archive / 'ɑːkaiv/ 档案，公文
usable floor area 可用面积
expenditure / iks'penditʃə, eks- / 支出，花费
accession / æk'seʃən / 添加
periodical / ˌpiəri'ɔdikəl / 期刊
soundproof / 'saundpruːf / 隔音的
turnstile / 'təːnˌstail / 十字转门
give priority 给予优先
at peak times 在高峰期

重点剖析

— Upon registering in the IIEP, students are given a placement exam to determine their proficiency in English. Assignments to levels of instruction are based upon the results of these examinations. Students are required to attend all classes in which they are placed. 学生们在IIEP注册登记后，将举行分班（定位）考试，以确定他们的英语水平如何。指导等级作业将按照考试结果来确定。要求学生们参加所有的分班课。

— Students starting intensive English studies at the beginning level will normally acquire sufficient proficiency to begin academic work after three terms in the IIEP. Intermediate students usually require two terms, and advanced students normally require one term. The duration of intensive English study required for an individual student varies depending on personal motivation, level of proficiency, and aptitude.
参加初级阶段英语专训的学生一般在参加完IIEP举办的三个学期课程后就有足够能力开始学术课程的学习。参加中级课程的学生通常需要两个学期，参加高级课程的学生一般需要参加一个学期。英语专训的时间长度根据学生的个人目的、熟练程度和能力而定。

— At the end of the program, the IIEP issues a Certificate of Completion to students who have attended class regularly and have received passing grades. 课程结束时，IIEP将给学生颁发结业证书，但获取证书的前提是必须按时上课并通过级别考试。

— A $100 Reservation Deposit - This deposit is applied toward the tuition due for the first term of study; it is NONREFUNDABLE, although it can be transferred to a later term if a student is delayed in coming to the IIEP. 100元的预定押金，押金是用到第一学期的学费中的，不退还，但如果学生到IIEP就学的时间延误了，可以把此费用转移到随后学期的学费中。

— A controlled entry policy operates, with turnstiles triggered by the University/Library Card, in order to give priority for use of facilities to members of the University. 有一个进入管制政策，十字转门用图书馆专用卡打开，以便让大学的人员优先使用这些设施。

— The cost of a standard A4 copy is 6p. Over 3.5 million self-service copies are made each year. 复印一张标准A4纸价格是6分钱，每年用户自行复印的超过350万张之多。

（V20 真题题源）

18. International Student Admissions Frequently-Asked Questions

大学招生介绍

How many students attend Sul Ross State University?

Approximately 2,400 students are enrolled in the fall semester of each year. Graduate students comprise 38% of the total student body. Sul Ross is residential campus with approximately 500 residence hall rooms, apartments, and married student housing.

What is the deadline for applying for admission to Sul Ross State University?

International student applicants must submit all documents one month prior to the anticipated date of registration.

What makes a person an international student?

An admission applicant who does not hold the United States citizenship or permanent resident status and who has not graduated from a United States high school must fulfill international student admission requirements. Admission to Sul Ross State University is for full-time degree-seeking students only.

What are the requirements for a student wanting to pursue an undergraduate degree?

1. Submit a completed application form for admission
2. Send official transcript of credits form each college or university attended, or a secondary school transcript. **English language interpretation must accompany transcripts.**
3. Achievement test scores when required
4. Test of English as a Foreign Language (TOEFL) score of 520 or an official transcript showing completion of two full semesters (24 Semester credit hours) from a regionally accredited American college or university with a C average or better.
5. **Evidence of ability to support him/herself while studying in the United States.**
6. A housing deposit of $100.00 (US currency)
7. An application fee of $50.00 (US Currency)

Can international students receive financial assistance?

Undergraduate international students are not eligible to receive financial assistance through the Office of Financial Assistance. You should plan on having adequate funds available for your entire time in school.

Graduate international students may apply for teaching and research assistantships through the individual graduate programs. You will need to visit with a graduate adviser for additional information.

Citizens of Mexico may be eligible for financial assistance through a program called PROGRAMA DE ASISTENCIA ESTUDIANTIL (PASE) Mexican citizens are eligible for the Programa de Asistencia Estudiantil (PASE) under which they qualify for in-state tuition and fees. Only Mexican citizens are eligible for PASE. **US citizens holding dual US/Mexican status are not eligible for PASE.**

Can you tell me something about the graduate program at Sul Ross State University?

Sul Ross State University provides graduate programs which will enable the student to enrich his or her study in a specialized field. The aim of the graduate program is to build greater breadth and depth of knowledge in the field of study. Advisors will provide direct counseling to students in their major field of study. Students desiring to pursue work in a teacher certification program at the graduate level are also advised by the Director of Teacher Education. **Each graduate student will be assigned a committee of faculty members prior to taking the comprehensive examination. The student shall complete all assigned work and receive recommendations of the committee and the Dean of the School and/or Division before a degree will be awarded.**

What is required for full admission to the Graduate Program?

A student seeking admission for the purpose of pursuing a master's degree must hold a baccalaureate degree from an institution approved by a nationally recognized accrediting agency. Official transcripts reflecting all college work attempted and degree(s) conferred should be on file in the Office of the Registrar at least ten days prior to initial registration as a graduate student.

There are two levels of admission to a master's program, full and probationary. Approval of the major department is required for admission at either level. The following criteria will be used in determining the eligibility for full admission.

Applicants must have official transcripts and test scores sent to the Office of the Registrar, Sul Ross State University. The Office of the Registrar will compile and tabulate the documentation submitted and submit a file on each applicant to the major academic department. Following the departmental review of the file, the Office of the registrar will communicate to the applicant the admission status to be granted. Both of the following criteria must be met for full admission status.

1. A 2.5 grade point average on a 4.0 scale calculated on the last 60 hours prior to the issuance of the bachelor's degree and a GRE score of 850 (verbal and quantitative) or GMAT score of 400.
2. Full admission may also be granted to applicants who hold a master's degree from accredited colleges or universities and who have the approval of the department in which they propose to do work.

Full admission status does not imply an absence of additional departmental requirements (leveling work, higher GRE scores, etc.). Reference should be made to the various departmental graduate programs in the Catalog for more information.

If I am not eligible to be fully admitted, are there other methods of admission?

Yes, probationary admission may be granted with the approval of the major academic department if a student has submitted transcripts of baccalaureate work, and GRE or GMAT scores, as well as having satisfied at least one of the requirements for full admission. The probationary student must satisfy all conditions which are required by the major department and must maintain a 3.0 grade point average on all courses attempted for graduate credit. Upon the completion of 12 semester credit hours with a 3.0 grade point average or higher, the student may be admitted to full admission status upon the recommendation of the chair of the major department and with the approval of the dean/director of the school or division. **Failure to maintain a 3.0 grade point average during the probationary period will result in dismissal from the graduate program.**

Probationary status also may be granted to any student who has not submitted GRE or GMAT scores to the Office of Admissions and Records. The GRE or GMAT must be taken prior to the **end of the first long semester** (fall or spring) after initial enrollment (summer terms included).

The responsibility for monitoring the probationary student's compliance with all conditions of admission (including the submitting of GRE or GMAT scores, the maintaining of a 3.0 GPA, and the satisfaction of other academic conditions imposed by the department) rests with the major department and the school or division in which the student is enrolled. The dean/director of the school or division will track all probationally admitted students each semester, secure information as necessary from the department chairs and the Office of the Registrar on each probationally admitted student, and communicate to the Office of the Registrar and the major department chairs changes of status which are made. During the entire probational period, the student is responsible for maintaining close communications with the major department and, as called upon, with the dean/director of the school or division.

Are there any other special requirements for an international student?

Yes, international students must meet the requirements for admission as stated previously. In addition, they must file the following items in the Office of the Registrar:

A. Evidence of Financial Responsibility. This may be satisfied by an Affidavit of Support (Immigration Service Form I-134) or a signed statement from a U.S. citizen or foreign national committing the necessary resources in U.S. dollars for student's expenses.

B. Evidence of English language proficiency as demonstrated by any one of the following:

1. A TOEFL score of 520; or
2. Twenty-four hours of undergraduate work with a C average at an accredited U.S. college or university, or 12 graduate hours with a B average at an accredited U.S. college or university; or
3. A bachelor's or master's degree from an accredited U.S. college or university; **or**
4. **Prospective students may petition the Director of Recruiting and Admissions in writing requesting an individual oral assessment of English proficiency. Applications granted an interview will be notified of the date, time, and location of the interview. The interview panel must deem the applicant's oral English proficiency adequate to successfully complete the program. The interview panel will file the results of the assessment in the Office of the Registrar. The Registrar will notify the student of the decision in writing.** In addition to the above requirements, students must submit the following:
5. An application fee of $50 in U.S. currency (non-refundable).
6. A housing deposit of $100 in U.S. currency.
7. Health insurance and immunization records.

(THE END)

graduate student 研究生
comprise / kəm'praiz / 包含
deadline / 'dedlain / 最终期限
applicant / 'æplikənt / 申请者
citizenship / 'sitizənʃip / 公民的身份
permanent resident status 永久性居民状态
accredited /ə'kreditid / 认证的，公认的
deposit / di'pɔzit / 押金
eligible / 'elidʒəbl / 符合条件的，合格的
probationary / prəu'beiʃənəri / 试用的
criteria 标准
tabulate / 'tæbjuleit / 把……制成表格
baccalaureate / ˌbækə'lɔːriit / 大学学士
affidavit / ˌæfi'deivit / 宣誓书
evidence of Financial Responsibility 资金责任证明
proficiency / prə'fiʃənsi / 熟练程度
immunization / ˌimjuːnai'zeiʃən / 免疫

重点剖析

— International student applicants must submit all documents one month prior to the anticipated date of registration. 国际学生申请者必须在预计注册之日前一个月提交所有文件。

— English language interpretation must accompany transcripts. 成绩单必须配上英文翻译件。

— Evidence of ability to support him/herself while studying in the United States. 资助他 / 她在美国学习期间的（资金）能力证明。

— US citizens holding dual US/Mexican status are not eligible for PASE. 持有美国/墨西哥双重国籍的美国公民没有资格享受 PASE。

— Each graduate student will be assigned a committee of faculty members prior to taking the comprehensive examination. The student shall complete all assigned work and receive recommendations of the committee and the Dean of the School and/or Division before a degree will be awarded. 在接受综合测试之前，每名研究生将被分配给一个教师团队委员会。在被授予学位之前，学生应完成所有安排的作业，得到该委员会和校长和 / 或系主任的推荐。

— Full admission status does not imply an absence of additional departmental requirements (leveling work, higher GRE scores, etc.). 完全录取状态不意味着不需要其他的系里要求（等级考核、较高的 GRE 分数等）。

— Failure to maintain a 3.0 grade point average during the probationary period will result in dismissal from the graduate program. 在试用期没有维持 3.0 平均分的学生将被开除出研究生课程。

— Prospective students may petition the Director of Recruiting and Admissions in writing requesting an individual oral assessment of English proficiency. Applications granted an interview will be notified of the date, time, and location of the interview. The interview panel must deem the applicant's oral English proficiency adequate to successfully complete the program. The interview panel will file the results of the assessment in the Office of the Registrar. The Registrar will notify the student of the decision in writing. 未来的学生可以向招生主任提交书面申请，要求进行个人英语水平口头测评。如果给予面试，面试的日期、时间和地点将通知给申请人。面试小组必须认定申请人的口语水平足以成功完成课程。面试小组将把测评结果在注册办公室备案。注册员将以书面方式把决定通知给学生。

六、公司管理类（5篇）

（V38真题题源）

1. A Balance Work and Life Research

职业妇女工作家庭冲突

The pursuit of a better work-life balance is at the root of calls for flexible hours, affordable childcare and paid paternity leave. More than ever before we demanding choice in our working lives. Gemma Lavender of the TUC explores the pressures and challenges.

The issue

If you're not careful, work can take over your life. People in Britain work longer hours than anywhere else in Europe. Too many workplaces are gripped by a long hours culture where everyone is expected to do hours of unpaid overtime every week. Astonishingly, people in Britain do ￡23 billion worth of unpaid overtime every year

—that would be a £4,000 wages boost for the average long-hours worker.

Hardly surprising, then, that there's an epidemic of workplace stress. **Contrary to some expectations, according to a recent TUC poll, Brits do actually enjoy their jobs. 85 per cent told us that they found their work enjoyable and fulfilling, yet slightly more than half said they also found it hard to cope with the pressure.**

Eight million people complain that pressure of work gives them headaches or migraines, 12 million say they get bad tempered and irritable at home, nearly three million need to take time off work and more than two-and-a-half million say they drink too much.

That is why work-life balance is the slogan of the moment. Unions, good employers and the government are all concerned —but much more needs to be done.

The pressures

The core agenda with work-life balance issues is still the family. And despite all the improvements in equality between the sexes, this is still largely perceived as an issue for women rather than men.

But times are changing. Mothers still take the greater responsibility for childcare but are also more likely to have paid jobs than ever before. **Seven out of ten women of working age now have jobs, and half of mothers with children aged under five are in work. Today's women are breadwinners.**

Men and women are both taking on multiple roles. Men are doing more of the care responsibilities (according to the Equal Opportunities Commission, a surprising 36% of couples say that the man is the main carer) and women are working more. **Polls show that fathers feel they are missing out on time with their children.**

With people living longer, more workers are experiencing care demands on elderly relatives as well as children. The fact that women are now having children later in life means that they may end up facing caring responsibilities for both ends of the age spectrum.

The attitude of female workers has also changed. Women are growing more ambitious as they become key players in the world of work, contributing to major company successes. Whether you're a Martha Lane Fox or a Marjorie Scardino, the impact of the female boss is considerably more powerful than ever before.

The pressure for women to achieve drives them to work harder and for longer, especially when wanting to prove themselves against their male counterparts.

Technology both helps and hinders. Email and the Internet gives people the potential to work flexibly. Some now work for themselves or for their employer entirely from home. This doesn't suit everyone—some find it far too isolating to be cut off from office networks, but working at home for part of the week can be a real help.

However, technology can also increase work pressure. The overflowing email inbox and the constantly ringing phone can really step up the stress levels.

Progress on work-life balance is likely to give individual employees much more choice about how and when they work. **Research shows that the more control you have over your own work, the less stressed you're likely to get. But organisations, as a whole, need to tackle the issue — it can't just be the sum of individual responses.**

And work-life balance issues are not just for carers. Everyone needs their personal space, and policies that only benefit parents or carers might cause antagonism with other colleagues.

The challenges

Flexitime, working at home, and crèches are available only to a minority, but they are on the increase. Falling unemployment in most parts of the country means that employers are having to put a bit more effort into retaining staff and providing good conditions designed to attract particular staff with skills and experience.

While flexitime and home-working options are not appropriate for every type of job, there is still room for imaginative approaches to choosing working hours.

The main obstacle is employer resistance. Too many think that progressive policies will cost them. Small companies, in particular, say it may be all right for big organisations but we don't have the same options to be flexible.

But the independent Institute of Employment Studies shows that some small and medium-sized businesses have saved up to £250,000 on their budget simply by using family-friendly work policies. This is mainly because people take less time off sick when they have a better balance in their life.

The benefits

Businesses benefit if they make the best use of their most valuable resource: their staff. The main advantage of balancing personal and professional life is that the workers are happier. If they are happy, they work better; if they work better, the

company profits. And if staff are happy they will stay.

In a tight labour market, employers need to retain and recruit good, hard-working, loyal staff, especially and increasingly women. Offering good working conditions cements the company's reputation as an employer of choice and will attract the best candidates for the job. **Workers are also holding companies more and more accountable for bad working conditions and inflexible practices.** The pressure is growing on employers.

Society demands choice in the 21st century—the choice to take the kids to school and then go to work, the choice to leave early to attend a language course or visit granny, the choice to return to work on a basis you want, the choice to take unpaid leave to travel somewhere new, to train, or to have more time to visit friends.

The facts

Family-friendly flexibility in the Australia:

- While 65% of employers claim to offer some kind of family-friendly working arrangements, including part-time working, only 10% of workplaces provide any practical help with childcare.
- Only 5% of employers provide four kinds of family-friendly practices: maternity benefits, paternity leave, childcare arrangements and non-standard working time.
- 17% of employers offer career breaks of at least three months. But only 12% of employers offer career breaks to both men and women.
- Only 5% of employers provide extended maternity leave with pay beyond the legal minimum. **Women are twice as likely to return to employers where extended maternity has been negotiated.**
- 31% of male employees are entitled to some form of paternity leave—usually paid and typically four days—around the time of birth.
- Fewer than one in three employers offer parents flexibility and extended leave around the time of birth.

(THE END)

work-life balance 职业—生活平衡
flexible hours 灵活的工作时间
affordable /əˈfɔːdəbl/ 足够的，能负担得起的
paternity leave 产假
take over 代替，占据
grip /grip/ 紧握，掌握
overtime /ˈəuvətaim/ 加班，超时工作

epidemic / ˌepiˈdemik / 流行的
poll 民意测验
complain / kəmˈplein / 抱怨
migraine / ˈmiːgrein, ˈmai- / 偏头疼
union / ˈjuːnjən / 工会
perceive / pəˈsiːv / 感觉
breadwinner / ˈbredwinə(r) /养家糊口的人
couple / ˈkʌpl / 夫妇
attitude / ˈætitjuːd / 态度
ambitious / æmˈbiʃəs /有雄心的，野心勃勃的
counterpart / ˈkauntəpɑːt / 同事
step up 升级，抬高
tackle / ˈtækl / 解决

重点剖析

— Contrary to some expectations, according to a recent TUC poll, Brits do actually enjoy their jobs. 85 per cent told us that they found their work enjoyable and fulfilling, yet slightly more than half said they also found it hard to cope with the pressure. TUC的调查表明，英国人实际上喜欢自己的工作，这与某些预期相反。85%的被调查者说自己的工作很有意思让人很充实。不过微过半数的被调查者说自己很难应对工作压力。

— Seven out of ten women of working age now have jobs, and half of mothers with children aged under five are in work. Today's women are breadwinners. 十名在工作年龄的妇女中有七人都在工作，五岁以下孩子的母亲中有一半在工作。如今妇女承担了养家糊口的重任。

— Polls show that fathers feel they are missing out on time with their children. 调查表明父亲们感到他们没有与孩子呆在一起的时间。

— With people living longer, more workers are experiencing care demands on elderly relatives as well as children. The fact that women are now having children later in life means that they may end up facing caring responsibilities for both ends of the age spectrum. 随着人们寿命的增长，越来越多的工作族正经历着"上老有、下有小"的生活。现在的女性要孩子较晚，这就意味着她们既要照顾老人，又要看管孩子。

— The pressure for women to achieve drives them to work harder and for longer, especially when wanting to prove themselves against their male counterparts. 成就动机驱使女性工作更努力、工作时间更长，尤其当她们想证明自己的能力不比男性差时更是如此。

— Research shows that the more control you have over your own work, the less stressed you're likely to get. But organisations, as a whole, need to tackle the issue —it can't just be the sum of individual responses. 研究表明,个体越能控制自己的工作,感到的压力就越小。但总的来说,单位要介入这个问题的解决——毕竟这不全是员工自己的问题。

— The main obstacle is employer resistance. Too many think that progressive policies will cost them. Small companies, in particular, say it may be all right for big organisations but we don't have the same options to be flexible. 主要的障碍来自雇主的抵制,他们大多认为实施这种改良政策的成本太高。尤其是小公司的雇主更是这样认为,他们觉得大公司也许可以实行弹性工作制,但他们自己没有这种能力。

— Businesses benefit if they make the best use of their most valuable resource: their staff. The main advantage of balancing personal and professional life is that the workers are happier. If they are happy, they work better; if they work better, the company profits. And if staff are happy they will stay. 公司如果能最优化利用人才这一最宝贵资源,将会大大受益。平衡员工的个人生活和工作,最主要的好处是会让员工更快乐。快乐的员工会更卖力地工作;如果员工工作更努力,公司就会获益。而且,快乐的员工愿意留在公司(而不愿跳槽)。

— Workers are also holding companies more and more accountable for bad working conditions and inflexible practices. 员工也会认为公司应负责处理不好的工作条件和不灵活的规章制度。

— Women are twice as likely to return to employers where extended maternity has been negotiated. 如果公司与女职员就产假延长问题协商妥当,那么该职员将来重返该公司的可能性就增加了一倍。

（V29真题题源）

2. Corporate Management

公司的管理

Our proposal demonstrates that there is a problem with the employee retention rate at McDonald's fast food restaurants. In order to make up for their recent financial loss, our group proposes that McDonalds hold a convention that will retrain the franchise managers and give them new strategies in dealing with their employees. The managers will attend programs to teach them skills so that eventually the employee retention rate will increase. **When an employee's "life span" at the restaurant is increased, the costs of interviewing, hiring, and training new employees will decrease.**

Despite McDonalds success as a fast food restaurant, there are still some apparent weaknesses. McDonalds is a public company in which many people have brought stock and witnessed its growth. Unfortunately, the shares have dropped nearly two percentage points since 1985 and they have only been growing with the rate of inflation. **The reason that McDonalds is not growing at the pace they were in the past is not only because of their lack of consistent, quality service as indicated by a University of Michigan study; McDonald's inconsistency also comes from the large employee**

turnover rate. Eighty percent of the employees work part time, and there is a three hundred percent turnover rate annually just within the United States. A high turnover rate financially impacts McDonalds because they spend too much money replacing employees. As a result, their rate of growth has decreased over the past ten years. Wages are low, as well as, there are few chances for promotions within the individual franchises because McDonalds functions in a way that each position within the restaurant is almost identical, thus eliminating the amount of promotions. Another reason for such a disproportionate turnover rate is that seventy percent of McDonald's employees are under the age of twenty, also, now more than ever there is more competition for young employees. It is a challenge to keep students working when there are opportunities elsewhere with higher salaries and more chances for promotions. If something can be done about the high turnover rate, McDonalds will be able to witness more growth as they have in the past.

Proposal

In order to increase the employee retention rate, we propose a change in the way the managers interact with the workers at the franchises. First the proposal should be tested in many different geographical and economical settings to determine its effectiveness. We propose that McDonalds should hold a convention for franchise managers to attend, which will retrain the managers to make the employee environment better at McDonald's restaurants. **The convention consists of many different training sessions with the objectives of creating more employee sensitivity, handling promotions and incentives, and incorporating teamwork in the atmosphere.**

The first point to the convention is to assist the managers in becoming more sensitive to their employees. In these sessions, the managers will learn to ask the workers questions about their families, hobbies, talents, accomplishments, and lifetime goals so that good relationships can be developed within the McDonalds franchises. **Skills to make the workers feel valued are important for the managers to learn. In addition, the managers will learn how to ask for feedback from their employees. For example, managers should ask questions such as what they like most and least about their job. Then together they can brainstorm and plan ways to make the workplace more interesting. The manager's employees will then have more respect for McDonald's and want to stay.**

In addition to employee sensitivity, it is important for managers to promote healthy

competition among their employees. To develop a healthy competition, managers will be taught how to reward effectively. Obviously every employee cannot be rewarded monetarily; however, it is possible to give rewards like a certificate of praise for good work. If every worker receives positive feedback and a big deal is not made when employees win actual prizes of monetary value, a healthy competition is then created. In addition, everyone can work together instead of sabotaging his or her co-workers efforts. When employees receive praise, they know that more hard work will eventually yield the monetary awards that they want, thus encouraging the employees to work at McDonald's longer. Another way to control the competition is by using the money for many little prizes instead of a few larger ones. For example, incentives can be given in theater tickets, gift certificates, thank you notes for a job well done, flowers, and negotiated discounts at local retailers. Items such as these are effective because people can look forward to getting them more often throughout the year. With many little, but meaningful prizes, the employees will always look forward to receiving something, which creates more of an incentive to stay at McDonalds, thus achieving the goal of a higher employee retention rate.

It is known that teamwork among employees satisfies customers more because it increases quality and efficiency, which creates a better atmosphere within the restaurant. By increasing "team spirit" within McDonalds, the employees will feel more valuable. When a person gets more attention somewhere, they associate positive thoughts with being at that place. The McDonalds managers will be taught to give each employee attention and make them feel that without them the restaurant cannot succeed in their ultimate goal of pleasing the customers. **Being part of a team and feeling needed will become a characteristic unique to working at McDonald's.**

Conclusion

Through extensive managerial training and hard work, McDonalds should be able to achieve a better employee retention rate. Each employee will have the opportunity to feel they are a part of something important. They will look forward to working because of the friendlier environment. Eventually there will be more repeat customers and the amount of complaints will diminish. Our proposed idea should, in turn, generate more revenue, more employees, and a better organizational structure for everyone.

(THE END)

必备词汇

demonstrate / ˈdemənstreit / 证明，论证
retention rate 留住率
franchise manager 特许经营经理人
eventually / iˈventjuəli / 最终
strategy / ˈstrætidʒi / 策略，战略
deal with 对待，处理
employee / ˌemplɔiˈiː, imˈplɔii / 员工
despite / disˈpait / 不管，尽管
apparent weakness 明显的缺点
inflation / inˈfleiʃən / 通货膨胀
lack of 缺乏，缺少
inconsistency / ˌinkənˈsistənsi / 不一致，矛盾
turnover rate 周转率
promotion / prəˈməuʃən / 升职，晋升
identical / aiˈdentikəl / 同样的，一样的
eliminate / iˈlimineit / 排除
disproportionate / ˌdisprəˈpɔːʃənit / 不成比例的
challenge / ˈtʃælindʒ / 挑战
interact with 和……交流，交互
incentive / inˈsentiv / 激励
teamwork / ˈtiːmwəːk / 团队合作
sensitivity / ˈsensiˈtiviti / 敏感性，灵敏度
hobby / ˈhɔbi / 业余爱好
accomplishment / əˈkɔmpliʃmənt / 成就，造诣
brainstorm / ˈbreinˌstɔːm / 集体讨论
team spirit 团队精神
ultimate / ˈʌltimit / 最终的
characteristic / ˌkæriktəˈristik / 特有的，典型的
extensive / iksˈtensiv / 广泛的
repeat customer 回头客
in turn 反过来
revenue / ˈrevinjuː / 收入

— Our proposal demonstrates that there is a problem with the employee retention rate at McDonald's fast food restaurants. 我们的提案证明，麦当劳快餐店的员工留住率有问题。

— When an employee's "life span" at the restaurant is increased, the costs of interviewing, hiring, and training new employees will decrease.当员工在店里的"工作生涯"增加时，面试、聘用和培训新员工的费用会下降。

— The reason that McDonalds is not growing at the pace they were in the past is not only because of their lack of consistent, quality service as indicated by a University of Michigan study; McDonald's inconsistency also comes from the large employee turnover rate. 麦当劳公司的发展速度放慢了，原因之一正如密歇根大学的某研究所指出的，是因为缺乏稳定的优质服务；另外一个原因就是高员工流动率。

— In order to increase the employee retention rate, we propose a change in the way the managers interact with the workers at the franchises. 为提高员工的留住率，我们建议改变经理和员工的交流方式。

—The convention consists of many different training sessions with the objectives of creating more employee sensitivity, handling promotions and incentives, and incorporating teamwork in the atmosphere. 会议包括各种训练科目，目标是提高员工敏感度、完善升迁和激励机制、营造团队协作气氛。

— Skills to make the workers feel valued are important for the managers to learn. In addition, the managers will learn how to ask for feedback from their employees. 让员工明白自己的价值所在是管理者特别要学习的技能。此外，管理者要学习如何通过询问员工以获取反馈信息。

— For example, managers should ask questions such as what they like most and least about their job. Then together they can brainstorm and plan ways to make the workplace more interesting. The manager's employees will then have more respect for McDonald's and want to stay. 比如，管理者可以问员工这样的问题：最喜欢、最不喜欢工作的是哪些。然后一起来讨论如何使工作变得更为有趣。这样员工将会更为尊重麦当劳，喜欢继续留在公司。

— In addition to employee sensitivity, it is important for managers to promote healthy competition among their employees. To develop a healthy competition, managers will be taught how to reward effectively. Obviously every employee cannot be rewarded monetarily; however, it is possible to give rewards like a certificate of praise for good work. 除了员工敏感性外，管理者学会如何促进员工的良性竞争也很重要。为此，管理者需要学会如何有效奖励员工。显然，不是每位员工都需要物质上的奖励。不过，对工作表现好的员工可以给他们颁发表彰证书什么的。

— Being part of a team and feeling needed will become a characteristic unique to work ing at McDonald's. 让员工成为团队的一部分，让员工觉得自己有用，这将成为在麦当劳工作的重要特色。

(V39真题题源)

3. What is Innovation?

创业与革新的不安

The Latin root of innovation is novus, meaning "new". Innovation means "bringing into effect new and more effective products, services, or approaches." **Continuous innovation allows companies to adapt to constantly changing conditions—both positive and negative. It makes companies more resilient and cost effective. Breakthrough innovations make headlines, but in fact successful organizations value incremental innovation as well. In order to stay in synch with the times, they must develop new markets, products, and services; find ancillary uses for existing products; latch on to new economic trends; and grow or streamline operations as needed.**

That said, companies have to strike a balance between innovation on one hand and order/organization on the other. Innovation to a company is like cell renewal in the human body. Without it there is stagnation and death, so it is absolutely vital. **On the other hand, no company can stand unrestrained innovation. There has to be some degree of order, organization, and control or costs will go wild and chaos will reign. Profitability demands efficiency, and efficiency demands repetition, which can put short-term profits at odds with the longer-term growth provided by innovation.**

Whether the natural tension between innovation and order turns into paralyzing con-

flict or creative interplay really depends on how the company is led. Each company needs to find its own balance between life-giving innovation and life-sustaining organization.

So all companies need to be innovative at some level?

Yes! I don't want to torture the metaphor, but a company really is like a living organism. It has to renew itself to adapt to changing conditions. **Most of the big companies that we now see as pillars of stability were founded on innovative ideas and have had innovative shifts of direction along the way. A lot of other companies that were giants in their day failed to adapt effectively and are history.**

Why is innovative thinking important under current conditions?

Innovation helps companies to:

- Find creative ways of keeping the same level of service without using the same level of resources.
- Retain top performers. People get a sense of satisfaction from creating something new (breakthrough) or making something better (incremental). I personally stayed with a company six years longer than I had planned because of the variety of projects I had there and the level of creativity my management encouraged.
- Enhance teambuilding efforts. Teamwork and innovation go hand-in-hand. Where you have innovation, you almost always find cross-functional and specialist teams working to carry it out. **I would also support the notion that a truly team-based organization is more likely to foster an innovative environment.**

Today, are companies giving more weight to their stable side in order to make stakeholders, employees, and customers feel more secure?

These are obviously unusual times and leaders can't be faulted for feeling anxious. Companies will have reactions to stress as varied as individuals have. Some are paralyzed by the slightest threat; I have seen companies doing things akin to applying the brakes to a car that is already stopped, as if that will somehow help. Others are naturally agile or are shaken out of their complacency, and they take advantage of the turmoil to try something new. Overall, I sense a kind of uneasy optimism right now, as if the nascent economic recovery is like wet cement that we hope will dry soon before too much graffiti gets scrawled into it.

What can a company do to foster innovation?

Some people are always innovative and some people never are. Most people are somewhere in the middle. I firmly believe that those in the middle take their cues from the overall environment and their immediate leaders. Companies and their leaders need to send a clear message that innovation is valued, refrain from micromanaging employees (because nothing kills the urge to innovate faster), and give employees recognition for their ideas. Since innovation is never a sure-fire thing, some level of failure must be tolerated.

That is the dilemma. Our business world is results oriented, but much of the experimentation that eventually leads to successful innovation is unsuccessful; there's a lot of "failure" involved in success. Companies that understand that are more likely to give innovators the time, resources, and political support they need to produce something new and better. **Companies that are impatient or superficial in their support of innovation remind me of the Chinese proverb about the farmer who felt that his crops were growing too slowly so he decided to help them along by pulling on the roots.**

What is the task of an innovative leader?

Independent of whether the leadership of a company openly supports innovation or transmits signals against change, I think that individual people experience the same ambivalence toward innovation that organizations experience. **People are often skeptical of new things at the same time that they are excited by them. The job of the innovator is to minimize the perception of risk on the one hand and maximize the perception of benefit on the other. Perception of risk is minimized by helping others see that change is not necessarily loss.** Risk is also minimized by familiarizing people with the change so that it is not seen as so strange after all. It takes a lot of communicating, and successful innovators are usually great lobbyists in their organizations.

Increasing perception of benefit involves helping the individual constituencies affected by the innovation to see how their goals will be met by its implementation. It is about answering the question "what's in it for me—or others?"

(THE END)

必备词汇

innovation /ˌinəuˈveiʃən/ 革新，创新
adapt to 适应
resilient /riˈziliənt/ 有弹性的
approach /əˈprəutʃ/ 方法，途径
strike a balance between 在……之间达成平衡
renewal /riˈnju(ː)əl/ 更新，补充
stagnation /stægˈneiʃən/ 停滞
unrestrained /ˈʌnrisˈtreind/ 无限制的
chaos /ˈkeiɔs/ 混乱
profitability /ˌprɔfitəˈbiliti/ 收益性
repetition /ˌrepiˈtiʃən/ 重复，循环
at odds 不和谐，不相称
tension /ˈtenʃən/ 紧张，不安
paralyzing /ˈpærəlaiziŋ/ 瘫痪的
conflict /ˈkɔnflikt/ 冲突
interplay /ˈintə(ː)ˈplei/ 相互影响
torture /ˈtɔːtʃə/ 拷问，折磨
metaphor /ˈmetəfə/ 比喻，象征
pillar /ˈpilə/ 栋梁
akin /əˈkin/ 类似的
agile /ˈædʒail/ 敏捷的，灵活的
complacency /kəmˈpleisənsi/ 满足，安心
turmoil /ˈtəːmɔil/ 骚动，混乱
optimism /ˈɔptimizəm/ 乐观主义
fault /fɔːlt/ 挑剔
refrain from 节制，避免
sure-fire thing 做好的熟饭
tolerate /ˈtɔləreit/ 忍受，容忍
dilemma /diˈlemə, dai-/ 进退两难的局面，困难的选择
ambivalence /æmˈbivələns/ 正反感情并存
skeptical /ˈskeptikəl/ 怀疑的
lobbyist /ˈlɔbiist/ 说客
constituency /kənˈstitjuənsi/ 支持者

重点剖析

— Continuous innovation allows companies to adapt to constantly changing conditions—both positive and negative. It makes companies more resilient and cost effective. Breakthrough innovations make headlines, but in fact successful organizations value incremental innovation as well. In order to stay in synch with the times, they must develop new markets, products, and services; find ancillary uses for existing products; latch on to new economic trends; and grow or streamline operations as needed. 不断的创新让公司能适应不断变化的环境——无论是积极环境还是消极环境。这会让公司更为灵活、更具有成本效益。突进式的创新可以成为新闻头条，但实际上成功的组织也很重视循序渐进的创新。为了与时俱进，它们必须开发新的市场、产品和服务；寻找现有产品的补充用途；顺应新的经济潮流；必要时扩大或使经营流水化。

— That said, companies have to strike a balance between innovation on one hand and order/organization on the other.也就是说，公司应该在创新和秩序/组织两方面达到平衡。

— On the other hand, no company can stand unrestrained innovation. There has to be some degree of order, organization, and control or costs will go wild and chaos will reign. Profitability demands efficiency, and efficiency demands repetition, which can put short-term profits at odds with the longer-term growth provided by innovation. 另一方面，没有一个公司能够承受无限制的创新。创新需要有一定程度的秩序、组织和控制，否则成本就会超出范围而导致失控，这种混乱就会搞垮公司。利润率需要有效率，效率需要有循环往复，这些会使短期利润和创新带来的长期发展互不调和。

— Whether the natural tension between innovation and order turns into paralyzing conflict or creative interplay really depends on how the company is led. Each company needs to find its own balance between life-giving innovation and life-sustaining organization. 创新和秩序之间天然的紧张关系是转化成毁灭性的冲突还是创造性的相互影响其实取决于公司如何被领导。每个公司都需要找到生存赋予的创新和维持生计的组织之间的平衡。

— Most of the big companies that we now see as pillars of stability were founded on innovative ideas and have had innovative shifts of direction along the way. A lot of other companies that were giants in their day failed to adapt effectively and are history. 今天看到的大多数稳定的大公司是建立在创新观念之上的，它们一直都有创新性的方向转变。其他许多公司也曾一度叱咤风云，但由于没能有效适应新形势而成为过眼云烟。

— I would also support the notion that a truly team-based organization is more likely to foster an innovative environment. 我也认可真有具有团队精神的组织更能孕育创新的氛围这一观点。

— These are obviously unusual times and leaders can't be faulted for feeling anxious. Companies will have reactions to stress as varied as individuals have. Some are paralyzed by the slightest threat; I have seen companies doing things akin to applying the brakes to a car that is already stopped, as if that will somehow help. Others are naturally agile or are shaken out of their complacency, and they take advantage of the turmoil to try something new. Overall, I sense a kind of uneasy optimism right now, as if the nascent economic recovery is like wet cement that we hope will dry soon before too much graffiti gets scrawled into it. 这显然是个不寻常的时代，不能因为焦虑而挑管理者的错。公司应像个人一样灵活处理压力。有些公司因为一点小小的威胁就一蹶不振，我见到有些公司面临威胁时的反应，就像是对一辆停着的

汽车踩刹车，好像那样会有用。其他公司能自如灵活地做出应对，或者摆脱自我满足，它们会利用混乱尝试一些新招数。总得来讲，我现在感到一种不安的乐观主义，似乎刚刚露头的经济复苏就像那湿润的水泥，我们希望它在有太多的乱涂乱抹者出现之前就能很快干燥。

— Companies that are impatient or superficial in their support of innovation remind me of the Chinese proverb about the farmer who felt that his crops were growing too slowly so he decided to help them along by pulling on the roots. 那些没有耐心或者浮皮潦草地支持创新的公司使我想起中国的一句谚语：揠苗助长。

— People are often skeptical of new things at the same time that they are excited by them. The job of the innovator is to minimize the perception of risk on the one hand and maximize the perception of benefit on the other. Perception of risk is minimized by helping others see that change is not necessarily loss. 人们通常对新事物持怀疑态度，但同时也为此感到兴奋。创新者的工作就是一方面把人们对风险的看法降到最低，另一方面把人们对获益的看法放到最大。通过让人们明白创新并不一定意味着损失利益而使风险意识最小化。

(V39真题题源)

4. The New Meaning of Older Workers

老龄职工对公司的作用

The 21st century may be known as the era of lifelong learning and lifelong working. Retirement, the end stage of a linear working life, may be replaced with a learning, working, leisure, working, learning life cycle. In a cyclical living and working model, participating in the work force never ceases but is interspersed with periods of leisure and learning. Full-time work may be interspersed with periods of flexible working arrangements such as part-time, seasonal, occasional, and project work. The traditional notion of retirement may be replaced with lifelong working in various positions and in varying amounts of time throughout adult life. In the future a declining birthrate may result in a shortage of skilled and knowledgeable employees, making the notion of retirement for older workers a serious drain on organizational productivity. **Increasing demands for work force productivity, a projected shortage of skilled and experienced workers, and older adults who are healthier and living longer than previous generations are powerful societal forces shaping future employment practices.**

Two decades ago, Sheppard and Rix (1977) forecast the changing nature of the workplace and suggested that keeping older persons in the work force would make sound economic and social policy sense. **Yet Ginzberg (1983) raised a most challenging question by asking to what extent is our society ready to make work for an increasing number of older adults who choose to remain in the workplace while also providing**

opportunities for young adults: if employment is not a possibility, then what is our obligation to provide adequate financial support? Morrison (1990) noted that social policies were needed to encourage and support employers retaining older workers. Today the fastest growing segment of the population is the older adult. Still, the decision to remain or leave the workplace is a function of organizational policy. This Digest examines this trend and looks at ways adult educators can create and sustain working environments supportive of the needs and capabilities of older workers.

New Patterns Of Work For Older Adults

The trend toward longer periods of employment is beginning to become evident. Forced retirements and early retirement incentives have contributed to the decline of expertise in the workplace. **Inflation, increasing health care costs, and inadequate pensions are propelling older adults to remain in or reenter the work force past the traditional retirement age.** Stein, Rocco, and Goldenetz (2000) proposed a model that identifies older workers as remaining in, retiring from, or returning to the workplace. These patterns require employers to provide a variety of learning programs to accommodate these older workers. In this model, retirement as a permanent separation from work becomes just a temporary choice.

Retirement as permanent separation from the workplace is being replaced with the idea of bridge employment. **Bridging is a form of partial retirement in which an older worker alternates periods of disengagement from the workplace with periods of temporary, part-time, occasional, or self-employed work.** The key aspect of bridging is that it is work in other than a career job. A career job is a position occupied by a worker for a substantial portion of the working life in a single setting or with a single employer. Among workers age 60, more than 50 percent retire from a career job but only one in nine actually disengages from the workplace. Bridging allows older workers to "practice" retirement, to fill labor market shortages, or to try a variety of occupational positions after an initial period of retirement.

Bridging is sometimes described as a second career. The American Association of Retired Persons received 36,000 responses to a working life survey, covering 375 job titles from workers age 50 plus who had returned to the workplace after an initial period of retirement. **The three most frequently cited reasons for returning included having financial need, liking to work, and keeping busy. However, closer examination of the data revealed that "financial need" included money to help the children as well as to meet basic needs.** "Liking to work" included feeling successful, enjoying the excitement of the workplace, and making a contribution. "Keeping busy" included working with a spouse, staying healthy, or fulfilling a social need. Reasons cited for remaining or returning to the workplace expressed the social meaning of work. Ginzberg (1983) proposed that work provides income, status, and personal achievement; structures time; and provides opportunities for interpersonal relationships. In the study by Stein, Rocco, and Goldenetz (2000), older workers remaining in or returning to the workplace mentioned not planning wisely, the need to contribute, appreciation from others, and the desire to create something as reasons for not retiring from the workplace. Work is more than earning a living. It is a way to live.

To some extent older workers remain in the workplace because they are healthier, cognitively able, and want to remain engaged. In a review of older worker studies, Rix (1990) concluded that many aging workers continue to work at peak efficiency and that there is usually much more variation within age groups than among age groups. Shea (1991) summarized the studies on older workers by pointing out that "age-related changes in physical ability, cognitive performance, and personality have little effect on workers' output except in the most physically demanding tasks." Farr, Tesluk, and Klein (1998) found that there is no consistent relationship between age and performance across settings. **Among faculty in the sciences, age had a slight negative relationship to publishing productivity. Some studics have shown a stronger negative relationship between age and work performance for nonprofessional and low-level clerical jobs than for higher-level craft, service, and professional jobs.**

With declining birthrates and an anticipated shortage of new entrants to the work force, early retirement will become an issue for organizations to explore in more detail. Organizations will need to assess the consequences to profits and productivity of encouraging talented and wise elders to exit the work force. As a society we need to recognize all of the costs of supporting a nonworking population capable of productive work and living healthier and longer lives.

Organizations need to rethink allocating opportunities to older workers as well as changing the attitudes and expectations of managers and younger employees toward an increasing number of older workers. There is a growing interest among organizations to reengineer the work environment to account for physiological changes due to aging and to reorganize work schedules to account for seasonal or contingent labor pools composed of older workers. Few positions in our information society remain static and do not require some type of education. Education and job redesign are the means by which the older segment of the community can enter, reenter, and advance in the workplace.

Adult Education Implications

This inquiry suggests that older workers are situated in a dynamic pattern of periods of active employment, disengagement from the workplace, and reentry into the same or a new career. Older workers exhibit different work patterns at different stages. The workplace becomes a dynamic space for older workers rather than a unidirectional journey leading to retirement. An adult education perspective for the third stage of working life—eyond the traditional retirement age—ill view the older worker as an active agent negotiating various roles within the workspace. The roles, depending on life circumstances, might include the decision to remain in, retire from, or return to periods of part-time, full-time, or part-season work. These work choice patterns will challenge adult educators to develop training, career development, and organizational development strategies appropriate to a third stage of working life.

An aging and changing work force may cause us to reexamine and revalue the meaning and necessity of work for older workers. An aging work force might influence workplace cultures and values in ways that change our notions of the meaning and necessity of work. A workplace that blends training opportunities, flexible employment patterns, and policies supportive of the life needs of an aging work force may become a workplace that embraces older workers as capable, productive, and knowledgeable lifelong workers. Older workers will need organizational and social supports to encourage the extension of the work life.

Older workers represent a rich source of experience, accumulated knowledge, and wisdom. The quality and sensitivity of an institution's program for counseling, training, retraining, and preparing older workers for life and career transition might be the means by which organizations recruit and retain valued and productive workers.

(THE END)

lifelong / ˈlaiflɔŋ / 终生的
retirement / riˈtaiəmənt / 退休
intersperse / ˌintə(:)ˈspə:s / 点缀
full-time 全日的
part-time 兼职的
declining birthrate 下降的出生率

result in 导致
decade / ˈdekeid / 十年
forecast / ˈfɔːkɑːst / 预见，预测
workplace 工作场所
sound / saund / 健全的，合理的
expertise / ˌekspəˈtiːz / 专门技术
forced retirement 强制性退休
inflation / inˈfleiʃən / 通货膨胀
propel / prəˈpel / 驱使，推动
bridge employment 过渡就业
physically demanding task 对身体条件要求很高的工作
entrant / ˈentrənt / 新到者，进入者
reengineer / ˌriːendʒiˈnɪə(r) / 再设计
compose of 包括，由……组成
blend / blend / 混合
embrace / imˈbreis / 包容
represent / ˌrepriˈzent / 代表

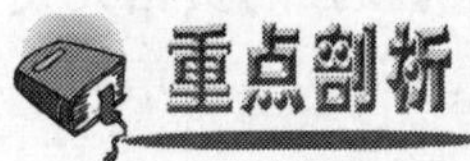

重点剖析

— Increasing demands for work force productivity, a projected shortage of skilled and experienced workers, and older adults who are healthier and living longer than previous generations are powerful societal forces shaping future employment practices. 对劳动力生产效率日益增强的要求、预期的熟练工人的短缺、比从前几代人更健康更长寿的老年人是影响将来就业情势的强大社会力量。

— Yet Ginzberg (1983) raised a most challenging question by asking to what extent is our society ready to make work for an increasing number of older adults who choose to remain in the workplace while also providing opportunities for young adults: if employment is not a possibility, then what is our obligation to provide adequate financial support? 然而，Ginzberg（1983）提出了一个更具挑战性的问题，他问道，我们的社会应做何准备才能为那些仍然要工作的日益增多的老年人提供工作岗位，而同时还要考虑年轻人的要求：如果老年人可能不再就业，那么我们给他们提供足够财政支持的义务会是什么呢？

— Inflation, increasing health care costs, and inadequate pensions are propelling older adults to remain in or reenter the work force past the traditional retirement age. 通货膨胀、医疗保健费用的日渐增加以及养老金的捉襟见肘驱使老年员工在过了传统退休年龄后重返就业大军。

— Bridging is a form of partial retirement in which an older worker alternates periods of disengagement from the workplace with periods of temporary, part-time, occasional, or self-employed work. 过渡是部分退休的一种形式，即老年员工改变了他们从职场中脱离的阶段，代之以临时的、兼职性的、偶尔的、或自己当老板的工作。

— The three most frequently cited reasons for returning included having financial need, liking to work, and keeping busy. However, closer examination of the data revealed that "financial need" included money to help the children as well as to meet basic needs. 最常引用的重返职场的三个原因：财政需要、喜欢工作、保持忙碌。然而，对数据经过更细致的检查发现，“财政需要”包括帮助孩子和满足基本生活需要的资金。

— Among faculty in the sciences, age had a slight negative relationship to publishing productivity. Some studies have shown a stronger negative relationship between age and work performance for nonprofessional and low-level clerical jobs than for higher-level craft, service, and professional jobs. 在科学的各学科中，年龄与工作效率只呈微弱的负相关关系。某些研究显示，非专业性的和低级别的文书工作比起较高级别的工艺、服务性和专业性的工作，年龄和工作业绩之间有较强的负相关关系。

— This inquiry suggests that older workers are situated in a dynamic pattern of periods of active employment, disengagement from the workplace, and reentry into the same or a new career. Older workers exhibit different work patterns at different stages. 调查显示，老年职工生活在一个积极就业、脱离工作场所、重新进入相同的或新职业的动态周期模式中。他们在不同的阶段显示出不同的工作模式。

— Older workers represent a rich source of experience, accumulated knowledge, and wisdom. 老年职工具有丰富的经验、知识和智慧。

(V34真题题源)

5. Office Space: A Tool, Status Symbol or a Cost Center?

工作职务与空间

Who among us has not compared the size, location, appearance, components, layout and degree of enclosure of our own individual offices to those of our colleagues or competition? **Offices have political, symbolic and functional importance. They can also have a dramatic impact on the bottom line, as offices represent the greatest percentage of occupied real estate in white-collar environments.**

Typically, people represent 65 percent to 80 percent of an organization's costs to be in business, while technology ranges from 10 percent to 20 percent, and facilities or real estate are 5 percent to 20 percent. **Efficiently planned offices can save valuable real estate and, more importantly, well-designed workplaces can enhance the effectiveness of the people responsible for growing a business.**

Offices as status symbols

Traditionally, offices in corporate America have been viewed as opportunities to minimize costs and to reward employees.

The result is often the top 10 percent to 15 percent of the organization in large, enclosed offices that provide beautiful views to the outside, while the balance of the organization resides in somewhat less desirable, efficiently planned offices and open workstations.

There is no denying entitlement and minimizing overall occupancy costs are valid considerations in most organizations. **In fact, for certain types of relationships, it can be critical that offices reinforce status and/or space efficiency.**

In a survey of Fortune 500 companies I conducted 10 years ago, 60 percent of the respondents indicated that office assignments were based solely on entitlement. Just this past summer, I posed that same question to 175 Fortune 500 companies and the responses were considerably different, with only 30 percent of participants assigning space solely by entitlement, another 30 percent making assignments by function and 40 percent doing so by a combination of entitlement and function.

Most importantly, 65 percent of the respondents said decisions about office assignments were based on what best aligned with the core business strategy like recruiting and retaining the best people and enhancing speed to market.

Offices as tools

Offices planned as tools consider status and space efficiency, but focus more on function, emphasizing individual activities, group workflow, operational relationships, amenity functions, the ambient environment, brand and identity.

Individual activities are the daily tasks that people perform in their assigned offices. There are 15 functional job types that describe the activities performed by about 95 percent of the people in corporate America. With each job type is a unique pattern of activities and corresponding space requirements. **Among numerous variables, meeting activities, storage, privacy, display needs and desktop tasks are the primary drivers of space requirements.**

Fortunately, the unique descriptions generate only four ranges of office sizes:

- 40- to 70-square-foot workstations.
- 80- to 100-square-foot workstations or offices.
- 110- to 150-square-foot offices.
- 160- to 200-square-foot offices.

Thus, most companies can create four basic office standards, within which a full range of task-supportive components can be provided.

Types of work

There are three categories into which eight different workflow types can be described as separate, independent teams. Groups whose individuals work separately do so for security reasons or because there is little or no need for face-to-face contact. The vast majority of groups work independently, with individuals coming together at planned times to exchange information.

A growing trend is groups that work as teams. Members of true teams work together throughout the day on a series of tasks that require everyone's input. For teams, the primary office is a centrally- located, shared place where people can work together. In all workflow types, it's absolutely critical that individuals have control over when to concentrate alone or communicate with the group.

Offices designed as tools consider places like fitness or wellness centers, cafeterias, break areas, day care and related amenities as opportunities for people to perceive an entire building as their office.

Bringing it all together

Recently, a Fortune 500 company redesigned its product-development processes from functional disciplines to product categories. Spatially, five responses were critical to supporting the new processes. The first step was to move people from sales, marketing, finance, IT and R&D into each category.

Within the groups, 90-square-foot workstations, each equipped with one of 10 component options, were provided to everybody. Employees also could conduct desktop videoconferencing, control task lighting, air movement and sound levels. In addition, there was a series of retreat rooms for one person, huddle rooms for two to four people and various conference rooms for up to 25 people.

Workstations were designed in clusters around a central team space called a living room. Finally, amenities were added including running trails, bank, wellness, cafeteria and outdoor interaction areas.

The financial benefit to the company has been huge as product development times have been reduced by 10 percent and the number of new or refined products developed has increased by 15 percent over the last three years. Occupancy costs are down 5 percent.

The bottom line is an office environment that is a tool of facility efficiency and, more importantly, organizational effectiveness.

(THE END)

layout / 'lei,aut / 布置，规划
colleague / 'kɔliːg / 同事
competition / kɔmpi'tiʃ ən / 竞争
symbolic / sim'bɔlik / 象征性的
impact / 'impækt / 影响，冲击
bottom line 底线
white-collar 白领
enhance / in'hɑːns / 增强
effectiveness / i'fektivnis / 效力
traditionally 传统上
minimize / 'minimaiz / 将……减到最小
reinforce / ˌriːin'fɔːs / 加强
Fortune 500 companies 《财富》500强公司
respondent / ris'pɔndənt / 应答者，回答者
entitlement 权利
identity / ai'dentiti / 身份

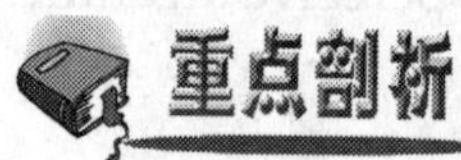

— Offices have political, symbolic and functional importance. They can also have a dramatic impact on the bottom line, as offices represent the greatest percentage of occupied real estate in white-collar environments. 办公室具有政治、象征和功能的重要性。它们还对底线价值具有重大的影响，因为办公室代表着白领环境中已占有不动产的最大比例。

— Efficiently planned offices can save valuable real estate and, more importantly, well-designed workplaces can enhance the effectiveness of the people responsible for growing a business. 经过有效规划的办公室可以节约宝贵的不动产，更重要的是，设计良好的办公场所可以提高那些负责增加公司业务的人员的工作效力。

— The result is often the top 10 percent to 15 percent of the organization in large, enclosed offices that provide beautiful views to the outside, while the balance of the organization resides in somewhat less desirable, efficiently planned offices and open workstations. 结果组织中10%~15%的人员在大而密闭的办公室里，从那里可以欣赏美妙的窗外风光。其他人员则在不那么合意、规划不那么有效的办公室里和公共的工作间里。

— In fact, for certain types of relationships, it can be critical that offices reinforce status and/or space efficiency. 事实上，对于某些关系来说，办公室加强身份和(或)空间效率的作用很重要。

— Most importantly, 65 percent of the respondents said decisions about office assign ments were based on what best aligned with the core business strategy like recruiting and retaining the best people and enhancing speed to market. 最重要的是，有65%的回答者说怎样布置办公室是基于那些和公司核心业务战略相一致的内容如招聘、留住最好的员工，提高打入市场的速度等来决定的。

— Offices planned as tools consider status and space efficiency, but focus more on function, emphasizing individual activities, group workflow, operational relationships, amenity functions, the ambient environment, brand and identity. 对作为工具的办公室的规划考虑了地位和空间效率，但更多地关注于功能，强调个人活动、团队工作流程、工作关系、礼仪功能、周边环境、品牌和身份。

— Among numerous variables, meeting activities, storage, privacy, display needs and desktop tasks are the primary drivers of space requirements. 在无数个变量之中，会见活动、存储、隐私、展示需求和桌面任务是空间要求的主要推动力。

— The bottom line is an office environment that is a tool of facility efficiency and, more importantly, organizational effectiveness. 办公环境的基本功用是体现设备效率，更重要的是体现组织有效性。

七、建筑结构类（8篇）

（New version真题题源）

1. Aswan High Dam Controls World's Longest River

阿斯旺水坝

Just north of the border between Egypt and Sudan lies the Aswan High Dam, a huge rockfill dam which captures the world longest river, the Nile, in one of the world third largest reservoirs, Lake Nasser. The dam, known as Saad el Aali in Arabic, was completed in 1970 after 18 years of work.

Egypt has always depended on the water of the Nile River. The two main tributaries of the Nile River are the White Nile and the Blue Nile. Lake Victoria is the source of the White Nile and the Blue Nile begins in the Ethiopian Highlands. **The two tributaries converge in Khartoum, the capital of Sudan where they form the Nile River. The Nile River has a total length of 4,160 miles (6,695 kilometers) from source to sea.**

Before the building of a dam at Aswan, Egypt experienced annual floods from the

Nile River which deposited 4 million tons of nutrient-rich sediment which enabled agricultural production.

This process began millions of years before Egyptian civilization began in the Nile valley and continued until the first dam at Aswan was built in 1889. **This dam was insufficient to hold back the water of the Nile and was subsequently raised in 1912 and 1933. In 1946, the true danger was revealed when the water in the reservoir peaked near the top of the dam.**

In 1952, the interim Revolutionary Council government of Egypt decided to build a High Dam at Aswan, about four miles upstream of the old dam. In 1954, Egypt requested loans from the World Bank to help pay for the cost of the dam (which eventually added up to US$1 billion). Initially, the United States agreed to loan Egypt money but then withdrew their offer for unknown reasons. Some speculate that it may have been due to Egyptian and Israeli conflict. The United Kingdom, France, and Israel had invaded Egypt in 1956, soon after Egypt nationalized the Suez Canal to help pay for the dam.

The Soviet Union offered to help and Egypt accepted. The Soviet Union's support was not unconditional, however. Along with the money, they also sent military advisers and other workers to help enhance Egyptian-Soviet ties and relations.

In order to build the dam both people and artifacts had to be moved. Over 90,000 Nubians had to be relocated. Those who had been living in Egypt were moved about 28 miles (45 km) away but the Sudanese Nubians were relocated 370 miles (600 km) from their homes. The government was also forced to develop one of the largest Abu Simel temple and dig for artifacts before the future lake would drown the land of the Nubians.

After years of construction (the material in the dam is the equivalent to 17 of the great pyramid at Giza), the resulting reservoir was named for the former president of Egypt, Gamal Abdel Nasser, who died in 1970. The lake holds 137 million acre-feet of water (169 billion cubic meters). About 17 percent of the lake is in Sudan and the two countries have an agreement for distribution of the water.

The dam benefits Egypt by controlling the annual floods on the Nile River and prevents the damage which used to occur along the floodplain. The Aswan High Dam provides about a half of Egypt's power supply and has improved navigation along the river by keeping the water flow consistent.

There are several problems associated with the dam as well. Seepage and evaporation accounts for a loss of about 12% — 14% of the annual input into the reservoir.

The sediments of the Nile River, as with all river and dam systems, has been filling the reservoir and thus decreasing its storage capacity. This has also resulted in problems downstream.

Farmers have been forced to use about a million tons of artificial fertilizer as a substitute for the nutrients which no longer fill the flood plain. **Further downstream, the Nile delta is having problems due to the lack of sediment as well since there is no additional agglomeration of sediment to keep erosion of the delta at bay so it slowly shrinks.** Even the shrimp catch in the Mediterranean Sea has decreased due to the change in water flow.

Poor drainage of the newly irrigated lands has led to saturation and increased salinity. Over one half of Egypt's farmland in now rated medium to poor soils.

The parasitic disease schistosomiasis has been associated with the stagnant water of the fields and the reservoir. Some studies indicate that the number of individuals affected has increased since the opening of the Aswan High Dam.

The Nile River and now the Aswan High Dam are Egypt's lifeline. About 95% of Egypt's population lives within twelve miles from the river. **Were it not for the river and its sediment, the grand civilization of ancient Egypt probably would have never existed.**

(THE END)

Aswan High Dam 阿斯旺大坝（位于埃及和苏丹的边界）
Nile River 尼罗河
rockfill / ˈrɔkfil / 废石填充，填石
capture / ˈkæptʃə / 拦截，捕获
reservoir / ˈrezəvwɑː / 水库，蓄水池
tributary / ˈtribjutəri / 支流
converge / kənˈvəːdʒ / 汇合
deposit / diˈpɔzit / 沉积，堆积
nutrient-rich sediment 富含营养的沉积物
hold back 阻拦，截住
peak / piːk / 顶峰，高峰
upstream / ˈʌpˈstriːm / 向上游，逆流
eventually / iˈventjuəli / 最终
speculate / ˈspekjuˌleit / 猜想，推测
nationalize / ˈnæʃənəlaiz / 使国有化
Suez Canal 苏伊士运河
unconditional / ˈʌnkənˈdiʃənəl / 无条件的
tie / tai / 关系，联系
relocate / ˈriːləuˈkeit / 重新安置，移民
drown / draun / 淹没
floodplain / flʌdplein / 涝原，泛滥平原
seepage / ˈsiːpidʒ / 渗流
artificial fertilizer 人造化肥
substitute / ˈsʌbstitjuːt / 代替物
agglomeration / əˌglɔməˈreiʃən / 凝结，聚集

shrimp / ʃrimp / 虾
drainage / 'dreinidʒ / 排水
saturation / ˌsætʃə'reiʃən / 饱和
salinity / sə'liniti / 盐分，盐度
parasitic disease 寄生虫疾病
schistosomiasis / ˌʃistəsəu'maiəsis / 血吸虫病
lifeline / 'laɪflaɪn / 生命线

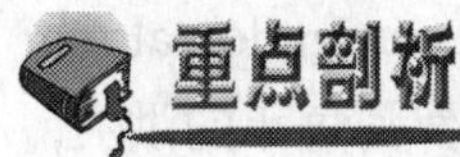

重点剖析

— Just north of the border between Egypt and Sudan lies the Aswan High Dam, a huge rockfill dam which captures the world's longest river, the Nile, in one of the world's third largest reservoirs, Lake Nasser. 阿斯旺大坝高高耸立在埃及和苏丹交界以北，是一个用废石填充的大坝，在世界三大水库之一的纳赛尔湖那里把世界最长的河流——尼罗河拦腰截住。

— The two tributaries converge in Khartoum, the capital of Sudan where they form the Nile River. The Nile River has a total length of 4,160 miles (6,695 kilometers) from source to sea. 两大支流在苏丹首都喀土穆汇合形成尼罗河。尼罗河从源头到入海口全长4160英里（6695公里）。

— Before the building of a dam at Aswan, Egypt experienced annual floods from the Nile River which deposited 4 million tons of nutrient-rich sediment which enabled agricultural production. 在阿斯旺建造大坝前，埃及每年都遭受尼罗河的洪灾泛滥，洪灾带来了400万吨营养丰富的沉积物，使埃及的农业生产受益多多。

— This dam was insufficient to hold back the water of the Nile and was subsequently raised in 1912 and 1933. In 1946, the true danger was revealed when the water in the reservoir peaked near the top of the dam. 大坝不足以拦住尼罗河的洪水，所以在1912年和1933年分别进行了加高。1946年，水库中洪水的洪峰一度接近大坝顶端，真正的危险凸现了。

— In 1952, the interim Revolutionary Council government of Egypt decided to build a High Dam at Aswan, about four miles upstream of the old dam. In 1954, Egypt requested loans from the World Bank to help pay for the cost of the dam (which eventually added up to US$1 billion). Initially, the United States agreed to loan Egypt money but then withdrew their offer for unknown reasons. Some speculate that it may have been due to Egyptian and Israeli conflict. 1952年，埃及临时革命委员会决定在旧坝上游大约四英里处的阿斯旺建造一个高坝。1954年，埃及向世界银行申请贷款以支付大坝的费用（最后增加到10亿美元）。起初，美国同意向埃及支付贷款，但最后取消了意向，其中的原因不为人所知。有人猜想是由于埃及和以色列的战争冲突引起的。

— In order to build the dam both people and artifacts had to be moved. Over 90,000 Nubians had to be relocated. 为建造大坝，人和文物不得不搬迁。有9万多努比亚人需要重新安置。

— The dam benefits Egypt by controlling the annual floods on the Nile River and prevents the damage which used to occur along the floodplain. The Aswan High Dam provides about a half of Egypt's power supply and has improved navigation along the river by keeping the water flow consistent. 大坝控制住了尼罗河每年的洪灾，使埃及大大受益，防止了给沿涝原的地区造成损失。阿斯旺大坝给埃及提供了一半左右的电力供应，由于水流稳定，从而改善了沿尼罗河的航行条件。

— There are several problems associated with the dam as well. Seepage and evaporation accounts for a loss of about 12%—14% of the annual input into the reservoir. The sediments of the Nile River, as with all river and dam systems, has been filling the reservoir and thus decreasing its storage capacity. This has also resulted in problems downstream. 但大坝也同样带来了一些问题。渗流和蒸发造成了水库中补水量的损失，大约相当于每年补水量的12%—14%。尼罗河以及其他河流和大坝系统的沉积物填满了水库，引起了储水量的下降。在下游，也出现了问题。

— Further downstream, the Nile delta is having problems due to the lack of sediment as well since there is no additional agglomeration of sediment to keep erosion of the delta at bay so it slowly shrinks. 在更远的下游，因为缺乏沉积物，尼罗河三角洲遇到了问题，因为没有额外的沉积物积聚来阻止海湾处三角洲的侵蚀，所以海湾面积慢慢地收缩了。

— Poor drainage of the newly irrigated lands has led to saturation and increased salinity. Over one half of Egypt's farmland in now rated medium to poor soils. 新灌溉的土地排水条件很差，使土壤饱和，盐度增加。埃及有近一半农田目前被标定为中等到贫瘠土壤。

— Were it not for the river and its sediment, the grand civilization of ancient Egypt probably would have never existed. 如果不是因为有尼罗河和它带来的沉积物，也许伟大的古埃及文明就不会产生。

(V35真题题源)

2. Microwave Technology of Detecting Bridges

桥梁微波检测技术

The primary types of sensors used for vibration testing are piezoelectric or piezoresistive seismic accelerometers. For experimental modal analysis applications piezoelectric accelerometers are most commonly used. They have adequate signal-to-noise ratio, bandwidth, and are usually small enough relative to the structure being tested so as not to alter the structure's dynamic properties.

Piezoelectric accelerometers are relatively inexpensive (typically in the range of 250—1000 Dollars US, 1997) and accurate. **However, there are problems associated with these devices particularly when they are applied to the vibration testing of very large structures, when they are used in hazardous environments, and when the mass of the accelerometer is significant relative to the mass of the structure being tested. Although mode shape and operating shapes of a structure are routinely measured with conventional accelerometers, these sensors do not provide a direct measurement of displacement, which is often of interest for the study of a structure's operating vibration shapes (the superposition of many mode shapes).**

Accelerometers must be mounted at the appropriate locations that are representative of the structure's motion, and access may be a problem, particularly if the tests are being performed in hazardous environments such as radiation or high voltage areas. Also, use of these transducers requires hardwiring from the transducer to the data acquisition system. When the structure is large, the effort associated with mounting and wiring the accelerometers is typically the most time-consuming task associated with the test, and can subject the test crew to hazardous conditions. As an example, the mounting and wiring of 26 accelerometers on a 130 m (425 ft) segment of the bridge discussed in this paper required approximately 30 person-days (much of this time was spent on narrow catwalks 6.1～12 m (20～40 ft) above the ground), while an actual test took only 2～3 hours.

There are non-contact, near-field and far-field displacement transducers that are commercially available. The near-field non-contact transducers include feedback-type capacitive devices, eddy current transducers, mutual inductance devices, variable reluctance devices, and fiber-optic sensors. **Because of the need for a fixed reference location to mount the near-field noncontact sensors, these devices do not offer any significant advantage over conventional accelerometers when testing large structures or structures in hazardous environments and, hence, will not be discussed further. Laser based systems are primarily used for far-field non-contact motion sensors. The principles of operation for these far-field transducers fall into one of three categories: 1) linear encoders for motion transverse to the laser beam, 2) optical interference for motion in the direction of the laser beam, or 3) the laser Doppler effect, again for motion in the direction of the laser beam. The encoders and the interferometers generally use some type of fringe counters to obtain a displacement reading. Some encoders also employ gratings to measure displacement. The laser Doppler unit is based upon the well known Doppler shift of frequency, but for a laser light frequency rather than an audio frequency. Generally, these commercial units meet the measurement specifications needed for the vibration analysis application, but they also have drawbacks. First, each type requires the mounting of a special reflector at the point of interest, and second, they are, in general, too expensive for multiple channel applications making mode shape measurement impractical. Scanning laser vibrometers can alleviate this problem. However, the scan area of these devices limits them to measuring relatively small areas of a large structure.**

This article will describe a non-contact vibration sensor that overcomes some of the problems associated with other types of commercially available far-field non-contact vibration measurement devices. The sensor is based on a microwave interferometer that has been previously developed to detect the motion of people in monitored areas. Application of these sensors to vibration monitoring of a bridge and comparisons of modal properties identified by these sensors with comparable quantities obtained from standard piezoelectric accelerometer measurement-s are presented.

The microwave interferometer consists of an aluminum parabolic dish, with an X or K band microwave source/receiver horn mounted at the focus. The microwave source is similar to that used for intruder alarms and automated door openers and, hence, it posed no safety hazard to people. The horn may have a commercial Gunn diode transceiver unit ("Gunnplexer") attached to it, or it may be connected by a wave guide to other microwave source and receiver components.

One primary advantage of this system over commercially available far-field non-contact vibration measuring devices is that for common construction materials the microwave interferometer does not require a target to be mounted on the monitored surface. This feature is advantageous when working in hazardous environments and when access to the target surface is difficult. The sensor has been tested on metallic surfaces and concrete, both of which have shown adequate reflectivity. The focused area of the microwave will be approximately equal to the size of the parabolic dish. Therefore, the displacement being measured is an average of the target surface over an area approximately equal to the size of the dish.

Two microwave interferometers that used a Gunnplexer microwave source and a 61cm diameter (24-in dia.) parabolic dish were used during vibration testing of the I- 40 bridge over the Rio Grande in Albuquerque, NM. The I- 40 bridges over the Rio Grande that were tested consisted of twin bridges, one for each traffic direction, each made up of a concrete deck supported by two welded-steel plate girders and three steel stringers. Loads from the stringers were transferred to the plate girders by floor beams located at 6.1 m (20 ft) intervals. Cross-bracing was provided between the floor beams. Each bridge was made up of three identical sections. Except for the common pier located at the end of each section, the sections were independent. A section had three spans; the end spans were of equal length, approximately 39.9 m (131 ft), and the center span was approximately 49.7 m (163 ft) long. Five plate girders were connected with four bolted splices to form a continuous beam over the three spans. The portions of the plate girders over the piers had increased flange dimensions, compared with the mid-span portions, to resist the higher bending stresses at these locations. Figure 1 shows the bridge that was tested.

Forced vibration tests using a hydraulic shaker mounted on the bridge deck were first performed on the bridge in its undamaged state. Next, damage was introduced into one plate girder incrementally and the vibration tests were repeated. The damage that was introduced was intended to simulate cracking that has been observed in plate girder bridges. Four levels of damage were introduced to the middle span

of the north plate girder close to the seat supporting the floor beam at mid-span. Damage was introduced by making various torch cuts in the web and flange of the girder. The first level of damage consisted of a 61-cm-long (24 in.) cut approximately 0.95-cm-wide (0.38-in.-wide) centered at mid-height of the web. Next, this cut was continued to the bottom of the web.

During this cut the web, on either side of the cut, bent out of plane approximately 3 cm (1 in.). The flange was then cut half way in from either side directly below the cut in the web. Finally, the flange was cut completely through leaving the top 120 cm (48 in.) of the web and the top flange to carry the load at this location.

Fig.1 The microwave interferometer to measure the response of a plate girder

The microwave sensors supplemented 26 conventional accelerometers that were also used to measure the vibration response of the bridge at locations shown in Fig. 2. Also shown in Fig. 2 are the location of the shaker, the damage location, and the locations of the microwave interferometers. These sensors measured the response of the bottom flange of the two main plate girders at the center of the mid-span of portion of the bridge that was tested. Experimental modal analyses using data from the accelerometers were performed before any damage had been introduced, and immediately after each stage of damage.

Concluding comments

A microwave interferometer that overcomes the need for a mounted target was developed for remote, non-contact displacement vibration measurements. The sensors were coupled with homodyne detection hardware and software to measure the vibration response at two locations on a bridge structure. A comparison of the modal frequencies identified from microwave interferometer data to modal frequencies identified from data obtained with conventional accelerometers shows that the modal information being obtained with the interferometer is as accurate as that obtained with the conventional accelerometers. Complete mode shape data can beobtained if more interferometers are placed along the length of the beam at similar locations as the accelerometers. An obvious improvement to the analysis of data obtained from the interferometers would be to feed a calibrated analog displacement —time history from the interferometer directly into a data acquisition system. Then this signal could be digitized and analyzed with the more refined commercial modal analysis and digital signal processing software that is currently available.

(THE END)

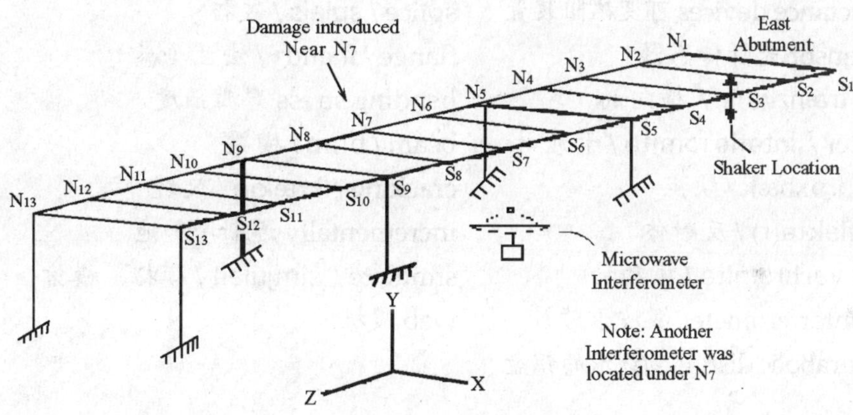

Fig. 2 Sensor locations for the bridge test

必备词汇

sensor / 'sensə / 传感器
vibration testing 振动测试
piezoelectric / paiˌiːzəui'lektrik / 压电的
piezoresistive / paiˌiːzəuri'zistiv / 压电电阻的
seismic / 'saizmik / 地震的
accelerometer / ækˌselə'rɔmitə / 加速计
signal-to-noise ratio 信噪比
bandwidth / 'bændwidθ / 带宽
dynamic / dai'næmik / 动态的
properties 属性，特性
inexpensive / ˌiniks'pensiv / 便宜的
displacement / dis'pleismənt / 位移
superposition / ˌsjuːpəpə'ziʃən / 重叠
accurate / 'ækjurit / 精确的
mount / maunt / 安装
motion / 'məuʃən / 运动
access 接近，进入

radiation / ˌreidiˈeiʃən / 辐射
transducer / trænzˈdjuːsə / 传感器
hardwiring 硬接线，硬连线
acquisition / ˌækwiˈziʃən / 获得
catwalk / ˈkætwɔːk / 狭小通道
time-consuming 耗费时间
non-contact 非接触
near-field 靠近现场
far-field 远离现场
feedback-type capacitive device 反馈式电容装置
eddy current transducers 涡流传感器
mutual inductance devices 互感装置
variable reluctance devices 可变磁阻装置
fiber-optic sensor 光纤传感器
transverse / ˈtrænzvəːs / 横向的
interferometer / ˌintəfiəˈrɔmitə / 干涉计
drawback / ˈdrɔːˌbæk / 缺点
reflector / riˈflektə(r) / 反射体
vibrometer / vaiˈbrɔmitə / 振动计
microwave interferometer 微波干涉计
aluminum parabolic dish 抛物线形的铝盘
band / bænd / 波段
horn / hɔːn / 喇叭天线
focus / ˈfəukəs / 焦点
intruder alarm 侵入警报器
automated door opener 自动门开启器
concrete / ˈkɔnkriːt / 混凝土
reflectivity / ˌriːflekˈtiviti / 反射率
deck / dek / 桥面，甲板
girder / ˈgəːdə / 梁，钢桁的支架
stringer / ˈstriŋə / 桁条
bracing / ˈbreisiŋ / 支柱
pier / piə / 桥墩
span （桥墩间的）墩距，跨距
splice / splais / 铰接
flange / flændʒ / 法兰（盘）
bending stress 弯曲强度
beam / biːm / 横梁
cracking / ˈkrækiŋ / 裂缝
incrementally 逐渐增加地
simulate / ˈsimjuleit / 模拟，模仿
web 腹板

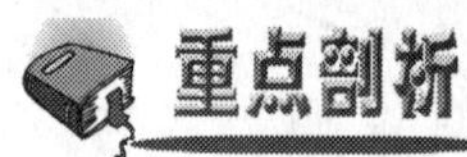

重点剖析

— The primary types of sensors used for vibration testing are piezoelectric or piezoresistive seismic accelerometers. For experimental modal analysis applications piezoelectric accelerometers are most commonly used. They have adequate signal-to-noise ratio, bandwidth, and are usually small enough relative to the structure being tested so as not to alter the structure's dynamic properties. 用于振动测试的主要传感器是压电或压阻地震加速计。在实验模型分析应用中，压电加速计最为常用。它们有足够的信噪比、带宽，通常比测试的结构物尺寸要小得多，所以不会改变结构物的动态特性。

— However, there are problems associated with these devices particularly when they are applied to the vibration testing of very large structures, when they are used in hazardous environments, and when the mass of the accelerometer is significant relative to the mass of the structure being tested. Although mode shape and operating shapes of a structure are routinely measured with conventional accelerometers, these sensors do not provide a direct measurement of displacement, which is often of interest for the study of a structure's operating vibration shapes (the superposition of many mode shapes). 然而，用这些设备出现了一些相关的问题，尤其是当它们被应用在对很大型结构物的振动测试上，以及用在有危险的环境下时，当加速计的质量大于被测试结构物的质量时，这些问题更加突出。虽然结构物的样式外形和工作外形通常是用传统的加速计来测量的，但这些传感器不提供对位移的直接测量，但对位移进行直接测量通常是对结构物工作振动外形（多个样式外形的重叠）的研究兴趣所在。

— Accelerometers must be mounted at the appropriate locations that are representative of the structure's motion, and access may be a problem, particularly if the tests are being performed in hazardous environments such as radiation or high voltage areas. Also, use of these transducers requires hardwiring from the transducer to the data acquisition system. 加速计必须被安装在能代表结构物运动的适当位置，而且接近它也是个问题，尤其当测试是在危险的环境中如辐射或高压区来进行时。此外，使用这些传感器需要在传感器到数据采集系统之间进行硬接线。

— Because of the need for a fixed reference location to mount the near-field noncontact sensors, these devices do not offer any significant advantage over conventional accelerometers when testing large structures or structures in hazardous environments and, hence, will not be discussed further. 因为需要有固定参照位置来安装靠近现场的非接触传感器，这些装置在测量大型结构物或测量处在危险环境中的结构物时，并不比传统的加速计有什么大的优势。所以在此不予考虑。

— Laser based systems are primarily used for far-field non-contact motion sensors. The principles of operation for these far-field transducers fall into one of three categories: 1) linear encoders for motion transverse to the laser beam, 2) optical interference for motion in the direction of the laser beam, or 3) the laser Doppler effect, again for motion in the direction of the laser beam. The encoders and the interferometers generally use some type of fringe counters to obtain a displacement reading. Some encoders also employ gratings to measure displacement. The laser Doppler unit is based upon the well known Doppler shift of frequency, but for a laser light frequency rather than an audio frequency. 基于激光的系统主要用在远离现场的非接触运动传感器。这些远离现场的传感器工作原理有三类：1）用于和激光束横向的运动的线性编码器；2）在激光束方向上运动的光学干涉；3）激光多普勒效应，也是用于沿激光束方向上的运动的。编码器和干涉计通常使用某种边缘计数器来获得位移读数。有些编码器也使用光栅来测量位移。激光多普勒设备根据著名的多普勒

频率变换，但是用于激光的频率而不是声音的频率。

— Generally, these commercial units meet the measurement specifications needed for the vibration analysis application, but they also have drawbacks. First, each type requires the mounting of a special reflector at the point of interest, and second, they are, in general, too expensive for multiple channel applications making mode shape measurement impractical. Scanning laser vibrometers can alleviate this problem. However, the scan area of these devices limits them to measuring relatively small areas of a large structure. 通常，这些商用设备满足振动分析应用所需的测量规范，但它们也有缺点。第一，所有的类型都需要在分析地点安装一个特殊的反射体；第二，它们通常在多通道应用中费用很高，使得样式外形测量变得不切实际。扫描激光振动计可以减轻这一问题。但是，这些装置的扫描区域把它们限制在只能测量大型结构物相对小的区域。

— This article will describe a non-contact vibration sensor that overcomes some of the problems associated with other types of commercially available far-field non-contact vibration measurement devices. 本文将描述一种非接触式振动传感器，它克服了市场上其他类型的远离现场的非接触式振动测量装置的一些相关问题。

— The microwave interferometer consists of an aluminum parabolic dish, with an X or K band microwave source/receiver horn mounted at the focus. The microwave source is similar to that used for intruder alarms and automated door openers and, hence, it posed no safety hazard to people. 微波干涉计包括一个抛物线形的铝盘、带有X或K波段微波源/接收器喇叭天线，天线安装在抛物线焦点的位置。微波源和侵入警报器及自动门开启器使用的微波源类似，所以不会给人的安全带来危险。

— One primary advantage of this system over commercially available far-field non-contact vibration measuring devices is that for common construction materials the microwave interferometer does not require a target to be mounted on the monitored surface. This feature is advantageous when working in hazardous environments and when access to the target surface is difficult. 和市场上的远离现场非接触式振动测量装置相比，该系统的一个主要优点是，对于普通的建筑材料，微波干涉计不需要把目标安装在被监视表面。当在危险的环境下工作或当进入目标的表面有困难时，这就显示出它的优势。

— Two microwave interferometers that used a Gunnplexer microwave source and a 61-cm diameter (24-in. dia.) parabolic dish were used during vibration testing of the I-40 bridge over the Rio Grande in Albuquerque, NM. The I-40 bridges over the Rio Grande that were tested consisted of twin bridges, one for each traffic direction, each made up of a concrete deck supported by two welded-steel plate girders and three steel stringers. 在位于Albuquerque的Rio Grande I-40桥的振动测试中，使用了两个微波干涉计，干涉计采用Gunnplexer微波源和61厘米直径的抛物线形盘。被测试的I-40桥由两座桥组成，一个干涉计用于一个车流方向，每座桥都包括混凝土桥面，桥面由两个焊接的钢桁支架和三根钢桁条所支撑。

— Loads from the stringers were transferred to the plate girders by floor beams located at 6.1 m (20 ft) intervals. Cross-bracing was provided between the floor beams. Each bridge was made up of three identical sections. Except for the common pier located at the end of each section, the sections were independent. A section had three spans; the end spans were of equal length, approximately 39.9m (131 ft), and the center span was approximately 49.7 m (163 ft) long. Five plate girders were connected with four bolted splices to form a continuous beam over the three spans. The portions of the plate girders over the piers had increased flange dimensions, compared with the mid-span portions, to resist the higher bending stresses at these locations. Figure 1 shows the bridge that was tested. 来自桁条的载荷由间隔为6.1米的地面横梁传递给钢桁支架。每座桥都由三个相同的部分组成。除了各部分终端的普通桥墩外，各部分都是独立的。一个部分有三个跨距；终端跨距长度相等，大约为39.9米，中央跨距的长度大约为49.7米。五个钢桁支架用四个螺栓铰接连起来，在三个跨距上形成连续的横梁。与中跨距部分相比，钢桁支架在桥墩上的部分提高了法兰的尺寸，以抵抗在这些位置上较高的弯曲压力。图1显示的是被测的桥梁。

— Forced vibration tests using a hydraulic shaker mounted on the bridge deck were first performed on the bridge in its undamaged state. Next, damage was introduced into one plate girder incrementally and the vibration tests were repeated. The damage that was introduced was intended to simulate cracking that has been observed in plate girder bridges. 首先，在桥处于未损坏状态时，把一个液压震动器安装在桥面上，对桥进行强迫振动测试。接下来，对钢桁支架逐渐加力进行破坏，并重复进行振动测试。引入破坏是为了模拟在钢桁支架桥上观察到的裂缝。

— Four levels of damage were introduced to the middle span of the north plate girder close to the seat supporting the floor beam at mid-span. Damage was introduced by making various torch cuts in the web and flange of the girder. The first level of damage consisted of a 61-cm-long (24 in) cut approximately 0.95-cm-wide (0.38-in-wide) centered at mid-height of the web. Next, this cut was continued to the bottom of the web. 给靠近北边支座的钢桁支架的中间跨距引入了四个级别的损坏，支座支撑着中间跨距上的桥面横梁。破坏是利用各种火把切割钢桁支架的腹板和法兰来达到的。第一级别的破坏包括一个61厘米长的切口，宽大约为0.95厘米，切口围绕着腹板的中间高度。接下来，把这个切口继续切到腹板的底端。

— The microwave sensors supplemented 26 conventional accelerometers that were also used to measure the vibration response of the bridge at locations shown in Fig. 2. Also shown in Fig. 2 are the location of the shaker, the damage location, and the locations of the microwave interferometers. These sensors measured the response of the bottom flange of the two main plate girders at the center of the mid-span of portion of the bridge that was tested. 微波传感器用26个传统加速计来补充，它们也被用来测量在图2所示的位置处桥梁的振动反应。图2还显示了震动器的位置、损坏位置及微波干涉计的位置。这些传感器测量出被测桥梁部分中间跨度中央处两个主钢桁支架底端法兰的反应。

— Experimental modal analyses using data from the accelerometers were performed before any damage had been introduced, and immediately after each stage of damage. 在进行损坏实验前，采用加速计得来的数据进行了实验模型分析，在各个损坏阶段之后也立即进行了分析。

(V65真题题源)

3. Flip Ship and Hinge Ship

垂直翻转船与铰链船

The scene of the sinking TITANIC from the latest film version, must be one of the more frightening images that many of us carry in our collective memory. Who can ever forget the chilling moment when the ship reared up like a huge monster above the cold and black waves and for a few minutes stood on its end? Who can ever forget the film scene when the two young lovers clanged to each other as they held to the rear railings of the ship, immediately before it plunged straight into the bosom of the sea.

Well, strangely enough, that ship's manoeuvre of rearing up on its end before plunging into the sea, may be one of the new technological means of exploring the deep blue ocean. Scientists and other interested persons (including, possibly tourists) could be soon (that is in a couple of years time) waiting in line to take the plunge... this time, most willingly and with great expectations of the thrills of visiting the fantastic world beneath the waves.

In the first half of the 1960s, there were a number of bold initiatives to construct deep underwater platforms, in which people may stay for a couple of weeks, while exploring the fascinating sea floor. No less than three underwater stations had been built up by then within the US Sealab programme. By the end of the 1960s people were staying on the ocean floors nearly 200 m beneath the surface, and experiencing the thrills of this relatively unexplored habitat. During this same period, the epic Apollo space programme was in high gear and people were very much interested in exploring both the outside as well as the inner space (that is, the sea). The promise of new knowledge and new gains from the utilisation of a number of resources on the sea floor was beckoning humankind to go down.

Unfortunately, this call of the mythical sirens was not powerful enough and most of these early technological attempts were discontinued, partly due to lack of funding.

But things may possibly change now. New technological ventures are awaiting on the drawing boards of a number of research foundations and institutions, which may well find their way into real life, within the next five to ten years.

One of the more promising ideas of how to reach the seafloor with the minimum of fuss and with the present technological capabilities, is that of flipping a long ship through 90 degrees, so that it actually sinks straight into the ocean, until its rear end is just above the ocean floor. Looks like the TITANIC all over again! Doesn't it?

The American Ocean Technology Foundation has plans to build up such a flipping ship within the next 10 years, and even before, if funds are made available. Picture 1 shows how this new way of getting down onto the ocean floor, may work out. **The ship will first sail to the place to be explored. Then its tubular structure will be weighed down by allowing water to flood a number of rear tanks, so that its rear end will sink, pulling the tubular structure through a 90 degree flip. Once vertical, almost 300 metres of the ship will be submerged (more than the height of the Eiffel Tower) while the front end, with the bridge and front cabins, staying afloat, complete with control rooms and helicopter pad.**

People can then move down the vertical shaft (by elevator) until they reach the lower decks. These would include research laboratories as well as observation decks for paying tourists!

The biggest advantage of this novel idea, would be that all persons reaching the seafloor would still be exposed to atmospheric pressure and therefore would not require any decompression procedures, or even swim suits!

Another similar idea would be to have a normal ship (such as a second-hand oil tanker) equipped with a long shaft, which would be attached to its front end by a hinge-like structure. The shaft will then be lowered into position by rotating it through 90 degrees, just like a jack-knife blade. This second version could in fact be more economically feasible to develop, since second-hand oil tankers are not so difficult to come by! Further, the FLIP ship will cost more than 200 millions, whereas the second version will just spend a little more than 60 million, you know.

You see, diving straight down into the abyss may not necessarily remain a frightening experience, reminiscent of the tragedy of the TITANIC. It may well be an experience of a lifetime... if you have the money.

(THE END)

必备词汇

TITANIC / təi'tænik / 泰坦尼克
plunge into 跳进，投入
bosom / 'buzəm / 胸，胸怀
afloat / ə'fləut / 漂浮的，在海上的
platform / 'plætfɔːm / 平台
beckon / 'bekən / 引诱
manoeuvre / mə'nuːvə / 策略，调动
initiative / i'niʃiətiv / 计划，主动
US Sealab Programme 美国海底实验室计划
American Ocean Technology Foundation 美国海洋技术基金会
Eiffel Tower （巴黎的）艾菲尔铁塔
shaft / ʃɑːft / 井筒
observation deck 观察甲板
decompression / ˌdiːkəm'preʃən / 减压
blade / bleid / 刀片，刀刃
economically feasible 经济上可行的
abyss / ə'bis / 深渊
reminiscent / remi'nis(ə)nt / 回忆往事的

— Well, strangely enough, that ship's manoeuvre of rearing up on its end before plunging into the sea, may be one of the new technological means of exploring the deep blue ocean. 嗯，奇怪的是，在一头栽进大海之前船的一端会倒立起来，这可能是探索海洋深处的最新技术之一。

— Unfortunately, this call of the mythical sirens was not powerful enough and most of these early technological attempts were discontinued, partly due to lack of funding. 不幸的是，呼唤“神秘女郎”的声音还不够强大，大多数早期的技术尝试后来都中止了，部分原因是缺乏资金。

— One of the more promising ideas of how to reach the seafloor with the minimum of fuss and with the present technological capabilities, is that of flipping a long ship through 90 degrees, so that it actually sinks straight into the ocean, until its rear end is just above the ocean floor. 关于如何在利用现在技术手段，把人们的紧张降低到最小的情况下到达海底，更有前途的想法就是把一艘长长的大船倾斜90度，这样船实际上就垂直沉入海中，直到船的尾部触到海底。

— The ship will first sail to the place to be explored. Then its tubular structure will be weighed down by allowing water to flood a number of rear tanks, so that its rear end will sink, pulling the tubular structure through a 90 degree flip. Once vertical, almost 300 metres of the ship will be submerged (more than the height of the Eiffel Tower) while the front end, with the bridge and front cabins, staying afloat, complete with control rooms and helicopter pad. 船首先航行到考察地点。然后通过让船尾的储水罐装满水而让船尾下沉，这样一来船的管状结构也会随重量增加而下降并在推力作用下呈90度角翻转。船体一旦垂直，将有300多米没入水中（超过了艾菲尔铁塔的高度），而船桥、前船舱、控制室和直升机起落台所在的船头将浮在水面上。

— People can then move down the vertical shaft (by elevator) until they reach the lower decks. These would include research laboratories as well as observation decks for paying tourists! 然后，人们可以沿垂直的井筒（乘电梯）下行，直抵较低的甲板上。当然，研究实验室和供付费游客观光的观察甲板也可以一同送下来。

— The biggest advantage of this novel idea, would be that all persons reaching the sea floor would still be exposed to atmospheric pressure and therefore would not require any decompression procedures, or even swim suits! 这个新颖主意的最大好处是，人在到达海底后仍旧暴露在大气压力下，所以不需要经过任何减压程序，甚至无需穿游泳衣!

— Another similar idea would be to have a normal ship (such as a se-cond-hand oil tanker) equipped with a long shaft, which would be attached to its front end by a hinge-like structure. The shaft will then be lowered into position by rotating it through 90 degrees, just like a jack-knife blade. This second version could in fact be more economically feasible to develop, since second-hand oil tankers are not so difficult to come by! 另一个类似的主意是让一艘普通的船只（比如二手油轮）装上一个长长的井筒，用铰链似的结构固定到船的前端。然后把井筒旋转 90 度下放到预定位置，就像一把折叠匕首的刀片一样。第二种想法实际在经济上可能更为可行，因为二手油轮不是那么难弄到手!

(New Version 真题题源)

4. Margam Castle

法 国 城 堡

History and design

Margam Castle, a typical French mansion was, with it's service buildings and courtyards, built between 1830 and 1840 and it is listed Grade I as a building of exceptional quality and with some spectacular features such as the staircase.

It was not until the 1820's that Christopher Rice Mansel Talbot (1803—1890) determined to build a new house at Margam.

The Margam estate had been in his family since 1536, however Thomas Mansel Talbot had demolished the original mansion house in 1787 to replace it with the magnificent Orangery that can be seen in the gardens today. **Proud of this ancient family lineage Christopher Rice Mansel Talbot had always been attracted to romantic Margam. He wished to rebuild a suitable country residence which would compliment Margam's illustrious history.**

The site was deliberately chosen for its historic associations and picturesque position at the foot of a wooded historic hill, Mynydd-y-Castell, itself the site of Margam's earliest habitation, with the ruins of the Cistercian Abbey and the eighteenth century Orangery visible to the West. The prospect of the house, rising above the Orangery and monastic remains to the west is unique in Wales.

Whilst the recognised and accredited architect is Thomas Hopper (1776 — 1856), it is rather interesting to find that another distinguished architect was closely involved with the project and almost certainly influenced the finished house with work on the interior and exterior, the stables, terraces and lodges, the Shrewsbury architect Edward Haycock (1790—1870). Thus we have two distinguished 19th century architects involved with Margam.

However there is a third person who was to greatly influence the architectural style and finished design and this was C.R.M.Talbot who was greatly influenced by the architecture of two family homes borrowing elements from Lacock Abbey in Wiltshire, ancestral home of the Talbots and residence of his cousin W.H.Fox Talbot and the idea of the octagonal tower from Melbury House in Dorset, the seat of his mother's family, the Fox-Strangeways, Earls of Illchester.

Margam was really designed by three men Hopper, Haycock and Talbot and influenced by two earlier houses Laycock and Melbury whilst presenting an unique creation in sympathy with its sylvan surroundings, evocative of a rich and illustrious past — which is exactly what C.R.M.Talbot had in mind.

The Building

The irregular plan and pinnacled, chimneyed and castellated skyline of the house give it a Romantic appearance. The house was built around a complex of three courtyards, one in the centre of the main block and two former service courts to the east forming an oblong site with four elevations, three of which included the most decorated parts of the main house. There are two main storeys, with a gabled third storey. The surfaces of the building are ornamented with carvings and sculpted heraldic panels, the great number of shields and coat of arms of the branches of the Mansel family show the owner's pride in his family history, which are seen in the stonework.

A dramatic octagonal tower with attached stair turret (the stair turret is not the original height, decorative parapet stonework has appeared to have been removed) is situated in the centre of the building, it rises two storeys above the main house and at the top is a viewing room.

The house is aligned east-west, with the main entrance front on the north. The drive approaches from the southeast, dividing just before the house. The southern branch leads to the stable court on the east end of the house and the main drive runs through a short cutting between grass banks and to the forecourt with central grass circle in front of the main entrance.

This entrance is a two-storey gabled porch, with a four-centred arched door and a Gothic traceried window over it. The long, irregular south front, with protruding bays, oriel windows and another arched door, overlooks the wide terrace which also extends along the west front. Inside there is a spectacular stone staircase rising up the first two storeys of the tower.

Most of the building work was completed by 1836 when the interior decoration began, the gothic style continued in the entrance and staircase halls. Whilst the exterior may have been impressive, it gave little indication of the elaborate finishes within. It had a spacious library, a drawing room, dining room, study and muniment room.

The staircase hall was flagged and fitted with a fleu-de-lys and riband carpet in pink on a rich brown. Later a set of fitted gothic stalls were installed around the edge of the staircase hall each carved with a back panel set with monograms of C.R.M. Talbot, above were carved lifelike figures of the animals seen on the park.

The library, drawing and dining rooms were sumptuously decorated with carved woodwork and panelling, stained glass windows, gilded plasterwork and handsome marble fireplaces. Bedroom suites were treated in various ways, including the then fashionable Chinese style, another was decorated with tapestries and some contained fireplaces of the popular, local, Mumbles marble. Gold leaf, carved marble, fine furniture, French rococo panelling, crystal chandeliers, Chinese lacquer screens, porcelain vases, paintings by Rubens, Canaletto, all completed the opulent furnishing of the rooms. C.R.M.Talbot was an avid collector. He brought many sculptures, paintings and antiques back from Italy. Margam was soon filled with fine furniture, paintings and object d'art.

To the east of the main block are the Grade II* service buildings clustered around a cobbled and flagged service court, with a screen wall on the north side topped with stepped crenellations. The entrance to the courtyard is through a massive, higher archway topped with a heraldic panel at the west end of the north side. Kitchens and domestic offices, including laundry, bakehouse and brewery, are ranged around all but the south side which is bounded by a wall with a door in it leading through to a smaller yard of stores and larders. To the east is the boiler house, laundry-maids sitting room and gun room, to the south of which is a long, single-storey Gothic building with arched doorways in the end walls and small three-light windows with shallow buttresses between them. Further to the east continuing the main axis of the house is the stable court, an L-shaped area with an entrance on the north side and a bounding wall on the south.

The mansion is mostly built of a local sandstone, Pyle ashlar, which has mellowed beautifully over the years. Inside, use was made of a harder stone for the staircase hall whilst bricks were used extensively for the internal walls, the cellars and other parts of the building.

Oak and pine were used for rafters and flooring, with an ingenious use of cast iron railway lines to support the stone landings of the main staircase. Elsewhere cast iron was used for the drainage system, for grilles and ventilation covers. The guttering and water pipes were of lead, with the Talbot crest embellishing each hopper above the downpipes. The complicated roof was of lead and Cornish slate and was constructed at so many levels and angles that it was always necessary for a small army of men to regularly sweep out the gutters and gullies whilst the onset of snow saw estate workmen sweeping the roofs clean. The great number of elaborate chimney stacks, all in variations of the Tudor style were especially made in Bedfordshire and brought to Margam.

Christopher Rice Mansel Talbot died in 1890, his only son Theodore Mansel Talbot had died in 1876 and his daughter Miss Emily Charlotte Talbot inherited her father's Margam and Penrice estates. **She made various changed to the house, new bathrooms and plumbing was installed, the heating improved and in 1891— electricity was installed.** The billiard room was added, being built over the small inner courtyard. Jacobean in style it became the popular haunt of gentlemen guests invited to her large house parties in the late 19th and early 20th centuries. A large skylight of plain coloured glass lit the room. The fireplace had an elaborately carved mantle bearing the date 1892 and the initials ECT, Emily Charlotte Talbot. Miss Talbot maintained a large retinue of servants in the house and on her estate including an army of gardeners.

(THE END)

castle / 'kɑːsl / 城堡

mansion / 'mænʃən / 大厦，官邸，公寓

staircase / 'steəkeɪs / 楼梯

courtyards / 'kɔːtjɑːd / 庭院

spectacular / spekˈtækjulə / 引人入胜的，壮观的
estate / iˈsteit / 财产，不动产
demolished 推倒，拆除
lineage / ˈliniidʒ / 血统
compliment / ˈkɔmplimənt / 称赞，恭维
picturesque / ˌpiktʃəˈresk / 风景如画的
prospect / ˈprɔspekt / 景色，景观
accredited / əˈkreditid / 公认的，著名的
distinguished / disˈtiŋgwiʃt / 著名的，杰出的
architect / ˈɑːkitekt / 建筑师
octagonal tower 八角形的塔
sympathy / ˈsimpəθi / 同情
irregular plan 不规则的平面图
pinnacled 小尖塔般耸立的
castellated / ˈkæsteleitid / 造成城型的，有城的
skyline / ˈskailain / 轮廓线
complex / ˈkɔmpleks / 联合体
oblong / ˈɔblɔŋ / 长方形的
elevation 高地
gabled / ˈgeibld / 有山墙的，人字板制作的
carving / ˈkɑːviŋz / 雕刻
stonework / ˈstəunwɜːk / 石雕工艺
stair turret 楼梯塔楼
parapet / ˈpærəpit / 栏杆，扶手，胸墙
porch / pɔːtʃ / 门廊，走廊
traceried 窗饰，花饰窗格
protruding bay 突出的耳房
monogram / ˈmɔnəugrɑːf / 字母组合
gilded plasterwork 镀金的灰泥工程
marble fireplace 大理石壁炉
stepped crenellation 可行走的开垛口
archway / ˈɑːtʃwei / 拱门，拱道
laundry / ˈlɔːndri / 洗衣店
bakehouse / ˈbeɪkhaus / 面包屋
brewery / ˈbruːəri / 酿酒厂
heraldic panel 刻有纹章的饰板
rafter / ˈrɑːftəz / 椽
flooring / ˈflɔːrə / 地板
gutter / ˈgʌtəs / 排水沟
gully / ˈgʌlis / 檐槽
mantle / ˈmæntl / 壁炉架

重点剖析

— Margam Castle, a typical French mansion was, with it's service buildings and courtyards, built between 1830 and 1840 and it is listed Grade I as a building of exceptional quality and with some spectacular features such as the staircase. 马加姆城堡是典型的法国式官邸建筑，它包括有服务楼和庭院，建于1830年和1840年之间。由于其质量卓越、风格独特（如别致的楼梯）而被列为一级建筑。

— Proud of this ancient family lineage Christopher Rice Mansel Talbot had always been attracted to romantic Margam. He wished to rebuild a suitable country residence which would compliment Margam's illustrious history. Christopher Rice Mansel Talbot一直以自己的家族遗风而引为自豪，对浪漫的马加姆情有独钟。他希望重建一个乡村式院落来颂扬马加姆的伟大历史。

— Whilst the recognised and accredited architect is Thomas Hopper (1776-1856), it is rather interesting to find that another distinguished architect was closely involved with the project and almost certainly influenced the finished house with work on the interior and exterior, the stables, terraces and lodges, the Shrewsbury architect Edward Haycock(1790-1870). Thus we have two distinguished 19th century architects involved with Margam. 伟大的建筑师Thomas Hopper主持了城堡的设计，但有趣的是另一名杰出的建筑师Edward Haycock也与该工程有紧密联系，并且在很大程度上影响了房屋的完工。他设计了房屋的室内外主体、马厩、阳台和小屋。所以在马加姆项目中，两大著名建筑师都参与其中。

— The irregular plan and pinnacled, chimneyed and castellated skyline of the house give it a Romantic appearance. The house was built around a complex of three courtyards, one in the centre of the main block and two former service courts to the east forming an oblong site with four elevations, three of which included the most decorated parts of the main house. 房屋具有不规则的平面造型，轮廓线呈现出高耸的小尖塔、烟囱和山墙，从而具备了罗马式的建筑外观。房屋是围着三个庭院组成的联合体建造的，一个庭院位于主街区的中心，另两个庭院以前是服务性庭院，它们位于东边，并和四个高的建筑一起形成一个长方形的场地，其中的三个高建筑中包括有主房屋重点装饰的内容。

— The house is aligned east-west, with the main entrance front on the north. 房屋呈东西走向，前面的主要入口位于北面。

— The drive approaches from the southeast, dividing just before the house. The southern branch leads to the stable court on the east end of the house and the main drive runs through a short cutting between grass banks and to the forecourt with central grass circle in front of the main entrance. 车道从东南面进入，在房屋前部分开。南面的部分通向房屋东端的庭院，主车道穿过草坪上的一条小道，到了前院。前院中有圆形的中央草坪，中央草坪位于主入口前面。

— This entrance is a two-storey gabled porch, with a four-centred arched door and a Gothic traceried window over it. The long, irregular south front, with protruding bays, oriel windows and another arched door, overlooks the wide terrace which also extends along the west front. Inside there is a spectacular stone staircase rising up the first two storeys of the tower. 入口是一个两层的山形墙门廊，有一个拱形门，顶端是哥特式花饰窗户。朝南的前端很长，形状不规则，有突出的耳房、凸出壁外的窗和另一扇拱形门，俯瞰着宽大的阳台，阳台西边的前端，也是伸出来的。里面的石头楼梯造型独特，建在塔楼的前两层上。

— Most of the building work was completed by 1836 when the interior decoration began, the gothic style continued in the entrance and staircase halls. Whilst the exterior may have been impressive, it gave little indication of the elaborate finishes within. It had a spacious library, a drawing room, dining room, study and muniment room. 建筑工程的大部分是在1836年底完工的，这时内部装修刚刚开始，还在继续修建哥特式的入口和楼梯大厅。虽然外观相当引人入胜，但内部具体的装饰如何却无从知晓。马加姆城堡中还建有一间宽敞的图书馆、一间画室、一间餐厅、一间书房和一间保安室。

— She made various changed to the house, new bathrooms and plumbing was installed, the heating improved and in 1891—electricity was installed. 她对房屋进行了多处改造，新修了浴室，改进了供暖系统，还于1891年通了电。

(V33真题题源)

5. Pagodas

中国和日本的塔

Visitors to Kyoto and Nara, Japan's ancient capitals, invariably retain in their memories the evocative silhouette of a wooden pagoda—at times towering gracefully above the tiled rooftops of an old neighborhood, at times rising abruptly from the midst of a huddle of modern buildings. Most people familiar with the Kansai region will know the stately five-story pagoda of Kyoto's Toji (Kyoo Gokokuji) temple, clearly visible from the Shinkansen bullet train, or the pagoda of Nara's Kofukuji, standing at the edge of Sarusawa Pond.

At 55 meters in height, the pagoda of Toji is the tallest such structure in Japan. It is far from the tallest pagoda ever built, however. The octagonal nine-story pagoda of Kyoto's Hoshoji was 83 meters tall, and the seven-story pagoda of Shokokuji, also in Kyoto, is said to have risen a full 108 meters. These towering structures, along with many other wooden pagodas built over the centuries, were destroyed by fire—generally either struck by lightning or caught in the crossfire of civil war.

Because of their wood construction, Japan's pagodas have always been extremely

vulnerable to fire. At the same time, these tall, slender towers, built of interlocking posts and beams, are so resistant to earthquakes and typhoons that Japan's long architectural history records only a very few instances of their collapsing. Some 1,300 years after it was built, the five-story pagoda of Horyuji in Nara, recently added to UNESCO's "world heritage" list of cultural assets, shows not the slightest sign of instability.

Although built primarily of wood, pagodas are by no means lightweight structures. Like most traditional wood-frame architecture in Japan, they display wide eaves, giving considerable prominence to the tiled roof. If we compare the charming octagonal Yumedono, or "Dream Hall" of Horyuji with the octagonal pagoda of Fogongsi temple in China's Shansi Province, the difference is instructive: The eaves overhang of the Yumedono is 3 meters, more than one-fourth the building's total diameter of 11 meters. The pagoda of Fogongsi, which measures 29 meters across, has an overhang of only 2.5 meters—less than one-tenth the building's diameter.

The jutting eaves of Japan's wooden pagodas lend a powerful rhythm to their silhouette, but their purpose is by no means solely aesthetic.

A wide overhang means a larger roof relative to the rest of the structure. The large roof, consisting of clay and tiles laid on top of wood rafters, is extremely heavy. A heavy roof relative to the size of the building is one of the main characteristics of traditional Japanese wood architecture. With five such overhanging roofs, a five-story pagoda is a heavy structure indeed.

Why such pagodas, despite their height and weight, have remained upright and intact through numerous earthquakes and typhoons is something that no one has been able to explain satisfactorily from the standpoint of modern architectonics. **This is because building science evolved in the West as a discipline dealing with the structural mechanics of rigid bodies, that is, buildings of stone, brick, or concrete.** In the article that follows, architect Ueda Atsushi elucidates the ingenious techniques by which the Japanese of earlier times built their pagodas to withstand even the strongest winds and earthquakes.

Of course, high towers have been built in the West ever since the Middle Ages. In all cases, however, the material is masonry—stones or bricks joined to form a single mass of wall capable of withstanding this or that impact from without. **In the case of Japan's wooden pagodas, however, each story is structurally independent.**

Each story of the pagoda is basically a square box with no bottom, built around twelve outer pillars, or gawabashira. The pagoda as a whole is, in essence, five stacked boxes. Since each story is smaller than the one beneath it, the placement of the gawabashira moves inward as one proceeds up the pagoda, meaning that horizontal beams are needed to support the gawabashira of each story above the first. In fact, these pillars rest on horizontal bases, which in turn are supported by taruki—slanting beams that run from the inside of the structure diagonally downward to the outside, where they support the eaves.

The weight of the upper story, pushing down on the inner ends of the taruki, would cause the outer ends to rise if there were no counterweight. The heavy tiled roof of the eaves performs precisely this function. In short, the taruki functions as a lever arm, while the top of the gawabashira serves as the fulcrum.

The story above bears down on the inner end of the lever, and the overhanging roof balances this load at the outer end. Or, to put it another way, the heavy eaves are in effect supported by the story above. When one reaches the uppermost level, of course, there is no story above to counterbalance the overhang. Here, however, the tall copper or iron spire, or finial, performs that function. The finial of the Horyuji pagoda, we are told, weighs a full three tons.

Ueda explains in detail how this lever construction ensures that, during typhoons and earthquakes, pagodas swing and sway but almost never collapse. Built not to resist the forces of nature head-on but to accept and absorb their impact, pagodas epitomize the ingenuity of traditional Japanese wood architecture. This solution to the problem of structural stability could be said to manifest the Japanese approach to nature—not only to observe it carefully but also to learn from it and coexist harmoniously with it.

Ueda's essay concludes with a discussion of the central pillar, or shinbashira, a feature absent in the wood pagodas extant in China, where the form originated, but present in virtually all Japanese pagodas. Ueda's theory regarding the changing religious and structural significance of this basically free-standing (or hanging) pillar provides much food for thought on the dynamics of Japan's adoption and transformation of mainland culture.

Pagoda followed Buddhism into China around the first century, and developed into pavilion-like pagoda on which one can view scenery after immediate combination with traditional Chinese architecture.

Most Chinese pagodas are multistoried ones. Early pagodas were usually wooden and had quadrangle, hexangle, ocatagonal and twelve sided ichnographies. During the Sui and Tang dynasties, pagodas tended to be stone and brick. In the Liao Dynasty, solid pagoda appeared. After, in the Song, Liao and Jin dynasties, flower pagodas were introduced which were decorated with assorted carved flowers, honeycombed shrines, animals and Buddha and disciple sculptures, looked like flowers. Generally speaking, pagodas became more and more decorative.

The main reasons early pagodas in China had many storeys were, first, since pagodas were originally built to preserve Buddhist relics, which were considered the most sacred objects in the world, representing Buddha, they should be majestic and striking in style. Second, multistoreyed buildings were traditionally used by the ruling class to show off its power and wealth; they were also believed to be the residences of the immortals; therefore they were most suitable for enshrining the mysterious Buddha, the highest saint among the immortals. Third, high buildings of many storeys were usually awe inspiring and mysterious looking.

(THE END)

必备词汇

invariably / in'veəriəb(ə)li / 总是
silhouette / ˌsilu(:)'et / 轮廓，侧面影像
towering / 'tauəriŋ / 高耸的
rooftop 屋顶
huddle / 'hʌdl / 拥挤，杂乱
stately / 'steitli /
pagoda / pə'gəudə / 宝塔
octagonal / ɔk'tægənl / 八边形的
vulnerable / 'vʌlnərəb(ə)l / 易受攻击的
interlocking / ˌintə(:)'lɔkiŋ / 联锁的
post / pəust / 柱
beam / bi:m / 梁
world heritage 世界遗产
by no means 绝不是
eave / i:v / 屋檐
jutting / 'dʒʌtiŋ / 突出的
aesthetic / i:s'θetik / 美学的
rafter / 'rɑ:ftə / 椽
upright / 'ʌprait / 垂直的，竖直的
intact / in'tækt / 完整无缺的
standpoint / 'stændpɔint / 立场，观点
architectonics / ˌɑ:kitek'tɔniks / 建筑学
elucidate / i'lu:sideit / 阐明，说明
ingenious / in'dʒi:njəs / 有独创性的
withstand / wið'stænd / 抵挡，经受得住
pillar / 'pilə / 柱子
slanting / 'slɑ:ntiŋ / 倾斜的
counterweight / 'kauntəweit / 平衡力，平衡物
lever arm 杠杆臂
fulcrum / 'fʌlkrəm / 杠杆的支点
finial / 'fainiəl / 顶尖
multistoried 多层的
quadrangle / kwɔ'dræŋgl / 四方形

hexangle / heks'æŋgjulə / 六方形
ichnographies / ik'nɔgrəfi / 平面图
assorted / ə'sɔːtid / 多种混合的
honeycombed shrine 蜂窝结构的神殿
sacred object 圣物
enshrine / in'ʃrain / 祭祀
immortal / i'mɔːtl / 不朽的

重点剖析

— Visitors to Kyoto and Nara, Japan's ancient capitals, invariably retain in their memories the evocative silhouette of a wooden pagoda — at times towering gracefully above the tiled rooftops of an old neighborhood, at times rising abruptly from the midst of a huddle of modern buildings. 到日本著名的古都京都和奈良观光的游客无不在记忆深处深深地留下木制宝塔的雄伟轮廓——有时静立在老街区的砖瓦屋顶上，有时突兀地高耸在纷乱的现代建筑的袅袅薄雾之中。

— At 55 meters in height, the pagoda of Toji is the tallest such structure in Japan. It is far from the tallest pagoda ever built, however. 东寺塔高 55 米，是日本最高的木塔。但它还远远不是曾经建造过的最高的宝塔。

— Because of their wood construction, Japan's pagodas have always been extremely vulnerable to fire. At the same time, these tall, slender towers, built of interlocking posts and beams, are so resistant to earthquakes and typhoons that Japan's long architectural history records only a very few instances of their collapsing. 由于是木制结构，日本的宝塔总是极易遭受火灾。同时，由于这些细而高的塔是用互相锁定的柱和梁建成的，对地震和台风的抵御能力非常强，所以在日本漫长的建筑史记录中，只有少数几次情况下塔才坍塌了。

— Although built primarily of wood, pagodas are by no means lightweight structures. Like most traditional wood-frame architecture in Japan, they display wide eaves, giving considerable prominence to the tiled roof. If we compare the charming octagonal Yumedono, or "Dream Hall" of Horyuji with the octagonal pagoda of Fogongsi temple in China's Shansi Province, the difference is instructive: The eaves overhang of the Yumedono is 3 meters, more than one-fourth the building's total diameter of 11 meters. The pagoda of Fogongsi, which measures 29 meters across, has an overhang of only 2.5 meters —less than one-tenth the building's diameter. 虽然主要是用木头建成的，但宝塔可不是轻量级的建筑结构。和日本大多数传统的木框架建筑一样，宝塔有宽大的屋檐，突出了铺瓦的屋顶。如果我们把位于法隆寺久负盛名的八角形"梦之厅"，和位于中国陕西省的佛宫寺八角形宝塔比较一下，差别是很明显的："梦之厅"的屋檐悬垂长 3 米，超过宝塔 11 米总直径的四分之一。

而佛宫寺宝塔的直径长达29米，但悬垂只有2.5米——还不到宝塔直径的十分之一。

— A wide overhang means a larger roof relative to the rest of the structure. The large roof, consisting of clay and tiles laid on top of wood rafters, is extremely heavy. A heavy roof relative to the size of the building is one of the main characteristics of traditional Japanese wood architecture. With five such overhanging roofs, a five-story pagoda is a heavy structure indeed. 宽大的悬垂相对宝塔的其他部分来说，意味着更大的屋檐。大屋顶，是由铺在木椽上的泥土和瓦建成的，分量非常重。较之宝塔的尺寸而颇显沉重的屋顶是传统日本木建筑的主要特点。有五个这样悬垂的屋顶，一座五层高的宝塔确实很重。

— This is because building science evolved in the West as a discipline dealing with the structural mechanics of rigid bodies, that is, buildings of stone, brick, or concrete. 这是因为在西方，建筑学是作为研究刚性体的结构力学的一门学科而发展起来的，也就是研究石头、砖和混凝土的建筑。

— In the case of Japan's wooden pagodas, however, each story is structurally independent. 日本的木制宝塔，每一层的结构都彼此独立。

— The story above bears down on the inner end of the lever, and the overhanging roof balances this load at the outer end. Or, to put it another way, the heavy eaves are in effect supported by the story above. 上面的一层压在杠杆的向内端，而悬垂的屋顶在向外的端来平衡这个载荷。或者，换句话来说，沉重的屋檐实际是由上层的建筑来支撑的。

— Ueda's essay concludes with a discussion of the central pillar, or shinbashira, a fea ture absent in the wood pagodas extant in China, where the form originated, but present in virtually all Japanese pagodas. Ueda在文章结尾对中央圆柱进行了讨论。虽然木塔源于中国，但中国现存的木塔中并没有中央圆柱，而日本所有的木塔都有。

(New version 真题题源)

6. Taughened Glass: the Solution to Retail Owners' Security Concerns

强化玻璃

DuPont has done a great job of working with architects and the architectural glass industry to understand, develop and promote the use of taughened glass (safety glass) worldwide. Within the retail environment in particular, architects in all continents are using taughened glass for a diverse range of applications—not only for economic and functional reasons but also for the pure aesthetic delight of using the material.

Yet sadly, the general public in North America is still too often ignorant of the benefits taughened glass can bring—not only in shops but also in offices and homes. The material is still all too often perceived as vaguely "more expensive" and its wide range of benefits remains largely unknown. Sharing the benefits with building owners—from the business community to homeowners — has to be our next major challenge.

National Gate and Glass Corp. supplies storefront glass to retailers throughout North America, from nationwide chains to single outlet owners. However large or small, our customers have similar concerns when it comes to the storefront glass they use with regard to cost, appearance/aesthetics, security and service.

The good news is that in 99.9 percent of cases, we find that the installation of 6 mm + 6 mm taughened glass with an interlayer of 0.76 mm Butacite(r) PVB interlayer solves all of these concerns with ease! **Taughened glass is an ideal solution for modern retailers in terms of same day installation, security prevention, protection from the UV rays that cause the degradation of store displays and furnishings and the elimination of boarding following damage to the storefront.**

Time is money

Everyone in the retail construction value chain, from owners to foremen, are concerned with costs. We are able to address this first concern pretty quickly. In the USA, taughened glass costs almost exactly the same as tempered glass to purchase and install per square meter. In Australia and Europe, it can be significantly cheaper than tempered glass! In the case of breakage, the cost benefits of taughened glass can be seen very clearly; as store owners, managers and loss prevention departments know, time is money! Unlike tempered glass, taughened glass allows stores to stay open in the case of breakage since cracked or broken glass stays in the frame, adhered by the PVB interlayer. Smaller locations that are boarded up with plywood can leave customers with the impression that they are closed—and nobody can afford that. It's critically important that everyone knows that you are still open for business.

Better looking storefronts

The second major concern is aesthetics. Many of our retail customers located in downtown areas automatically assume that shutters will have to be installed to ensure adequate security after store opening hours. It is always a pleasure for me to see the relief on customers' faces when I tell them about the security benefits of taughened glass and how the material eliminates the need for shutters, allowing much better looking storefronts.

A real boost to the bottom line

A third concern is security. The loss prevention officers of major retailers understand perhaps better than anyone else the extent to which break-ins and vandalism negatively affect the bottom line. My retail customers tell me that the average cost of a break-in is US$ 30, 000. **This not only includes stolen goods but also takes account of the costs**

related to store downtime while repairs are effected, clean-up costs, inventory evaluation, and insurance assessment. Increasingly, retailers' loss prevention departments are prevailing in getting any broken glass in the store replaced with taughened glass. One retailer told me that over a three-year period, this policy has resulted in a 50 percent drop in damage from vandalism due to the added strength of taughened glass.

For the past five years, loss prevention officers have also been strongly in favor of getting taughened glass installed right from when the original storefront is specified. Because loss prevention is now recognized as such a major driver of profits and the bottom line, they are seeing their views prevail with owners. The task now is to help spread the word to commercial and residential owners everywhere regarding the optimal solutions that taughened glass solutions bring to them.

But What is Taughened (Safety) Glass

Toughened glass is produced by applying a special treatment to ordinary float glass after it has been cut to size and finished. The treatment involves heating the glass so that it begins to soften (about 620 degrees C) and then rapidly cooling it. This produces a glass which, if broken, breaks into small pieces without sharp edges. The treatment does increase the surface tension of the glass which can cause it to"explode" if broken; this is more a dramatic effect than hazardous.

Crystal reinforcement is used where there is a desire for security as well as containing the glass if it breaks. The cyrstal is embedded in the glass during manufacturing. When the glass is broken the bond between the glass and cyrstal keeps pieces for falling out. The cyrstal also stops someone from forcing their way through the broken glass as would be possible if there was just a thin layer of plastic.

It is important to note that the treatment must be applied only after all cutting and processing has been completed, as once "toughened", any attempt to cut the glass will cause it to shatter.

Sydney's Galleries Victoria: Old-world charm meets new-world glass technology

The Galleries Victoria shopping mall in Sydney (completed: August 2000) designed by Crone & Associates of Sydney, reintroduces the winding laneways and alleyways known to the city 150 years ago—but in a modern contextual form, with the inclusion of a floating, taughened glass roof, 22 meters above ground, creating a weather-protected, naturally ventilated series of spaces. In another traditional architectural feature, taughened heat strengthened glass is used for the traditional street awnings that project into the mall and out onto the sidewalk; there is also a large, flat skylight of taughened heat strengthened glass over the mall's main piazza.

Clear glazed walls of 10.38 mm taughened glass are incorporated to form enticing entrances to the laneways.

Greg Crone said: "We set about developing highly transparent entries to allow the building street facade to continue in the laneways. The benefits of architectural taughened glass are becoming more widely accepted, with architects now challenging and extending the boundaries for which it can materially improve the amenity of the built environment and contribute to architectural form. **Taughened glass also provides acoustic protection and fulfills safety requirements. The aesthetic variations are endless—from laminating in leaf forms to using tints or spandrel panels.** We have used the material many of our projects over the past 15 years, in shopping malls, high rise office buildings, hotels and apartment buildings, throughout Asia, the Middle East and China."

All the toughened glass for the Galleries Victoria Incorporates DuPont(tm) Butacite(r) PVB and was supplied by G. James Safety Glass of Australia.

(THE END)

必备词汇

taughened glass (safety glass) 强化玻璃（安全玻璃）
aesthetic / iːs'θetik / 美学的，审美的
perceive / pə'siːv / 感知，认识到
interlayer / 'intə(ː)ˌleiə / 夹层
in terms of 基于，根据
tempered glass 回火玻璃
plywood / 'plaiwud / 夹板
downtown / 'dauntaun / 市区的
shutter / 'ʃʌtə / 百叶窗
break-in 破窗而入，侵入
take account of 考虑
downtime / 'dauntaim / 停工时间
bottom line 账本底线
float glass 浮法玻璃
sharp edge 锋利的边缘
tension / 'tenʃən / 张力
explode / iks'pləud / 爆炸
hazardous / 'hæzədəs / 危险的
reinforcement / ˌriːin'fɔːsmənt / 增强，加强
crystal / 'kristl / 水晶
embed / im'bed / 嵌入，插入
bond / bɔnd / 结合力
laneway / 'leinwei / 巷道，通路

— Taughened glass is an ideal solution for modern retailers in terms of same day installation, security prevention, protection from the UV rays that cause the degradation of store displays and furnishings and the elimination of boarding following damage to the storefront. 强化玻璃是现代零售商们的理想用品，它具有如下优点：当天即可安装完毕、安全防护、防止紫外线辐射给橱窗展示品和家具造成品质下降、取消了对木板的使用，增强了店面的美观效果。

— This not only includes stolen goods but also takes account of the costs related to store downtime while repairs are effected, clean-up costs, inventory evaluation, and insurance assessment. Increasingly, retailers' loss prevention departments are prevailing in getting any broken glass in the store replaced with taughened glass.这不仅包括被偷去的货品，也考虑到了进行维修时店面关张期间损失的费用、清洁费用、存货评估及保险评估。零售商的损失防范部门正越来越倾向于把店中所有损坏的玻璃更换为强化玻璃。

— Toughened glass is produced by applying a special treatment to ordinary float glass after it has been cut to size and finished. The treatment involves heating the glass so that it begins to soften (about 620 degrees C) and then rapidly cooling it. This produces a glass which, if broken, breaks into small pieces without sharp edges. The treatment does increase the surface tension of the glass which can cause it to "explode" if broken; this is more a dramatic effect than hazardous. 强化玻璃的制造工艺是这样的: 把普通的浮法玻璃切割成一定的尺寸，成型后对它施加一种特殊的处理。在处理过程中，把玻璃加热使其软化（大约600摄氏度），然后快速冷却。这样出来的玻璃如果遇到破碎，将碎成没有尖锐边缘的小片。这种处理提高了玻璃的表面张力，在其破碎时造成“爆炸”的效果，这种效果比危险来说是一种进步。

— Crystal reinforcement is used where there is a desire for security as well as containing the glass if it breaks. The cyrstal is embedded in the glass during manufacturing. When the glass is broken the bond between the glass and cyrstal keeps pieces for falling out. The cyrstal also stops someone from forcing their way through the broken glass as would be possible if there was just a thin layer of plastic. 如果想更安全以及控制碎裂的玻璃碎片，可以使用水晶来强化。在制造过程中把水晶嵌入在玻璃中。当玻璃破碎后，玻璃和水晶之间的结合力会阻止碎片落下来。水晶还阻止有人强行通过碎裂的玻璃，因为如果仅有一薄层塑料这一情形是有可能发生的。

— It is important to note that the treatment must be applied only after all cutting and processing has been completed, as once "toughened", any attempt to cut the glass will cause it to shatter. 需要注意的是，强化处理必须是在所有的切割和处理完成后才能进行，因为一旦被"强化"，任何切割玻璃的企图都将使它变成一堆碎片。

— Taughened glass also provides acoustic protection and fulfills safety requirements. The aesthetic variations are endless—from laminating in leaf forms to using tints or spandrel panels. 强化玻璃还提供了隔音保护，满足了安全要求。美学上的变化没有穷尽——从树叶形状的层合到使用的色调或拱肩板。

(V27真题题源)

7. Two Dome Models

两种房屋之构造对比

Geodesic dome

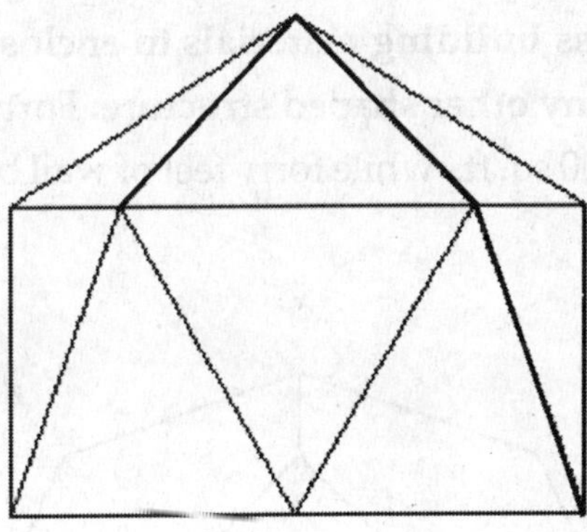

Geodesic dome

Designed by Professor Fuller, a geodesic dome is a type of structure shaped like a piece of a sphere or a ball. **This structure is comprised of a complex network of triangles that form a roughly spherical surface. The more complex the network of triangles, the more closely the dome approximates the shape of a true sphere. This assemblage of triangular trusses grows stronger as it grows larger.**

By using triangles of various sizes, a sphere can be symmetrically divided by thirty-one great circles. A great circle is the largest circle that can be drawn around a sphere, like the lines of latitude around the earth, or the equator. Each of these lines divides the sphere into two halves.

The dome is a structure with the highest ratio of enclosed area to external surface area, and in which all structural members are equal contributors to the whole. There are many sizes of triangles in a geodesic, depending on the frequency of subdivision of the underlying spherical polyhedron. The cross section of a geodesic approximates a great-circle line.

Well, the structures weigh less when completed because of the air-mass inside the dome. When it's heated warmer than the outside air, it has a net lifting effect (like a hot-air balloon).

This is almost unnoticeable in smaller structures, like houses, but, as with other things about geodesics, being as they're based upon spheres, the effect increases geometrically with size. So you'd be able to notice it in a sports stadium, and a sphere more than a half mile in diameter would be able to float in the air with only a l degree F difference in temperature!

As sphere is defined as the geometric shape that encloses the most volume with the least surface area, the geodesic dome is the safest, strongest and most energy efficient building. It takes less building materials to enclose usable living or working area in a dome than any other shaped structure. Forty feet of wall will enclose a 10 ×10 area measuring 100 sq. ft., while forty feet of wall built in a circle will enclose 127 sq. ft., a 27% increase.

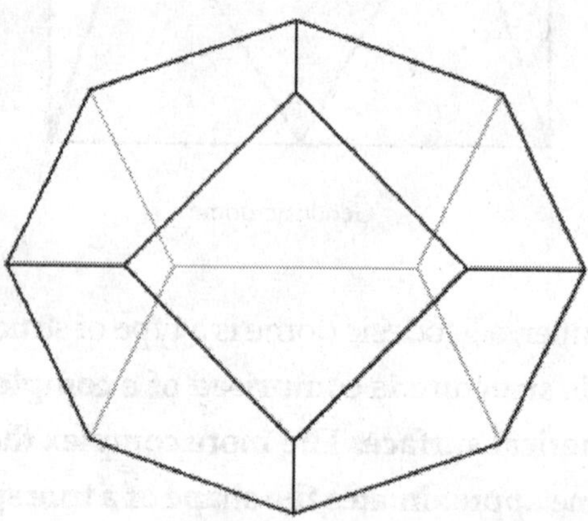

Geotangent dome

Geotangent domes

Mr. Craig Yacoe, a retired engineer, designed "geotangent dome". **He thinks, due to the structure of triangles, the geodesic dome allows no flexibility to arbitrarily change its height. So he designed this improved version to cope with this problem, while**

inheriting other advantages of its geodesic predecessor. Since geotangent dome is made up of pentagons and hexagons, it promises to be more versatile that its geodesic predecessor.

Geotangent dome is a kind of dome formed by a section of a polyhedral structure that approximates a non-spherical ellipsoid. The ellipsoid has an equator and two poles, the structure composed of two polar faces and at least three rings of polygonal faces. The polygonal faces have from 4 to 8 sides, including at least one ring closest to each pole and at least one ring at or adjacent the equator. Wherein each face in a ring is at the same latitude of the ellipsoid and each edge of each polygon is tangent to the approximated ellipsoid at one point. Each ring of polygons at or closest to the equator contains more faces than the most polar rings. It provides a broad range of height to diameter ratios for the enclosure of space.

Geodesic domes have, in the past, been used for a wide variety of structures. Spheres of approximately equilateral triangles in the geodesic pattern do, in fact, exhibit considerable strength. **However, a number of practical problems are inherent in building structures based on a three-way grid defining substantially equilateral triangles.** With either a spherical or hemispherical dome structure based on this pattern, each vertex intersection of surface planes represents the meeting of five or six triangular planes at a point. Such intersections require careful fitting and sealing. When a structure is patterned on a bisected sphere to form a dome, additional difficulties are encountered using equilateral triangles as the planar surfaces. These difficulties arise from the fact that alternate intersections of five or six triangles, in the geodesic pattern, define a surface which is either concave or convex with respect to the enclosed sphere. **As a result, the perimeter of a geodesic dome, at the point of meeting a horizontal surface or other plane, defines a zigzag pattern. Moreover, the faces at the edge of the dome do not meet the planar surface at a right angle. These considerations make it difficult to incorporate basic architectural elements such as doors and windows into a geodesic dome.**

Since Fuller's dome is based on a sphere, cutting it anywhere but precisely along its equator means that the triangles at the bottom will tilt inward or outward. In contrast, Yacoe's dome, which has a circular base, follows the curve of an ellipsoid. Builders can consequently pick the dimensions they need, Yacoe says. And his design ensures that the polygons at the base of his dome always meet the ground at right angles, making it easier to build than a geodesic dome. He hopes these features will prove mathematic flexibility when designers depict a dome. He says two potential uses exist: space station construction and energy-saving housing. Yacoe has also proposed that the National

Aeronautics and Space Administration consider a geotangent structure as part of a space station.

But some professionals in the construction industry have doubt. They think Yacoe's model leaves no room for door. Further, with the dome's height increasing, the foundation will hardly withstand the bearing thus arising. But Yacoe argues that he will upgrade his computer system and do more calculations to solve it. He still insists his dome model will expect good prospect of application.

(THE END)

必备词汇

dome / dəum / 圆顶屋
triangle / 'traiæŋgl / 三角形
spherical / 'sferikəl / 圆形的
trusse/ trʌs / 架构
latitude / 'lætitjuːd / 纬度
equator/ i'kweitə/ 赤道
member / 'membə / 构件
polyhedron / pɔli'hedrən / 多面体
cross section 横断面
flexibility / ˌfleksə'biliti / 灵活性
pentagon / 'pentəgən / 五角形
hexagon / 'heksəgən / 六角形
predecessor / 'priːdisesə / 前辈，前任
ellipsoid / i'lipsɔid / 椭球体
polygonal face 多边形表面
tangent / 'tændʒənt / 切线的，相切的
equilateral triangle 等边三角形
hemispherical / ˌhemi'sferik / 半球形的
vertex / 'vəːteks / 顶端
intersection / ˌintə(ː)'sekʃən / 交汇处
concave / kɔn'keiv / 凹的
convex / kɔn'veks / 凸的
bisected / ˌbai'sekʃə·n / 对切的，对开的
zigzag / 'zigzæg / 锯齿形的
tilt / tilt / 倾斜
upgrade / 'ʌpgreid / 改进，更新，升级

重点剖析

— This structure is comprised of a complex network of triangles that form a roughly spherical surface. The more complex the network of triangles, the more closely the dome approximates the shape of a true sphere. This assemblage of triangular trusses grows stronger as it grows larger. 该结构是由复杂的三角形网络构成的，形状像一个球体的表面。三角形网络越复杂，屋顶越接近真正的球体形状。此三角形构架越大，支撑力越强。

— By using triangles of various sizes, a sphere can be symmetrically divided by thirty-one great circles. A great circle is the largest circle that can be drawn around a sphere, like the lines of latitude around the earth, or the equator. Each of these lines divides the sphere into two halves. 使用尺寸不同的三角形，球体可以对称的分为31个大圆。大圆是围绕球体画出的最大的圆圈，样子像环绕地球或赤道的纬度线。这些线的每一条都把球体分割为两个半球。

— As sphere is defined as the geometric shape that encloses the most volume with the least surface area, the geodesic dome is the safest, strongest and most energy efficient building. It takes less building materials to enclose usable living or working area in a dome than any other shaped structure. 由于球体的几何形状，它以最小的表面积包容了最大的容积，所以网格球顶屋是最安全、最结实、最节能的建筑物。比其他形状的结构物而言，它使用更少的建筑材料来包容可使用的居住或工作空间。

— He thinks, due to the structure of triangles, the geodesic dome allows no flexibility to arbitrarily change its height. So he designed this improved version to cope with this problem, while inheriting other advantages of its geodesic predecessor. Since geotangent dome is made up of pentagons and hexagons, it promises to be more versatile that its geodesic predecessor. 他认为，由于网格球顶屋使用的是三角形，所以不能任意改变屋子的高度。所以他设计了改进型，但继承了网格球顶的其他优点（如，节能等）。他的屋子是由五角形和六角形构成的，所以有更大的灵活性。

— Geotangent dome is a kind of dome formed by a section of a polyhedral structure that approximates a non-spherical ellipsoid. The ellipsoid has an equator and two poles, the structure composed of two polar faces and at least three rings of polygonal faces. Geotangent 圆顶屋由多边形结构组成，类似于一个非球体状的椭圆体。椭圆体有一个赤道和两个极，包含有两个极表面的结构物和多边形表面的至少三个环。

— However, a number of practical problems are inherent in building structures based on a three-way grid defining substantially equilateral triangles. 然而，由等边三角形的三向栅格构成的建筑物有一些与生俱来的问题。

— As a result, the perimeter of a geodesic dome, at the point of meeting a horizontal surface or other plane, defines a zigzag pattern. Moreover, the faces at the edge of the dome do not meet the planar surface at a right angle. These considerations make it difficult to incorporate basic architectural elements such as doors and windows into a geodesic dome. 结果是，网格球底的周边，在水平表面或者其他平面汇合点处，出现了锯齿状的形状。而且，屋顶边缘的表面和平面的表面结合不是呈直角的。这些因素使得它难以包容基本的建筑成分，如门和窗户等。

— But some professionals in the construction industry have doubt. They think Yacoe's model leaves no room for door. Further, with the dome's height increasing, the foundation will hardly withstand the bearing thus arising. 但业内的其他专家提出了质疑。他们认为Yacoe的模型没有留出门的位置。而且，随着屋顶的高度增加，屋子的地基几乎不能承受压力。

(New version 真题题源)

8. Wind Power and the Pyramids

风力与金字塔

When people think about the building of the Egyptian pyramids, they probably have a mental image of thousands of slaves laboriously rolling massive stone blocks into place with logs and levers. But one Caltech aeronautics professor has set out to demonstrate that the task could have been accomplished by several people using a kite to move the heavy stones.

On June 23, Mory Gharib and his team raised a 6,900-pound (3132.6 kg), 15-foot (3.0 m) obelisk into vertical position in the desert near Palmdale by using only a kite, a pulley system, and a support frame. **Although the blustery winds were gusting up to 22 miles (35.4 km) per hour, the team set the obelisk upright on their second attempt.**

"It actually lifted up the kite flyer, Eric May, so we had to kill the kite quickly," said Gharib. "But we finished it off the second time."

Emilio Castano Graff, a Caltech undergraduate who tackled the problem under the sponsorship of the Summer Undergraduate Research Fellowship program, was also pleased with the results. "The wind wasn't that great, but basically we're happy with it," he said.

Despite the lack of a steady breeze, the team raised the obelisk in about 25 seconds, so quickly that the concrete-and-rebar object was lifted off the ground and swung free for a few seconds. Once the motion had stabilized, the team lowered the obelisk into an upright position. The next step is to build a bigger obelisk to demonstrate that even the mammoth 300-ton monuments of ancient Egypt, not to mention the far less massive building blocks of Egypt's 90-odd pyramids could have been raised with a fraction of the effort that modern researchers have assumed.

Project Born of a Passion

Clemmons' kite theory is a major departure from conventional thinking, which holds that thousands of slaves used little more than brute force and log-rolling to put the stone blocks and obelisks in place. No one has ever come up with a substantially better system for accomplishing the task, and even today the moving of heavy stones would be quite labour-intensive without power equipment.

As an indication of how little progress was made in the centuries after the age of the pyramids had passed, Gharib points out, the Vatican in 1586 moved a 330-ton Egyptian obelisk to St. Peter's Square. It is known that lifting the stone into vertical position required 74 horses and 900 men using ropes and pulleys.

Although Clemmons has no scientific or archaeological training, she has managed to marshal the efforts of family, friends, and other enthusiasts to work on a theory that could alter thinking about ancient engineering practices and the interpretation of ancient symbols.

Researching the tools available to the Egyptian pyramid builders, she discovered, for example, that a brass ankh, long assumed to be merely a religious symbol, makes a very good carabiner for controlling a kite line. And a type of insect commonly found in Egypt could have supplied a kind of shellac that helped linen sails hold wind.

For Gharib, the idea of accomplishing heavy tasks with limited manpower is appealing from an engineer's standpoint because it makes more logistical sense.

"I prefer to think of the technology as simple, with relatively few people involved," he explained.

Ancient Clues

No one has found any evidence that the ancient Egyptians moved stones or any other objects with kites and pulleys. But Clemmons has found some tantalizing hints that the project is on the right track. **On a building frieze in a Cairo museum, there is a wing pattern in bas-relief that does not resemble any living bird. Directly below are several men standing near vertical objects that could be ropes.**

Gharib's interest in the project is mainly to demonstrate that the technique may be viable. "We're not Egyptologists," he said. "We're mainly interested in determining whether there is a possibility that the Egyptians were aware of wind power, and whether they used it to make their lives better."

Now that Gharib and his team have successfully raised the four-ton concrete obelisk, they plan to further test the approach using a ten-ton stone, and perhaps an even heavier one after that. Eventually they hope to obtain permission to try using their technique to raise one of the obelisks that still lie in an Egyptian quarry.

An important question is: Was there enough wind in Egypt for a kite or a drag chute to fly? Probably so, as steady winds of up to 30 miles per hour are not unusual in the areas where pyramids and obelisks were found.

(THE END)

必备词汇

pyramid / 'pirəmid / (埃及)金字塔
aeronautics / ˌɛərə'nɔːtiks / 航空学
kite / kait / 风筝
obelisk / 'ɔbilisk / 方尖石块
pulley system 滑轮系统
support frame 支撑架
blustery / 'blʌstəri / 大风的
ankh / æŋk / T形十字章
carabiner / kærə'binə / 竖钩
shellac / ʃə'læk / 虫漆
linen / 'linin / 亚麻布

重点剖析

— When people think about the building of the Egyptian pyramids, they probably have a mental image of thousands of slaves laboriously rolling massive stone blocks into place with logs and levers. 当人们想到如何建造金字塔时，可能脑海中不由地就浮现出成千上万名奴隶艰难地用杠杆和圆木翻滚着巨大的石块这样的情境。

— But one Caltech aeronautics professor has set out to demonstrate that the task could have been accomplished by several people using a kite to move the heavy stones. 但一名航空学教授却向世人证明，这一任务是通过少数人使用风筝移动巨石来实现的。

— Although the blustery winds were gusting up to 22 miles (35.4 km) per hour, the team set the obelisk upright on their second attempt. 虽然风速达到每小时22英里，但研究组却在第二次把方石块垂直地举了起来。

— On a building frieze in a Cairo museum, there is a wing pattern in bas-relief that does not resemble any living bird. Directly below are several men standing near vertical objects that could be ropes. 在开罗一间博物馆里，有一个浮雕中刻有翅膀样图案，它不像任何现存的鸟类，在图案的下面是几个人站在竖直的物体下，这个物体可能是绳子。

八、医疗健康类(15篇)

(New versian真题题源)

1. Heat and Athletic Activity

体 育 运 动

Heat injuries endanger the health of many athletes each year. Those involved in athletics must know how to recognize and provide emergency aid to the athlete suffering from heat disorders. **Most importantly, we must know how to prevent heat injuries with proper attention to conditioning, clothing, fluid intake, and be familiar with the precautions for limiting play during times of high temperatures and humidity.**

Heat Regulation

A small gland in the brain called the hypothalamus carefully regulates body temperature; as body temperature rises, certain mechanisms are activated to promote heat loss. These mechanisms include conduction (transfer of heat from the warm body to a cooler object); convection (transfer of heat from the warm body to the cooler environmental air); evaporation (transformation of water on the body surface into a vapor); respiration (entrance of cooler air into the body via the lungs);

and radiation (transfer of heart from the warm body to the cooler environment). Physiologically, the body responds by dilating the blood vessels in the skin, enhancing blood flow to the skin, producing more sweat, and increasing the pulse and respiratory rates.

Heat Injuries

If these heat loss mechanisms fail to restore normal body temperature, the spectrum of heat injury syndromes can occur, including heat cramps, heat exhaustion, or heatstroke.

Heat cramps are the mildest form of hyperthermia or heat injury. The athlete with heat cramps complains of muscle twitching, cramps, and spasm. Treatment of the athlete with heat cramps typically consists of encouraging drinking to restore adequate hydration. The athlete should stop activity and should rest in a cool environment while replenishing fluids. Heat cramps frequently occur at the beginning of the hot weather season, before the athlete has had time to adequately condition for participation at high temperature or humidity. The body's ability to improve its response to heat exposure is called acclimatization.

The athlete with heat exhaustion, the next most severe of the heat injury syndromes, complains not only of muscle spasms and cramps, but also may complain of headache, fatigue, weakness, lack of coordination, and excessive thirst. He or she may be nauseated or have diarrhea. On physical examination, he may have slow mentations, weight loss, dry tongue and mouth, and elevated body temperature. His skin is typically ashen, cold, and clammy, and he may be sweating profusely. Treatment consist of removing the athlete to a cool place, sponging him with cool water, fanning him, and encouraging him to drink cool fluids if the athlete is able to do so. Placing ice packs in the axilla (underarm) and hip/groin area can be helpful. If the athlete is mentally confused and refuses to drink, intravenous fluids are needed.

The athlete with heatstroke, the most severe form of heat injury, may complain of all the symptoms of heat exhaustion (headache, dizziness, fatigue, vomiting, diarrhea), but his skin is hot and dry (i.e. no sweating), not cold and clammy, since the normal homeostatic sweating mechanism has been overwhelmed. In addition, he may be confused or disoriented and combative. He feels like he is burning up, and indeed, his body temperature may rise to 104 or 105 degrees Fahrenheit or greater.

Heatstroke is a medical emergency! If the athlete is not rapidly cooled, he can die. The high body temperature literally burns up tissues, and hence, alters function of the heart, lungs, brain, kidneys, and other organ systems. Treatment consists of rapid transport to an emergency room facility for administration of intravenous fluids and rapid cooling with either ice water lavages or ice water immersion as indicated. While waiting for transport, the athlete should be placed in a cool environment, his clothing removed, and ice packs placed about his body with fanning to speed cooling. If the athlete is alert, encourage him to drink fluids.

Prevention of Heat Injuries

Prevention should be everyone's first priority. Preseason conditioning improves athletes' ability workout when the environmental heat and humidity are high, processes know as acclimatization. **The amount of time an athlete takes to acclimatize can vary, and coaches and athletic trainers should be more cautious in the first few weeks of practice to make sure athletes are adjusting to surrounding conditions. Athletes should wear lightweight, light-colored, porous clothing, and should be allowed to change into dry clothes as often as necessary.**

Water should be readily available, with athletes encouraged to drink small amounts at frequent intervals (before, during and after practice), even if they are not thirsty.

Athletes should be taught to camel-up with fluids. Athletes lose 2% of body weight before becoming thirsty, and satisfying thirst only replaces 50% of the fluid that is needed, so it is impossible to catch-up with hydration once the athlete falls behind. Electrolyte solutions (i.e. sports drinks) can also be helpful to replace lost electrolytes, and some athletes may prefer sports drinks to help them take in adequate amounts of fluids. It may be helpful to weigh athletes before and after practice to ensure adequate hydration and to identify those particularly prone to fluid loss.

Whenever possible, practices should be held at cooler times of the day (early morning or late afternoon), with regular rest and water breaks. Those in charge of the practice should assess environmental conditions, taking into account not only the absolute temperature, but also the relative humidity, since the latter strongly influences the athlete's ability to sweat. (Remember, sweating is the body's most effective means of heat dissipation.) If heat and humidity add up to over 160 (i.e. temperature is 800C and 80% humidity) one should be cautious and think prevention.

While all athletes must be carefully monitored for signs of heat injury, certain athletes may be more prone to heat stress and deserve special consideration. Among these are out of shape athletes, obese athletes, athletes with chronic diseases such as diabetes and kidney disorders, athletes taking diuretics, antihistamines, antidepressants, and other medications; and athletes who are so eager to please the coach that they may ignore impending symptoms of heat illness. Athletes prone to profuse sweating are also at an increased risk. Remember, too, that children are much more susceptible to hyperthermia than adults because of their reduced ability to regulate body temperature. Children generate more metabolic heat per unit mass; therefore, their sweating capacity is lower. They also have less ability to transfer heat to the skin than adults do.

Remember, heat related injuries are preventable but require a commitment to the many issues outlined above. These measures will not only optimize athletic performance, but also improve overall sport safety.

This is provided for general information. It does not purport to encompass all risks associated with exercising in hot and humid weather, nor is it a substitute for your own good judgment and consultation with competent professional regarding specific fact situations.

(THE END)

必备词汇

endanger / in'deindʒə / 危及
athletic / æθ'letiks / 运动的
emergency aid 急救
disorder / dis'ɔ:də / 紊乱
conditioning / kən'diʃəniŋ / 条件作用，训练
intake / 'inteik / 吸入
precautions / pri'kɔ:ʃəs / 预防，防范
humidity/ hju:'miditi / 湿度
gland / glænd / 腺
hypothalamus / ˌhaipəu'θæləməs / 视丘下部
regulate / 'regjuleit / 调节
activate / 'æktiveit / 激活
dilate / dai'leit / 扩大，膨胀
syndrome / 'sindrəum / 综合症
preseason conditioning 赛前训练
workout / 'wə:kaut / 测验
acclimatization / əˌklaimətai'zeiʃən / 环境适应性
cautious / 'kɔ:ʃəs / 小心的，谨慎的
camel-up 补充
hydration / hai'dreiʃən / 水合作用
electrolyte solutions 电解液
prone to 倾向于
take into account 考虑
dissipation / ˌdisi'peiʃən / 散发

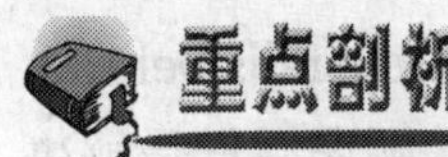

重点剖析

— Most importantly, we must know how to prevent heat injuries with proper attention to conditioning, clothing, fluid intake, and be familiar with the precautions for limiting play during times of high temperatures and humidity. 最重要的是必须了解如何防止热损伤，要适当注意训练、衣着和水份摄入，并熟知在高温高湿环境中进行运动和训练应该注意什么。

— A small gland in the brain called the hypothalamus carefully regulates body temperature; as body temperature rises, certain mechanisms are activated to promote heat loss. These mechanisms include conduction (transfer of heat from the warm body to a cooler object); convection (transfer of heat from the warm body to the cooler environmental air); evaporation (transformation of water on the body surface into a vapor); respiration (entrance of cooler air into the body via the lungs); and radiation (transfer of heart from the warm body to the cooler environment). 大脑中一个称为视丘下部的小腺体仔细地调节着体温；当体温升高时，它启动某些机制来促进热流失。这些机制包括传导（热从热的身体传递到较凉快的物体）；对流（热从热的身体传递到较凉快的环境空气）；蒸发（体表的水转化为水蒸汽）；呼吸（身体通过肺吸入较凉快的空气）；辐射（从热的身体到较凉快的环境的热转移）。

— If these heat loss mechanisms fail to restore normal body temperature, the spectrum of heat injury syndromes can occur, including heat cramps, heat exhaustion, or heatstroke. 如果这些热流失机制不能恢复正常的体温，就会出现热损伤综合症，包括热抽筋、热疲劳或热中暑。

— The amount of time an athlete takes to acclimatize can vary, and coaches and athletic trainers should be more cautious in the first few weeks of practice to make sure athletes are adjusting to surrounding conditions. Athletes should wear lightweight, light-colored, porous clothing, and should be allowed to change into dry clothes as often as necessary. 运动员进行环境适应花费的时间长度可能各不相同，教练和运动训练师应在训练的前几周更为谨慎，确保运动员能适应环境条件。运动员应穿轻便、浅色的、吸汗的衣服，应时常更换干衣服。

— Water should be readily available, with athletes encouraged to drink small amounts at frequent intervals (before, during and after practice), even if they are not thirsty. 水应该放在方便取的地方，运动员应隔一会儿（训练前、训练中、训练后）就喝少量水，即使不感到口渴也应如此。

— Athletes should be taught to camel-up with fluids. Athletes lose 2% of body weight before becoming thirsty, and satisfying thirst only replaces 50% of the fluid that is needed, so it is impossible to catch-up with hydration once the athlete falls behind. 应教会运动员补充 水份。运动员在感到口渴时已失掉2%的体重，解渴后只是解决了需要量一半的体液，所以一旦运动员失去体重，就不可能满足水合作用。

(V24真题题源)

2. Alternative or Complementary Therapies: the Appeal to General Practitioners

澳洲医疗与中医

(第1篇)

Recent articles and editorials in the Journal have highlighted the increasing demand for complementary and alternative medicine (CAM) by Australians, and its provision by general practitioners (GPs). **The findings of Pirotta et al that 1 in 5 Victorian GPs are using CAM in their practice support earlier data of the Royal Australian College of General Practitioners that 1 in 6 Australian GPs employed some form of CAM.** A secondary analysis of Health Insurance Commission data indicates that about 1 in 7 GPs in Australia use acupuncture. CAM is a billion-dollar industry in Australia, and a multibillion-dollar industry globally. Pirotta and others have emphasized the need for further research into the reasons behind GPs' use of CAM.

Reasons for GPs' use of CAM

My research in this area — a qualitative study involving GPs and alternative practitioners — produced two main explanations for the increasing use by GPs of CAM. **The first is that GPs are responding to increasing consumer demand for these therapies because of their clinical success. The second and more contentious finding is that consumers are demanding, and GPs are using, these therapies because of factors beyond clinical success—factors related to globalisation and the characteristics of the global market. These market characteristics include increased consumer choice, increased competition among providers, a resultant power shift from provider to consumer, and a return to and commercialisation of nature, history, and tradition.**

The GPs I interviewed cited reasons for incorporating CAM into their practices that fall into three broad categories:

- **Last resort:The use of or referral to practitioners of CAM to treat patients with chronic conditions unresponsive to orthodox medicine.**

- **Integrated approach: A considered choice to regularly incorporate CAM, in addition to orthodox biomedical therapies.**

- **Ideological conversion:** The adoption of CAM as the main treatment practice. GPs who fall into this category also tend to use diagnostic techniques similar to those of alternative practitioners.

The prevalence of the last two categories, at least among the GPs I have interviewed formally and conversed with informally, contradicts the conclusion by Bensoussan, in a Journal editorial, that simple pragmatism — among both patients and doctors — adequately accounts for the dramatic increase in the use of CAM.

Clinical legitimacy

Bensoussan, rightly and with apt humour, criticizes recent articles that narrowly attribute patient demand for CAM to "postmodern" or "new age" values usurping scientific rationalism. He notes that a considerable segment of the medical profession has recognized this consumer demand, and that chronic sufferers and the elderly account for a large portion of the patients who request or accept CAM. He suggests that common sense indicates that medical practitioners, the elderly, and the chronically ill are not likely to embrace the naivety of "new age" thought or the jargonistic obscurity of postmodernism; instead, Bensoussan and others suggest that simple pragmatism among both doctors and patients provides a more satisfactory explanation for the dramatic increase in the use of CAM.

Other writers have coined the term "clinical legitimacy" to explain the links among consumer demand, pragmatism, and increased GP provision of CAM. That is to say, CAM is effective, particularly in the treatment of chronic conditions, regardless of the lack of scientific explanation or validation. This clinical success, aside from gratifying both patient and doctor, ensures continuing consumer demand, and thereby increases the financial viability of GPs who incorporate CAM, whether directly or through referrals.

Data from my research show that GPs acknowledge that, regardless of the deficit of scientific evidence for how or why, CAM does achieve clinical results.

Ideological motivations

GPs note that, in addition to being pragmatic, their patients want healthcare options, and some are indeed ideological in their increasing demand for "natural" therapies and their concomitant mistrust of pharmaceuticals and invasive surgery, a phenomenon described by one GP interviewed as the "greening of medicine".

GPs who offer CAM are keenly aware of this demand for "natural" therapy, and clearly do respond partly as pragmatists catering to consumer demand. However, my interviews reveal that GPs are not acting entirely as economic rationalists responding to market forces. GPs who resort to CAM, like their patients, are often ideological in their motivations. Many are genuinely disillusioned with their biomedical training and with the reality of general practice. They are genuinely seeking a more rewarding approach to primary healthcare, for themselves as well as their patients. For example, some GPs recommend CAM even to patients who prefer or expect synthetic drugs — a practice described by one doctor interviewed as "good medicine", particularly in light of antibiotic overprescribing.

Therefore, while my findings validate the roles of both therapeutic and market pragmatism in the increasing use of CAM by Australian GPs, these same findings suggest that this increase involves factors beyond simple pragmatism. The interview data support the sociological hypothesis that a broad cultural shift is occurring in late capitalist societies such as Australia, the United States, the United Kingdom and Western Europe, and GPs, like consumers, are not immune to this sweeping social change. **Arguably, GPs who use CAM are not just influenced by this social change, they contribute to it.**

Traditional Chinese Medicine (TCM) in Australia

（第2篇）

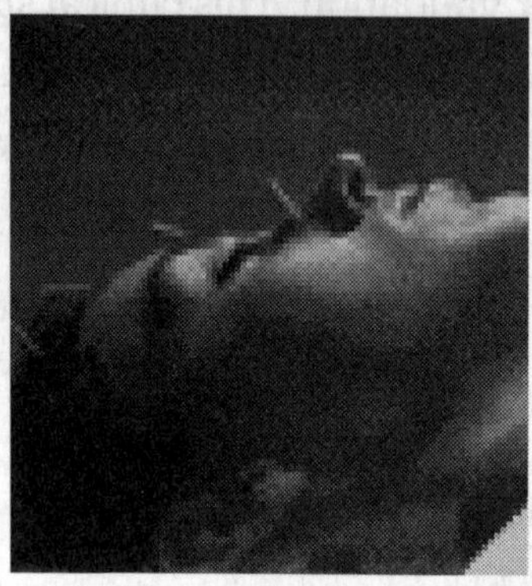

By far the major component of Chinese medical therapy is herbal medicine. This may come as a surprise to us in Australia, where acupuncture was the first modality to be introduced and practiced by non-Chinese practitioners. There are several thousand different medicinal substances used by Chinese herbalists, most of which are derived from plants. Minerals and animal parts are also used, however most of these are restricted by the Australian health authorities, specifically those that may be toxic, or that may involve the destruction of an endangered species.

In modern China, TCM is both taught as well as practiced alongside orthodox Western medicine. All of the major hospitals have Western and traditional Chinese departments, and patients are often referred from one department to the other. Thus Chinese patients are able to receive the best that each system has to offer, with combined Chinese herbal and Western drug therapy in serious cases. **This has proven to be an extremely successful approach, with remarkable results being achieved in such areas as cancer care, recovery from stroke, arthritis, skin diseases, heart disease, chronic degenerative diseases, post operative care, etc.**

TCM in Australia

In the last three decades there has been a steady growth of TCM in Australia. Several major universities now offer degree courses in TCM. Chinese herbal medicines have been subject to clinical trials for treating conditions such as hepatitis-C, irritable bowel syndrome, menopause, heart disease, etc. **In recent years an increasing number of doctors regularly refer patients to qualified TCM practitioners and many people have found help and relief with TCM after the failure of conventional methods.**

Recognition by government has resulted in higher standards for practitioners and consistent quality and purity of the Chinese herbal medicines that are imported into this country. Now, more than ever before, it is possible for patients to make an informed choice and have the benefit of well trained TCM practitioners and high quality medicines.

(THE END)

必备词汇

complementary and alternative medicine (CAM)补充医学和替代医学(CAM)
general practitioners (GPs) 全科医生(GP)
acupuncture / 'ækjupʌŋktʃə(r) / 针灸
qualitative study 定性研究
alternative practitioner 替代医生
pragmatism / 'prægmətizəm / 实用主义
ideological conversion 意识形态的转变
prevalence / 'prevələns / 流行
contradict / kɔntrə'dikt / 与……矛盾
legitimacys / li'dʒitiməsi / 合理性,合法性
rightly / 'raitli / 公正地
narrowly / 'nærəuli / 勉强地
usurp / ju(ː)'zəːp / 篡夺,侵占
rationalism / 'ræʃənəlizəm / 唯理论,理性主义
validation / væli'deiʃən / 确认,验证
aside from / in addition to 除了
gratify / 'grætifai / 取悦,满足
viability / ˌvaiə'biliti / 生存能力
deficit / 'defisit / 赤子,缺少
motivation / ˌməuti'veiʃən / 动机
pragmatic / præg'mætik / 注重实际的,务实的
keenly 敏锐地
cater to 迎合
overprescribing / ˌəuvəpri'skripʃən / 处方过量
immune / i'mjuːn / 免疫的,免除的
by far 到目前为止
herbal medicine 中药
modality / məu'dæliti / 形式,形态
herbalist / 'həːbəlist; (*US*) ɜːr- / 中医师
orthodox / 'ɔːθədɔks / 传统的

重点剖析

— The findings of Pirotta et al that 1 in 5 Victorian GPs are using CAM in their practice support earlier data of the Royal Australian College of General Practitioners that 1 in 6 Australian GPs employed some form of CAM. Pirotta等人的调查表明,在5名维多利亚全科医生中,有1名在他们的行医中采用CAM,这和皇家澳大利亚传统医学院的早先数据相吻合,后者的数据显示,在6名澳大利亚传统医生中,有1名采用某种形式的CAM。

— The first is that GPs are responding to increasing consumer demand for these therapies because of their clinical success. The second and more contentious finding is that consumers are demanding, and GPs are using, these therapies because of factors beyond clinical success—factors related to globalisation and the characteristics of the global market. These market characteristics include increased consumer choice, increased competition among providers, a resultant power shift from provider to consumer, and a return to and commercialisation of nature, history, and tradition. 第一，由于这些疗法在临床上获得了成功，医生要应对消费者不断高涨的需求。其二更有争议的发现是，消费者的要求越来越苛刻，医生之所以使用这些疗法是因为一些临床成功之外的因素 —— 和全球化及全球市场特点有关的因素。这些市场特点包括消费者更多选择、供应商之间竞争加剧、权力从卖方到消费者的转移、自然、历史及传统的回归和商业化。

— Last resort: The use of or referral to practitioners of CAM to treat patients with chronic conditions unresponsive to orthodox medicine. 最后一招：使用或参考CAM以治疗那些对传统医疗无反应的慢性病患者。

— Integrated approach: A considered choice to regularly incorporate CAM, in addition to orthodox biomedical therapies. 整合性的措施：深思熟虑的选择，除把传统生物医学疗法包括进来之外，还通常把CAM也包括进来。

— Bensoussan, rightly and with apt humour, criticizes recent articles that narrowly attribute patient demand for CAM to "postmodern" or "new age" values usurping scientific rationalism. He notes that a considerable segment of the medical profession has recognized this consumer demand, and that chronic sufferers and the elderly account for a large portion of the patients who request or accept CAM. Bensoussan公正而略带些幽默地批评了最近的文章，认为，这些文章勉强地把患者对CAM的需求归结到“后现代”或“新时代”的价值观从而篡夺了科学的唯理论。他强调，医学行业中有相当多的人已经承认了这一消费者需求，慢性病患者和老年人占了要求或接受CAM治疗患者中的很大比例。

— Arguably, GPs who use CAM are not just influenced by this social change, they contribute to it. 正如论证的那样，采用CAM的医生不仅仅受到这一社会变革的影响，而且他们也是这一变革的始作俑者。

— By far the major component of Chinese medical therapy is herbal medicine. This may come as a surprise to us in Australia, where acupuncture was the first modality to be introduced and practiced by non-Chinese practitioners. 到目前为止，中医疗法的主要成分是草药。这对我们澳大利亚人来说可能是一件新奇的事，因为第一种被非中国人医生引进和使用的中医疗法形式是针灸。

— This has proven to be an extremely successful approach, with remarkable results being achieved in such areas as cancer care, recovery from stroke, arthritis, skin diseases, heart disease, chronic degenerative diseases, post operative care, etc. 经证明这是一种极其成功的手段，它们在癌症、中风康复、关节炎、皮肤病、心脏病、慢性退化性病变、术后保养等领域取得了显著的疗效。

— In recent years an increasing number of doctors regularly refer patients to qualified TCM practitioners and many people have found help and relief with TCM after the failure of conventional methods. 近年来，有越来越多的医生经常把患者推荐给高明的中医那里，许多人在传统疗法失败后已经从中医那里找到了帮助，缓解了病情。

(V43真题题源)

3. Australia Struggles with Skin Cancer

澳洲皮肤癌研究

The world is watching the 2000 Olympics unfold in Sydney, Australia, the country with the highest rates of skin cancer in the world.

Two out of three Australians will develop skin cancer, and an estimated 1,000 die from it every year. **The country has the highest skin cancer incidence rates because of its latitude and because it has a population with susceptible skin types, according to Ted Gansler, M.D., Health Content Director for the American Cancer Society (ACS).**

The main risk factors for skin cancer are ultraviolet (UV) radiation exposure and skin type, people who burn or freckle rather than tanning and have blond or red hair have higher risk, he says. (However, UV exposure also can cause skin cancers among people with darker skin.)

"The southern United States has very high rates for the same reason. Israel also has a skin cancer problem among immigrants of European background," Dr. Gansler adds.

"The rates aren't as high as in Australia because there are fewer Israelis with very light complexions," he says. "Rates in Scandinavia and Israel are similar because most Scandinavians have a more susceptible skin type, even though they are exposed to less UV radiation at home. And, vacationing in areas where UV exposure is more intense probably contributes to skin cancer risk among Scandinavians."

Public Education Campaign

Because of Australia's high rate of skin cancer, the Anti-Cancer Council of Victoria has started perhaps the most comprehensive public skin cancer education programs in the world.

"We clearly have the highest rates of skin cancer anywhere in the world and because of that we also probably have the longest running public health campaign around skin cancer control than just about anybody," says Craig Sinclair, campaign manager for the education campaign called SunSmart. "We've been running a campaign in Victoria for at least twenty years, and that's enabled us to develop a fairly sophisticated and well researched skin cancer control program."

The campaign's messages include a television ad called "Timebomb," in which a doctor removes a skin cancer nodule that has spread to the lymph node in a patient's underarm. **This ad appears to be working, despite the somewhat controversial manner in which the message is relayed.**

The aim of the ad, the latest in a series of media campaigns, is to show that sunburn can cause far greater damage below the skin's surface than above it and may plant a skin cancer "timebomb" that will go off at some later time, Sinclair says.

In addition to the media campaign, SunSmart works with schools to teach children about the dangers of the sun. "Eighty percent of all primary schools in the state of Victoria have a 'no-hat, play-in-the-shade' policy which means the kids can't go outdoors unless they're wearing a hat,"Sinclair says.

Another public education campaign originally developed in Australia has been adapted by the ACS for the United States. **The "Slip! Slop! Slap!" program offers this message: slip on a shirt, slop on sunscreen and slap on a hat to protect your skin.**

Research Monitors Trends, Attitudes

Research is another key function of the Victoria Anti-Cancer Council. "We've put a lot of emphasis into research to make sure we've got very good baseline data. We have a behavioral research unit attached to the program, so we have very good methods of monitoring trends and behavior and attitudes in skin cancer rates," Sinclair says.

There are a number of other Australian agencies and experts working at education and research domestically and worldwide. **Earlier this year, for example, the Australian Cancer Society released findings from a study finding that many Australians still mistakenly assume sunscreen will completely protect them from sunburn and skin cancer. This misconception means they use sunscreen to prolong their time in the sun, increasing their risk of developing melanoma, the most dangerous form of skin cancer.**

In January, a leading Australian cancer specialist suggested replacing sun protection factor (SPF) numbers on sunscreen products with descriptions of the level of protection, such as "low" or "ultra high." This could reduce confusion and encourage people to use sunscreens more appropriately. The recommendation was suggested by Brain Diffey of Newcastle (U.K.) General Hospital and published in the British Medical Journal.

Repeating, Recreating the Message

"The Australian population is very well informed in relation to the link between sun exposure and skin cancer," says Terry Slevin, Director of Education and Research for the Cancer Foundation of Western Australia. "People get bored with hearing the same message again and again, so we have to try and re-invent and recreate the prevention message on an ongoing basis."

"We are now attempting to influence policies in society in general to help to reduce sun exposure," Slevin adds. "For example, new buildings need to have a certain number of car parking spaces allotted to them. Along those same lines, we're advocating that new buildings also need to have an appropriate amount of shade provided so that the avoidance of exposure to the sun is easier. So not only are we saying to people you should avoid exposure to the sun, we're trying to make it easier for them to follow that advice."

(THE END)

latitude /ˈlætitjuːd/ 纬度
susceptible /səˈseptəbl/ 易受影响的，易得病的
incidence rate 发生率
ultraviolet (UV) radiation 紫外线辐射
complexion /kəmˈplekʃən/ 肤色
nodule /ˈnɔdjuːl/ 节结
lymph node 淋巴腺节点
underarm /ˈʌndərɑːm/ 腋下
controversial /ˌkɔntrəˈvəːʃəl/ 有争议的
melanoma /ˌmeləˈnəumə/ 黑素瘤
misconception /ˈmiskənˈsepʃən/ 误解
confusion /kənˈfjuːʒən/ 混乱
appropriately 适当地
advocate /ˈædvəkei/ 提倡

— The country has the highest skin cancer incidence rates because of its latitude and because it has a population with susceptible skin types, according to Ted Gansler, M.D., Health Content Director for the American Cancer Society (ACS). 美国癌症学会（ACS）健康内容主任 Ted Gansler 说，由于地处于高纬度，其人口的皮肤类型易患病，澳大利亚的最高皮肤癌发生率。

— The main risk factors for skin cancer are ultraviolet (UV) radiation exposure and skin type, people who burn or freckle rather than tanning and have blond or red hair have higher risk, he says. (However, UV exposure also can cause skin cancers among people with darker skin.) 导致皮肤癌的主要危险因素是暴露在紫外线辐射中和皮肤类型，皮肤被灼伤或有雀斑的要比晒成褐色的和长着金发或红发的人面临更大的危险较高，他说（但是，紫外线暴露也可以使具有较深皮肤色的人患皮肤癌）。

— This ad appears to be working, despite the somewhat controversial manner in which the message is relayed. 虽然这个广告在信息传递方式上有一些争议，但它起了作用。

— The aim of the ad, the latest in a series of media campaigns, is to show that sunburn can cause far greater damage below the skin's surface than above it and may plant a skin cancer "timebomb" that will go off at some later time, Sinclair says. Sinclair 说道，这个广告的目的，即一系列媒体宣传的最新手段，是为了显示，比起皮肤的表面，晒斑可以给皮肤表面的下部造成更大的伤害，可能种下一个皮肤癌的"定时炸弹"，它会在将来的某个时间爆发。

— The "Slip! Slop! Slap!" program offers this message: slip on a shirt, slop on sunscreen and slap on a hat to protect your skin. "穿！抹！戴"计划给了我们如下信息：穿裙、抹油、戴帽子，保护好你的皮肤。

— Earlier this year, for example, the Australian Cancer Society released findings from a study finding that many Australians still mistakenly assume sunscreen will completely protect them from sunburn and skin cancer. This misconception means they use sunscreen to prolong their time in the sun, increasing their risk of developing melanoma, the most dangerous form of skin cancer. 例如，今年较早的时候，澳大利亚癌症学会发表了一份研究结果，发现许多澳大利亚人仍旧错误地认为抹防晒油可以完全保护他们免受晒斑和皮肤癌。这个误解意味着，他们使用防晒油来延长在太阳下待的时间，从而提高了患上黑素瘤的危险，而这是最危险的一种皮肤癌。

（V67真题题源）

4. Drop Promotions

医生与药品推销

Legalised bribery is what some drug representatives call their employers' marketing. Despite much publicised recent efforts by drug-industry groups to curb the most egregious ministrations to doctors by representatives-curiously, more often than not pretty women-firms still spend billions trying to walk a fine line between product promotion and undue influence. Yet some of the oldest tricks in the marketing book do not seem to pay off as they used to-which is bad news indeed for the drug firms.

Selling prescription drugs is a curious business. Unlike other consumer-goods makers, which pitch their wares directly to the consumer, drug companies lavish most of their marketing money on doctors — medical middlemen — in an effort to persuade them to prescribe their products to consumers (i. e. , patients). Last year, drug firms spent nearly $9.4 billion on marketing to American doctors, according to Verispan, a market-research firm.

The traditional focus of drug marketing is the personal "detail", in which a sales representative sits down with a doctor to discuss the merits of a drug and often hands over free samples. But these details are under growing scrutiny. Last week, police in Verona raided the offices of Glaxo Smith Kline; now 40 staff and 30 doctors are under investigation for comparaggio—prescribing drugs in exchange for gifts, such as computers and lavish trips.

Many European countries besides Italy restrict the value of gifts that drug firms can bestow on physicians. As well as laws covering kickbacks and false claims, American regulators are working on further "voluntary guidance" for interactions between drug companies and doctors. PhRMA, the American industry's trade association, has introduced a new code of conduct for corporate largesse. Even the tradition of free samples can land firms in trouble: two years ago TAP Pharmaceuticals was fined $875m by the Department of Justice for dodgy marketing practices, including giving doctors thousands of dollars' worth of samples on the understanding that they would then bill the federal government. AstraZeneca's sales and marketing of one of its drugs, Zoladex, is being investigated by the Department of Justice.

Strictly speaking, it is "unethical" for representatives to take doctors to baseball games or buy them gifts. But, as one former representative confesses, when a doctor said he would ask a representative for a Palm Pilot, "I offered to buy it, as I knew if I didn't a competitor would." Her firm helped to "hide" the purchase. Drug firms have happily taken doctors to spas and golf courses for "consulting trips".

Experience has taught drug firms that the more representatives they deploy to push a product, the higher their sales, says David Blumberg, of Accenture. **As a result, the number of drug representatives in America alone has almost tripled since 1995, to some 90,000 last year, even though the number of doctors has barely budged.**

There is a growing sense among industry executives that this "arms race" is running out of steam for some mass-marketed drugs, says Alasdair Mackintosh, of Cap Gemini Ernst & Young. Rising patient rosters mean that doctors, particularly in Europe, have less time to spend with sales representatives. The average sales-representative call with a doctor now lasts less than five minutes. A fall in the number of new drugs launched, combined with a wave of industry mergers and co-promotional deals, means that more representatives are flogging fewer drugs, often "me-too" products whose comparative merits take some explaining. **The upshot, according to a recent study by Datamonitor, a consultancy, is that for every dollar spent on marketing (not exclusively by representatives), the industry's top 14 firms earned an average of only $17 in sales in 2001, down from $22 in 1998.**

Drug firms are starting to use more sophisticated techniques than a short skirt and a smile to peddle their pills. In America, they send their sales representatives into battle with sophisticated tools, such as Palm Pilots with fancy software, and rigorous training, to make their pitches. In America, detailed prescribing data can be bought from specialist research firms, which some drug firms are now beefing up with detailed information about why doctors prescribe as they do. For example, Eli Lilly uses the call-centres it runs for doctors who have questions about products to make a few inquiries of its own, and to build detailed profiles of doctors.

With face time ever harder to secure, several companies, such as iPhysicianNet, have sprung up to provide "E-detailing", which uses computer-based video-conferencing to reach doctors at their convenience. In America, where direct-to-consumer advertising is allowed, television commercials enable drug firms to turn patients into salesmen too, demanding specific brands from their doctors.

Teaching, not bribery

Drug firms are having to work harder to build relationships with doctors, repositioning themselves as providers of medical education, without this coming across as a bribe. **Firms are also focusing more on specialists who influence medical practice, using highly trained "medical science liaisons" to engage such doctors early in a drug's development so that they can spread the good word to their colleagues.**

Given the growing complexity of the market, many firms have called in experts from industries such as consumer goods or financial services to create and maintain their brands. Novartis, a Swiss drugmaker, has hired marketing personnel from the likes of Procter & Gamble and Gillette to smarten up its direct-to-consumer advertising and brand creation. Thomas Ebeling, its head of drug operations, was once a marketing manager at Pepsi.

But techniques for selling soap do not necessarily work for pills. Nobody attacks IBM for its marketing budget; but drugmakers are lambasted by some campaigning groups for spending as much on sales as they do on R & D. Drug firms that try to extend their product's reach can land in trouble: a recent article in the British Medical Journal suggested that researchers associated with Pfizer were inventing a new disorder, female sexual dysfunction, not least to expand the market for anti-impotence medicines.

Few expect drug firms to spend less on marketing. But they could spend more wisely; and more exciting and innovative marketing could help to maintain brand loyalty long after generic competitors have entered the market. Although cutting salesforces makes sense for some drugs, few firms are willing to take the first step. As Jaideep Bajaj, at ZS Associates, a sales-research firm, notes, "These firms are caught in a classic prisoner's dilemma. Unilaterally, no one is willing to call off the arms race." Non-proliferation may have to wait for a drastic reversal of company fortunes—or the strong arm of regulators. (THE END)

必备词汇

legalised bribery 合法的行贿
curb / kəːb / 禁止
trick / trik / 诡计，窍门
undue / ˈʌnˈdjuː / 不适当的
prescription drug 处方药
lavish / ˈlæviʃ / 慷慨给予，浪费
merit / ˈmerit / 优点
free sample 免费样品
scrutiny/ ˈskruːtini / 详细审查
raid / reid / 搜捕，袭击
bestow / biˈstəu / 给予
kickback / ˈkikbæk / 回扣，酬金
largesse / ˈlɑːdʒes, ˈlɑːdʒis / 慷慨
dodgy / ˈdɔdʒi / 善于骗人的
bill / bil / 给……开账单
unethical 不道德的
confess / kənˈfes / 承认，坦白
competitor / kəmˈpetitə / 竞争者
spa 温泉区，游乐胜地
budge / bʌdʒ / 移动
roster / ˈrəustə / 花名册
triple / ˈtripl / 增至三倍
upshot / ˈʌpʃɔt / 结果
sophisticated / səˈfistikeitid / 复杂的，先进的
peddle / ˈpedl / 叫卖
pitch / pitʃ / 竭力推销
profile / ˈprəufail / 简历
video-conferencing 视频会议
convenience / kənˈviːnjəns / 方便
repositioning 重新定位
specialist / ˈspeʃəlɪst / 专家
engage / inˈgeidʒ / 聘请
colleague / ˈkɔliːg / 同事
complexity / kəmˈpleksiti / 复杂
lambaste / læmˈbeist / 痛打，严责
land in trouble 遇到麻烦
generic / dʒiˈnerik / 一般的，普通的

重点剖析

— Selling prescription drugs is a curious business. Unlike other consumer-goods makers, which pitch their wares directly to the consumer, drug companies lavish most of their marketing money on doctors—medical middlemen—in an effort to persuade them to prescribe their products to consumers (i. e., patients). 销售处方药是一个奇怪的行业。不像其他消费品生产商是把货物直接摆在消费者面前，医药公司把大部分营销资金慷慨地给了医生——药品中间人，以说服他们把产品开给消费者（即病人）。

— Many European countries besides Italy restrict the value of gifts that drug firms can bestow on physicians. As well as laws covering kickbacks and false claims, American regulators are working on further "voluntary guidance" for interactions between drug companies and doctors. 欧洲许多国家除意大利之外都限制医药公司赠予医生的礼品的价值。正如法律对回扣和虚假申报做出规定一样，美国的管理者正在为医药公司和医生之间的相互关系制定更多的“自愿指导”。

— Strictly speaking, it is “unethical” for representatives to take doctors to baseball games or buy them gifts. 严格来讲，医药代表把医生带到棒球场或给他们买礼品是“不道德”的。

— As a result, the number of drug representatives in America alone has almost tripled since 1995, to some 90,000 last year, even though the number of doctors has barely budged. 结果，仅在美国，医药代表的人数自1995年就几乎增加到三倍，去年达到9万人左右，虽然医生的人数基本没变。

— The upshot, according to a recent study by Datamonitor, a consultancy, is that for every dollar spent on marketing (not exclusively by representatives), the industry's top 14 firms earned an average of only $17 in sales in 2001, down from $22 in 1998. 按照一家咨询公司Datamonitor的最新调查显示，医药行业前14大公司在2001年花费在营销上的每一个美元（不是惟独由医药代表开展的），平均只赚回17美元，比1998年的平均22美元下降了不少。

— Drug firms are starting to use more sophisticated techniques than a short skirt and a smile to peddle their pills. In America, they send their sales representatives into battle with sophisticated tools, such as Palm Pilots with fancy software, and rigorous training, to make their pitches. 医药公司正开始利用比短裙和微笑更为先进的技术来叫卖他们的药片。在美国，他们用先进的工具如奇妙的软件 Palm Pilots 把销售代表武装起来，对他们经过严格的培训，再让他们投入营销战斗，竭力推销药品。

— With face time ever harder to secure, several companies, such as iPhysicianNet, have sprung up to provide “E-detailing”, which uses computer-based video-conferencing to reach doctors at their convenience. In America, where direct-to-consumer advertising is allowed, television commercials enable drug firms to turn patients into salesmen too, demanding specific brands from their doctors. 由于面谈的时间越来越难安排，几家医药公司，如iPhysicianNet开始提供“E-detailing”，即利用以计算机为基础的视频会议，在医生方便的时候和他们取得联系。在美国，直接面向消费者的广告是允许的，所以电视商业广告可以让药品公司也把病人变成销售人员，要求从医生那里开出专门牌子的药品。

— Firms are also focusing more on specialists who influence medical practice, using highly trained “medical science liaisons” to engage such doctors early in a drug's development so that they can spread the good word to their colleagues. 医药公司

还更多地关注那些能影响医疗实践的专家，利用训练有方的“医药科学联络会”早早地在药品开发阶段就聘请这些医生，以便他们向同事们传达好听的话。

— Given the growing complexity of the market, many firms have called in experts from industries such as consumer goods or financial services to create and maintain their brands. 随着市场变得越来越复杂，许多医药公司开始从诸如消费品或金融服务等行业征召专家来建立和维护他们的品牌。

— But techniques for selling soap do not necessarily work for pills. Nobody attacks IBM for its marketing budget; but drugmakers are lambasted by some campaigning groups for spending as much on sales as they do on R & D. 但销售肥皂的窍门用到药品上不一定管用。没有人因为IBM的营销预算而抨击它，但制药商却由于在销售上的花费和在研发上的花费一样巨大而遭到一些组织的严厉声讨。

（V30真题题源）

5. Adverse Health Effects of Noise

噪声对人的影响

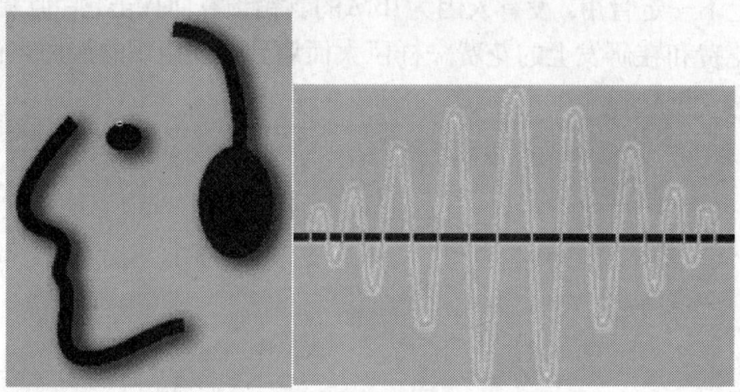

The perception of sounds in day-to-day life is of major importance for human well-being. Communication through speech, sounds from playing children, music, natural sounds in parklands, parks and gardens are all examples of sounds essential for satisfaction in every day life. Conversely, this document is related to the adverse effects of sound (noise). **According to the International Program on Chemical Safety (WHO 1994), an adverse effect of noise is defined as a change in the morphology and physiology of an organism that results in impairment of functional capacity, or an impairment of capacity to compensate for additional stress, or increases the susceptibility of an organism to the harmful effects of other environmental influences. This definition includes any temporary or long-term lowering of the physical, psychological or social functioning of humans or human organs.**

Noise annoyance is a global phenomenon. A definition of annoyance is "a feeling of displeasure associated with any agent or condition, known or believed by an individual or group to adversely affect them" (Lindvall & Radford 1973; Koelega 1987). **However, apart from "annoyance", people may feel a variety of negative emotions when exposed to community noise, and may report anger, disappointment, dissatisfaction, withdrawal, helplessness, depression, anxiety, distraction, agitation,**

or exhaustion. Thus, although the term annoyance does not cover all the negative reactions, it is used for convenience in this document.

Noise can produce a number of social and behavioral effects in residents, besides annoyance. The social and behavioral effects are often complex, subtle and indirect. Many of the effects are assumed to be the result of interactions with a number of non-auditory variables. **Social and behavioral effects include changes in overt everyday behavior patterns (e.g. closing windows, not using balconies, turning TV and radio to louder levels, writing petitions, complaining to authorities); adverse changes in social behavior (e.g. aggression, unfriendliness, disengagement, non-participation); adverse changes in social indicators (e.g. residential mobility, hospital admissions, drug consumption, accident rates); and changes in mood (e.g. less happy, more depressed).**

Although changes in social behavior, such as a reduction in helpfulness and increased aggressiveness, are associated with noise exposure, noise exposure alone is not believed to be sufficient to produce aggression. However, in combination with provocation or pre-existing anger or hostility, it may trigger aggression. It has also been suspected that people are less willing to help, both during exposure and for a period after exposure. **Fairly consistent evidence shows that noise above 80 dBA is associated with reduced helping behavior and increased aggressive behavior. Particularly, there is concern that high-level continuous noise exposures may contribute to the susceptibility of schoolchildren to feelings of helplessness.**

The effects of community noise can be evaluated by assessing the extent of annoyance (low, moderate, high) among exposed individuals; or by assessing the disturbance of specific activities, such as reading, watching television and communication. The relationship between annoyance and activity disturbances is not necessarily direct and there are examples of situations where the extent of annoyance is low, despite a high level of activity disturbance. **For aircraft noise, the most important effects are interference with rest, recreation and watching television. This is in contrast to road traffic noise, where sleep disturbance is the predominant effect.**

A number of studies have shown that equal levels of traffic and industrial noises result in different magnitudes of annoyance. This has led to criticism of averaged dose-response curves determined by meta-analysis, which assumed that all traffic noises are the same. Schultz (1978) and Miedema & Vos (1998) have synthesized curves of annoyance associated with three types of traffic noise (road, air, railway). In these curves, the percentage of people highly or moderately annoyed was related to the day and night continuous equivalent sound level, Ldn. For each of the three types of traffic noise, the percentage of highly annoyed persons in a population started to increase at an Ldn value of 42 dBA, and the percentage of moderately annoyed persons at an Ldn value of 37 dBA. Aircraft noise produced a stronger annoyance response than road traffic, for the same Ldn exposure, consistent with earlier analyses. However, caution should be exercised when interpreting synthesized data from different studies, since five major parameters should be randomly distributed for the analyses to be valid: personal, demographic, and lifestyle factors, as well as the duration of noise exposure and the population experience with noise.

Stronger reactions have been observed when noise is accompanied by vibrations and contains low frequency components, or when the noise contains impulses, such as shooting noise. Stronger, but temporary, reactions also occur when noise exposure is increased over time, in comparison to situations with constant noise exposure. **Conversely, for road traffic noise, the introduction of noise protection barriers in residential areas resulted in smaller reductions in annoyance than expected for a stationary situation.**

To obtain an indicator for annoyance, other methods of combining parameters of noise exposure have been extensively tested, in addition to metrics such as LAeq, 24h and Ldn. When used for a set of community noises, these indicators correlate well both among themselves and with LAeq, 24h or Ldn values. Although LAeq, 24h and Ldn are in most cases acceptable approximations, there is a growing concern that all the component parameters of the noise should be individually assessed in noise exposure investigations, at least in the complex cases.

The potential health effects of community noise include hearing impairment; startle and defense reactions; aural pain; ear discomfort speech interference; sleep disturbance; cardiovascular effects; performance reduction; and annoyance responses. These health effects, in turn, can lead to social handicap; reduced productivity; decreased performance in learning; absenteeism in the workplace and school; increased drug use; and accidents. In addition to health effects of community noise, other impacts are important such as loss of property value.

(THE END)

perception / pəˈsepʃən / 感知，察觉

day-to-day life 日常生活

essential / iˈsenʃəl / 必需的，必要的

conversely / ˈkɔnvɜːsli / 相反地

averse / ˈædvəːs / 不利的，有害的

morphology / mɔːˈfɔlədʒi / 形态学

physiology / ˌfiziˈɔlədʒi / 生理学
organism / ˈɔːgənizəm / 生物体，有机体
impairment / imˈpɛəmənt / 损害，损伤
compensate for 补偿，赔偿
stress/ stres / 压力，重压
susceptibility / səˌseptəˈbiliti / 易感性，感受性
psychological / ˌsaikəˈlɔdʒikəl / 心理的
annoyance / əˈnɔiəns / 烦恼，讨厌的事
phenomenon / fiˈnɔminən / 现象
displeasure / disˈpleʒə / 不愉快，不满意
negative / ˈnegətiv / 消极的，否定的
expose / iksˈpəuz / 暴露
disappointment / ˌdisəˈpɔintmənt / 失望
dissatisfaction / ˈdisˌsætisˈfækʃən / 不满
withdrawal / wiðˈdrɔːəl / 冷漠
depression / diˈpreʃən / 抑郁
anxiety / æŋˈzaiəti / 焦虑
distraction / disˈtrækʃən / 分心
agitation / ædʒiˈteiʃən / 激动
exhaustion 疲劳，疲惫
subtle / ˈsʌtl / 微妙的，敏感的
auditory / ˈɔːditəri / 听觉的，耳的
overt / ˈəuvəːt / 明显的，公然的
balcony / ˈbælkəni / 阳台
disengagement / ˌdisinˈgeidʒmənt / 脱离
admission / ədˈmiʃən / 入院人数
sufficient / səˈfiʃənt / 充分的，足够的
trigger / ˈtrigə / 激发，引发
predominant / priˈdɔminənt / 突出的，主要的
magnitude / ˈmægnitjuːd / 量极的
caution / ˈkɔːʃən / 小心，警惕
parameter / pəˈræmitə / 参数
demographic / deməˈgræfik / 人口统计学的
reaction / ri(ː)ˈækʃən / 反应
vibration / vaiˈbreiʃən / 震动
impulse / ˈimpʌls / 刺激
correlate / ˈkɔrileit / 和……关联
approximation / əˌprɔksiˈmeiʃən / 近似值
startle / ˈstɑːtl / 使（某人）吃惊
aural / ˈɔːrəl / 听觉的，听力的
absenteeism / æbsənˈtiːiz(ə)m / 矿工，旷课
handicap / ˈhændikæp / 障碍

重点剖析

— According to the International Program on Chemical Safety (WHO 1994), an adverse effect of noise is defined as a change in the morphology and physiology of an organism that results in impairment of functional capacity, or an impairment of capacity to compensate for additional stress, or increases the susceptibility of an organism to the harmful effects of other environmental influences. This definition includes any temporary or long-term lowering of the physical, psychological or social functioning of humans or human organs. 按照《化学品安全国际纲要》（世界卫生组织，1994年）的说法，噪声的危害有：生物体在形态和生理上发生变化，该变化导致的功能损伤或导致为缓解额外压力而造成的能力损害，或者提高了生物体对其他环境影响有害反应的易感性。此定义包括人体或人体器官在身体、心理或社交功能的任何临时性或长期性衰退。

— However, apart from "annoyance", people may feel a variety of negative emotions when exposed to community noise, and may report anger, disappointment, dissatisfaction, withdrawal, helplessness, depression, anxiety, distraction, agitation, or exhaustion. Thus, although the term annoyance does not cover all the negative reactions, it is used for convenience in this document. 然而，除了“烦恼”之外，当人们暴露在社区噪声中时，可能会产生各种消极的情绪，可能会易怒、失望、不满、冷漠、无助、沮丧、焦虑、激动或疲惫不堪。所以，尽管“烦恼”一词不能涵盖所有这些情绪，但本文为方便起见，就用该词统一代替。

— Social and behavioral effects include changes in overt everyday behavior patterns (e.g. closing windows, not using balconies, turning TV and radio to louder levels, writing petitions, complaining to authorities); adverse changes in social behavior (e.g. aggression, unfriendliness, disengagement, non-participation); adverse changes in social indicators (e.g. residential mobility, hospital admissions, drug consumption, accident rates); and changes in mood (e.g. less happy, more depressed). 社会和行为影响后果包括日常行为模式的明显改变（如关闭窗户、不使用阳台、把电视或收音机声音开得很大、重复地写东西、向官方投诉）；社会行为的有害变化（例如好斗、不友好、孤立、不合群）；社会指数的有害变化（例如，居民搬迁率、医院的入院率、药品消费量、事故率）以及情绪变化（例如，不太高兴、更多沮丧）。

— Fairly consistent evidence shows that noise above 80 dBA is associated with reduced helping behavior and increased aggressive behavior. Particularly, there is concern that high-level continuous noise exposures may contribute to the susceptibility of schoolchildren to feelings of helplessness. 比较一致的证据显示，等级在80分贝以上的噪声与助人行为的减少和攻击行为的增加有关。尤其是，有一种观点认为，连续暴露在高级别噪声中，学龄儿童倾向于产生无助感。

— For aircraft noise, the most important effects are interference with rest, recreation and watching television. This is in contrast to road traffic noise, where sleep disturbance is the predominant effect. 对飞机噪声而言，最重要的影响是对休息、娱乐和看电视的干扰。这和道路交通噪声形成了对比，后者的主要影响是干扰睡眠。

— Conversely, for road traffic noise, the introduction of noise protection barriers in residential areas resulted in smaller reductions in annoyance than expected for a stationary situation. 相反，对于道路交通噪声来说，在居民区引入噪声防护物的确使人们的烦恼减少了，但相当于人们对固定环境中烦恼程度的期望相比，这样的降幅实在是有点小。

— The potential health effects of community noise include hearing impairment; startle and defense reactions; aural pain; ear discomfort; speech interference; sleep disturbance; cardiovascular effects; performance reduction; and annoyance responses. These health effects, in turn, can lead to social handicap; reduced productivity; decreased performance in learning; absenteeism in the workplace and school; increased drug use; and accidents. In addition to health effects of community noise, other impacts are important such as loss of property value. 潜在的社会噪声对健康的影响有听力受损、震惊和防卫反应、耳朵疼痛、耳朵不适、语音受扰、睡眠干扰、心血管影响、成绩下降、烦恼反应。继而，这些对健康的影响会导致社交障碍、生产率下降、学习成绩下降、矿工旷课、药物用量增加及事故。除了对健康的影响外，其他影响也很重要，如财产价值损失。

（V16 真题题源）

6. Adolescence and Their Personality

青少年的人格与家庭

Adolescence is one of the most difficult transitions that teenagers have to go through in life. Anthropologists have suggested that physical and hormonal changes are not the only factors that affect teenagers because living in different cultural societies also has a great impact upon their lives.

Adolescence in Buenos Aires and Chicago

The effects on adolescents growing up in different societies are presented by the comparative studies, of Buenos Aires and Chicago adolescents, done by Dubois and Doll. **The studies have shown that due to the different cultural environments of the two places, Chicago youths are more resistant to authority, self-assertive and autonomous than Buenos Aires youths.** Moreover, Chicago youths see themselves as more active in their approach to the world than Buenos Aires youths. The North American culture is often said to promote earlier heterosexual interest and activity than the Latin-American culture, which tends to keep girls away from boys and to control adolescent heterosexual activity to a later age. **This conclusion was supported by the Needs Test dealing with heterosexual activity and affection which showed that Chicago adolescents are interested earlier and more openly in heterosexual activities than adolescents from Buenos Aires.** The Needs Test result is further backed by Robert Grinder who has written that adolescents' engagement in sexual practices does not only depend on their physical maturity. It also depends on where they were brought up. In fact, cross-cultural researchers have shown conclusively that the sexual behavior of children and adolescents varies immensely in different cultures. Some societies condone self-stimulation and sex-play. However, other societies are more restrictive. An example would be the typical middle-class parent in the United States.

Size of community and adolescence

Dubois and Doll also suggest that adolescents are affected by the size of the community that they live in because those adolescents from smaller communities tend to lead more active, diversified and organized leisure lives. On the other hand, adolescents living in large cities spend less time with their parents and report somewhat less congenial family relationships. They are more often either rebellious or overdependent on adult authority. Moreover, big city youngsters are much more likely than those from smaller communities to want to be the youngest in a group of older children. City youngsters do not hold jobs as often as boys and girls from smaller cities and towns, but when they do, they work longer hours and in more adult-like positions. City girls have heavier duties than girls in smaller communities, and they begin steady dating at an earlier age, although dating in general is more common and begins earlier in the smaller towns. City girls more often do not date at all or date only one boy. The complexity of life in a major city imposes certain pressures on the family and on parent-child relationships. Parents do not have the closer control of adolescent activity that comes with the parent-involving organized leisure and joint family activities that are common in smaller communities. The city child spends most of his free time beyond the range of control of parents and parent surrogates. (See additional information on sociological influences on adolescence.) The less active and less organized leisure of city children seems to reflect the fact that cities are not designed for children. This is one reason why city children seem so eager to arrive at adulthood, because the city offers most of its advantages to adults.

Adolescence in American and Chinese culture

The culture in which adolescents are brought up is also bound to affect them. One of the major characteristics of American culture is its inconsistency. Adolescents are profoundly affected by this. Fluidity of mores and customs do not provide a solid base upon which to guide young people in their decisions and choice of goals. In contrast, as Harold Bernard explains, Chinese adolescents are much less troubled by matters of obedience and respect for parents than their American counterparts. The former have generations of stable custom behind them and the problem of obedience simply does not arise. **A Chinese male is expected to follow his father's occupation while an American male is expected to make his own choice and rise to greater heights than his parents.** In some instances, it is as though the American youth was expected to take up from where his father left off. It is also pointed out that in rural communities, where face-to-face relations are intimate, youths are more firmly bound to community expectations in terms of employment. In the city, where face-to-face relations are impersonal, the pressure to maintain reputation is less influential.

Another great influence on adolescents in American culture is the appropriation of sex roles. **Boys are expected to be aggressive, explorative, rough and strong, and to dress plainly. Girls are expected to be polite, courteous and docile, and to dress in garments adorned with ribbons and lace.** However, the latter role conflicts with the increasing number of jobs for women outside the home. Furthermore, boys experience the greatest difficulty of assuming appropriate masculine roles because close association with a male model is denied.

Differences in culture and social class are seen to affect the physical development of adolescents. Robert Grinder has written that cultural differences and related social-class distinctions also account for discrepancies in the rate of growth because those of higher status seem to grow more rapidly. Tanner reports that children whose parents are in the professional and managerial classes are about an inch taller at three years of age and one and one-half to two inches taller at adolescence than children whose parents are unskilled laborers.

The value or importance placed upon body image by an adolescent depends to a great extent on the culture that surrounds him. Robert Grinder has written that: "For the adolescent, body image seems to be the product of real and fantasized experiences, which stem in part from his own physical development, from peer emphasis on physical attributes and from increasing awareness of cultural expectations". In American culture, advertising, magazines, movies, television and hero worship of athletes all contribute to a glorification of the ideal body. Unfortunately, for the adolescent whose body creates an unfavorable image, he may be discriminated against, ostracized, rejected by the opposite sex and even treated with contempt and hostility.

Anthropologists have discovered that the main factors affecting adolescents during their liminal state are: living in traditional and non-traditional societies, different cultures, size of the communities, family relationships, appropriation of family duties, definitive sex roles, different social-classes, cultural attitudes regarding sexuality and cultural body images. Culture has just as much importance as the biological processes in the development and transition that adolescents experience in life. As a discipline, anthropology plays a powerful and evolving role in helping us to understand the lives of adolescents, wherever they may be. (THE END)

必备词汇

adolescence / ˌædəuˈlesəns / 青春期
adolescent / ˌædəuˈlesnt / 青少年
transition / trænˈziʒən, -ˈsiʃ ən / 过渡
teenager / ˈtiːnˌeidʒə / 十几岁的青少年
anthropologist / ˌænθrəˈpɔlədʒist / 人类学家
hormonal change 荷尔蒙的变化
impact / ˈimpækt / 冲击，影响
profoundly / prəˈfaundli / 深深地，显著地
fluidity / flu(ː)ˈiditi / 流动性
in some instances 在某些情况下
intimate / ˈintimit / 亲密的
aggressive / əˈgresiv / 有闯劲的，好斗的
explorative / eksˈplɔːrətiv / 有开拓性的
courteous / ˈkəːtjəs / 有礼貌的
discrepancy / disˈkrepənsi / 差异，矛盾
hero worship 对英雄的崇拜
discriminate / disˈkrimineit / 歧视
ostracize / ˈɔstrəsaiz / 排斥
contempt / kənˈtempt / 轻视、轻蔑
hostility / hɔsˈtiliti / 敌视

重点剖析

— The studies have shown that due to the different cultural environments of the two places, Chicago youths are more resistant to authority, self-assertive and autonomous than Buenos Aires youths. Moreover, Chicago youths see themselves as more active in their approach to the world than Buenos Aires youths. 研究显示，由于两个地方不同的文化环境，比起布宜诺斯艾瑞斯的青少年，芝加哥的青少年更为反对权威、更为自信、更为独立。而且，芝加哥的青少年对世界的看待比布宜诺斯艾瑞斯的青少年更为积极。

— This conclusion was supported by the Needs Test dealing with heterosexual activity and affection which showed that Chicago adolescents are interested earlier and more openly in heterosexual activities than adolescents from Buenos Aires. 针对青少年异性交往、恋爱的Needs实验证实，芝加哥的青少年比布宜诺艾利斯的青少年更早涉足异性交往、恋爱，他们的这些行为也更公开。

— Dubois and Doll also suggest that adolescents are affected by the size of the community that they live in because those adolescents from smaller communities tend to lead more active, diversified and organized leisure lives. On the other hand, adolescents living in large cities spend less time with their parents and report somewhat less congenial family relationships. They are more often either rebellious or overdependent on adult authority. Moreover, big city youngsters are much more likely than those from smaller communities to want to be the youngest in a group of older children.

Dubois 和 Doll 也提出，青少年受到他们生活的社区的规模的影响，因为来自较小社区的青少年生活得更为积极、多样化、有组织、休闲。另一方面，生活在大城市的青少年和父母待在一起的时间较少，家庭关系不如前者融洽。他们通常要不就是反抗成人的权威，要不就是过分依赖成人。而且，比起那些来自较小社区的孩子来，大城市的孩子们在大孩子群体中更有可能希望扮演最小孩子的角色。

— A Chinese male is expected to follow his father's occupation while an American male is expected to make his own choice and rise to greater heights than his parents. 中国的男子一般要继承父亲的职业，而美国男子则希望自我选择，事业上比父母更胜一筹。

— Boys are expected to be aggressive, explorative, rough and strong, and to dress plainly. Girls are expected to be polite, courteous and docile, and to dress in garments adorned with ribbons and lace. 人们要求男孩有闯劲、有开拓性、粗犷，衣着随便。女孩要有礼貌、听话，衣着上有丝带和花边。

(New versian 真题题源)

7. A Historical Perspective: Health Care

医 疗 保 健

"Human life is priceless."

Discovery and innovation: an impressive history

In the 1930s, Bradford Hill persuaded the medical profession to accept the randomized clinical trial as the "gold standard" for deciding the efficacy of new drugs. Hill influenced Richard Peto, Henry Blackburn, Jerry Stammler and David Sackett, among others, who, by establishing the discipline of clinical epidemiology, made tremendous contributions toward studying disease and clinical interventions at the population level. Their advances ultimately produced quantitative methods of measuring disease which enabled the reliable assessment of treatment outcomes in various populations.

These advances led to a number of public health successes in the 20th century. Three notable examples: the successful eradication of hookworm from the southern United States, the global eradication of smallpox, and the Framingham Heart Study delineating risk factors for cardiovascular diseases.

Meanwhile, Vannevar Bush's highly influential 1945 report *Science — The Endless Frontier* was the prelude to unprecedented investments in basic scientific research in the United States of America following the Second World War. This report laid the foundations for the most important scientific advances of the second half of the 20th century.

Watson and Crick's discovery of the structure of DNA in 1953 heralded a "golden era" of biology. The astonishing achievements of biomedical science in prolonging human life and alleviating disease were further accelerated in 2001 with the sequencing of the entire human genome, and those of numerous human pathogens. With the promise of greater discoveries to come, investments in health research shot up dramatically, as seen in the doubling of the US National Institutes of Health budget and the generous philanthropy of the Bill and Melinda Gates Foundation.

The other side of the coin: more impact needed on public health

Towards the end of the 20th century, however, scientific advances alone proved insufficient to tackle the world's most pressing public health problems, particularly those in the developing world. Is science being increasingly driven by economic forces and ignoring its ethical, moral and social responsibility to give entire populations more equitable access to health care? This concern led to calls to shift some of the focus from the search for new interventions to the research process itself: to manage and align the health research process so that it could respond to global public health problems and issues more effectively.

Accepting the challenge, the 1990 Report of the Commission on Health Research for Development promoted a new vision of a global health research system. The Commission made four key recommendations: all countries should undertake essential national health research (ENHR), international partnerships should be set up to tackle priority health problems, more financial resources for research should be mobilized, and an international mechanism to monitor progress and generate support should be developed. The landmark report led to the establishment of the Council for Health Research and Development to focus on ENHR.

In 1996, the World Health Organization's Ad Hoc Committee on Health Research Relating to Future Intervention Options outlined a five-step priority-setting approach to decide how health research funds should be allocated. **It identified "best buys" for developing products and procedures in several key areas, including childhood infections, malnutrition, microbial threats, noncommunicable diseases and health systems.** The Ad Hoc Committee's report led to the setting up of the Global Forum for Health Research in 1998 to address the imbalance in global resources spent on health research.

Public-private partnerships that have been established over the past eight to ten years to accelerate the development of microbicides, diagnostics, drugs against malaria and tuberculosis, and vaccines against malaria, dengue and HIV/AIDS show that the global health research enterprise can be responsive to urgent public health needs.

Overall, however, progress has been slow and much more needs to be done to deal with major health challenges. The International Conference on Health Research for Development in Bangkok in 2000 reviewed achievements in health research and reaffirmed its importance, but also noted great disparities in research capabilities, performance and constraints between different countries. **The document prepared for the conference identified four key challenges for health research: values of ethics, equity and excellence, sustainable health research systems, favourable research environment, and knowledge production and application.** The document also noted that expectations have not been met, that the setting has changed and that the same key constraints identified by the Commission on Health Research for Development in 1990—weak human resources, institutional infrastructure and financing—are still major constraints in low-income countries. The 2000 conference presented a vision and an agenda for action based on equity, evidence, excellence and the view that knowledge is a "global public good". One of its key recommendations was to build a coalition of major organizations involved in health research to promote better global coordination of health research for development. Such a body, however, has yet to be set up.

Remarkable achievements but persisting inequities

The right to health is set forth in international human rights treaties and the WHO Constitution as the right to the "highest attainable standard of health". This right was reiterated in the Alma-Ata declaration, which was drafted in 1978 at the International Conference on Primary Health Care in the former USSR.

Today, the goals of Alma-Ata seem even more distant than they were a quarter of a century ago. Deep economic inequalities and social injustices continue to deny good health to many and persist as obstacles to continued health gains worldwide. There is also great variation in the pace and level of health achievements both between and within countries around the world. One possible explanation is that health sector reforms that began in the late 1980s as part of the structural adjustment programmes of the World Bank have not been conclusively shown to improve inequities; in some cases they may have worsened them. Attempts to foster equity by targeting services, fee exemptions and free insurance for the poor have shown mixed results. Moreover, the push towards privatization and user fees has sometimes undermined public health systems and public health, and may well have accentuated rather than attenuated health inequities.

Interventions not reaching those in need

The burden of disease has been reduced, quality of life improved and life expectancy increased. But as impressive as the achievements of health research have been, they are not reflected in the current state of global health. While one fifth of the world's population enjoys an average life expectancy approaching 80 years of age and a life comparatively free of disability, two thirds of the world's population living in the least well-off countries of Africa, Asia and Latin America suffer overwhelmingly from the world's burden of illness and premature death. Each year an estimated 15 million children—40,000 children per day—die from infection or malnutrition.

In an attempt to improve the state of global health, programmes and initiatives have been launched to better diagnose, treat, control or even eradicate diseases and other health problems. Principal among these are the Millennium Development Goals (MDGs), three of which (goals 4, 5 and 6) are directly health-related: reduce child mortality, improve maternal health, and combat HIV/AIDS, malaria and other diseases. However, there are some concerns that health-related MDGs may not be achieved for most of the world's population by 2015. Analysis of the reasons for such unsatisfactory progress suggests the existence of system-wide barriers and formidable challenges in implementation and scaling up because of weak health systems.

It is now a global imperative to find effective ways to strengthen health systems in order to improve the lives of people, to meet the MDGs and to prepare for what is to come. Health systems in developing countries are being identified as a key constraint to the implementation of major programmes such as the Global Fund to Fight AIDS, Tuberculosis and Malaria, the Global Alliance for Vaccines and Immunization (GAVI), and the 3 by 5 initiative to accelerate access to antiretroviral therapy to three million people by 2005.

The systems constraints relate not only to the realization that inadequate information or human resources may slow progress but also that the focus on priority problems may be distorting the existing systems with unintended negative consequences to "non-" or "low-priority" health problems.

To rise to the challenge, health systems and health research systems together should move into a learning and problem-solving mode, integrate innovation into their operations and better manage opportunities for future growth and development. There are no quick fixes, no simple solutions and much remains to be learnt. New methodologies are needed to study health systems; new structures and means to translate knowledge into effective interventions should be identified; new tools and delivery strategies that achieve effective and sustained coverage in diverse cultural and economic settings are needed. Basic health information is often lacking or unreliable. It will require new forms of interactions between researchers, funders, policy-makers, health service providers, patients and civil society, and a long-term commitment, political will and support from all WHO Member States. Such interactions have been shown to work at the national and global level in areas such as in responding to epidemics and curbing tobacco use respectively. If health systems and health research systems were more open to new opportunities and embraced a culture of learning and discovery, progress would be facilitated. (THE END)

必备词汇

persuade / pə'sweid / 说服
randomized clinical trial 随机性临床试验
efficacy / 'efikəsi / 功效
discipline / 'disiplin / 学科
epidemiology / ˌepiˌdiːmi'ɔlədʒi / 流行病学
eradication / iˌrædi'keiʃən / 根除
hookworm / 'hukwɜːm / 十二指肠病
smallpox / 'smɔːlpɔks / 天花
delineate / di'linieit / 描绘
cardiovascular diseases 心血管病
influential / ˌinflu'enʃəl / 有影响的
prelude / 'preljuːd / 序幕，先驱
herald / 'herəld / 宣布，预报
genome / 'dʒiːnəum / 基因组，染色体组
pathogen / 'pæθədʒin / 病原
pressing / 'presiŋ / 紧迫的
mobilize / 'məubilaiz / 动员
landmark / 'lændmɑːk / 里程碑
ad hoc / 'æd'hɔk / 临时的
malaria / mə'lɛəriə / 疟疾，瘴气
tuberculosis / tjuˌbəːkju'ləusis / 肺结核
vaccine / 'væksiːn / 疫苗
dengue / 'deŋgei / 登革热
disparity / dis'pæriti / 差别，不一致
yet to 还没有
reiterate / riː'itəreit / 重申
distant / 'distənt / 遥远
fee exemption 免费
privatization 私有化
accentuate / æk'sentjueit / 强调
attenuate / ə'tenjueit / 削弱
injustice / in'dʒʌstis / 不公正
life expectancy 生命预期
disability / ˌdisə'biliti / 残疾
approach / ə'prəutʃ / 接近
overwhelmingly 压倒性地，不可抵抗地
in an attempt to 试图，努力
initiative / i'niʃiətiv / 倡议，动议
mortality / mɔː'tæliti / 死亡率
maternal / mə'təːnl / 母亲的
formidable / 'fɔːmidəbl / 强大的，艰难的
distort / dis'tɔːt / 歪曲
unintended / ˌʌnin'tendid / 非故意的，无意识的

重点剖析

— In the 1930s, Bradford Hill persuaded the medical profession to accept the randomized clinical trial as the "gold standard" for deciding the efficacy of new drugs. 20

世纪30年代，Bradford Hill说服医学界把随机性临床试验确定为新药功效的“黄金标准”。

— Meanwhile, Vannevar Bush's highly influential 1945 report *Science—The Endless Frontier* was the prelude to unprecedented investments in basic scientific research in the United States of America following the Second World War. This report laid the foundations for the most important scientific advances of the second half of the 20th century. 在此期间，Vannevar Bush于1945年提交了一份非常有影响的报告，名为《科学——无止境》，它拉开了美国自二战后对基础科学研究空前投资的序曲。这份报告给20世纪后半叶最重要的一些科学发展打下了基础。

— Watson and Crick's discovery of the structure of DNA in 1953 heralded a "golden era" of biology. Watson和Crick于1953年发现了DNA的结构，宣告了生物学“黄金时代”的到来。

— It identified "best buys" for developing products and procedures in several key areas, including childhood infections, malnutrition, microbial threats, noncommunicable diseases and health systems. 报告确认了在几大领域开发产品和程序的“最佳采购”，这些领域是儿童感染、营养不良、微生物威胁、非传染性疾病和保健体系。

— The document prepared for the conference identified four key challenges for health research: values of ethics, equity and excellence, sustainable health research systems, favourable research environment, and knowledge production and application. 这份为会议准备的文件确认了健康研究中的四大挑战：道德的价值、公平和美德、可持续的健康研究体系、良好的研究环境及知识的产生和应用。

— Today, the goals of Alma-Ata seem even more distant than they were a quarter of a century ago. Deep economic inequalities and social injustices continue to deny good health to many and persist as obstacles to continued health gains worldwide. There is also great variation in the pace and level of health achievements both between and within countries around the world. One possible explanation is that health sector reforms that began in the late 1980s as part of the structural adjustment programmes of the World Bank have not been conclusively shown to improve inequities; in some cases they may have worsened them. 今天，Alma-Ata宣言的目标比起25年前反而离实现更为遥远了。深刻的经济不平等和社会不公正继续拒绝给许多人提供良好的健康，继续扮演全球持续性健康受益的障碍。全世界的国家间及国家内部在健康成就的步伐上和等级上仍有巨大的差异。一个可能的解释是开始于20世纪80年代作为世界银行结构性调整计划一部分的健康部门的改革还没有显示出改进不平等的结果；在某些情况下，它们反而让这些不平等更为严重了。

— To rise to the challenge, health systems and health research systems together should move into a learning and problem-solving mode, integrate innovation into their operations and better manage opportunities for future growth and development. There are no quick fixes, no simple solutions and much remains to be learnt. 为了应对挑战，保健体系和健康研究体系两者应向一个学习的和解决问题的模式推进，把创新包括进运作里面，更好地掌握未来发展的机遇。没有效果明显的锦囊妙计，没有简单的解决方法，只是有许多事情要去学习。

（V42真题题源）

8. Change of Blindness

人类视觉暂盲现象

I've been interested in how our brain makes sense of the world for a long time, probably about as long as I've been an atheist. **I think a lot of the supernatural experiences that people feel they've had are actually the result of perfectly natural phenomena which they've misinterpreted due to a lack of understanding of how their brain works. Everyone's familiar with the various optical illusions which demonstrate how easily our eyes can be fooled, but most never stop to consider that it's not our eyes that are being fooled; rather it's our brains that are being fooled.** Our eyes like all our other sensory organs are constantly transmitting a flood of information to our brain which, as it turns out, isn't as good at taking it all in as we'd like to believe.

We've all been told that the most amazing computer that has ever existed is the human brain, but that's not really true. **Our brains are pretty pathetic at processing all of the data they take in and so they compensate by cheating: taking shortcuts and ignoring a lot of the input.** Keep in mind that it's not just our senses that our brain has to worry about, it also runs all the bodily systems and is getting tons of feedback from internal sources which it has to respond to. Our lungs don't inflate and deflate on their own, they're controlled by a section of the brain. With all the crap it has to do every second of every day it's really no wonder that our brain has to cheat a little when interpreting all the external stimuli. It doesn't help that different parts of the brain handle different parts of the data processing.

For example, scientists have known for a long time that different regions of the brain are involved in the interpretation of color, shape and movement. What they didn't understand is how the brain puts all of that together in a seemingly perfectly synchronized manner that allows us to recognize, say, a red ball rolling across a table for what it is. This is called the "binding problem" as in "how does our brain bind all the different data together to allow us to see a red ball moving?"

Now scientists at the California Institute of Technology researching this issue have come up with a very simple optical illusion that answers the question. **Our brain cheats by making assumptions to fill in any gaps in data by drawing on past experience.** They did a segment on NPR the other day called Tricks the Brain Plays that includes the optical illusion so you can try it out for yourself. It opens a small browser window that has a field of random red and green dots that are moving up or down the screen. Within 8 inches of the display you'll think all the red dots are moving down and all the green ones are moving up, but if you shift your eyes to the left or the right of the image the direction of the dots will reverse. If you move back from your monitor you'll realize that the truth is there are three columns of dots. The ones on the left and right have the red dots moving up and the green ones down and the middle column is the reverse.

The illusion explained: What's happening is an example of a "binding problem" in the brain. Typically, color and movement are thought to be processed by different parts of the brain. But a red ball rolling across a table looks like a red ball rolling across a table because the brain puts the movement and color information together to form a coherent perception.

The brain is trying to do that in this illusion; it's incorrectly binding color and motion so it can tell us that all the red dots are moving in the same direction throughout our "world," in this case the animation display. The illusion breaks down if you stand several feet away from the monitor, and watch the illusion (a long mouse cable or a friend is necessary to do this.)

Even if you know ahead of time what the truth is that doesn't stop your brain from cheating. It's worse than that, though, some scientists have discovered that it's entirely possible for you to completely miss something that happens right in front of you or that things have changed. Professor Daniel Simons of the Visual Cognition Lab at the University of Illinois has done some amazing experiments on what he calls "change blindness" and "inattentional blindness." There was an interesting article printed earlier this month in The Daily Telegraph called *Did you see the Gorilla*? That talks about these experiments.

In one experiment, people who were walking across a college campus were asked by a stranger for directions. During the resulting chat, two men carrying a wooden door passed between the stranger and the subjects. After the door went by, the subjects were asked if they had noticed anything change.

Half of those tested failed to notice that, as the door passed by, the stranger had been substituted with a man who was of different height, of different build and who sounded different. He was also wearing different clothes.

Despite the fact that the subjects had talked to the stranger for 10-15 seconds before the swap, half of them did not detect that, after the passing of the door, they had ended up speaking to a different person. This phenomenon, called change blindness, highlights how we see much less than we think we do.

Working with Christopher Chabris at Harvard University, Simons came up with another demonstration that has now become a classic, based on a videotape of a handful of people playing basketball. They played the tape to subjects and asked them to count the passes made by one of the teams.

Around half failed to spot a woman dressed in a gorilla suit who walked slowly across the scene for nine seconds, even though this hairy interloper had passed between the players and stopped to face the camera and thump her chest.

However, if people were simply asked to view the tape, they noticed the gorilla easily. The effect is so striking that some of them refused to accept they were looking at the same tape and thought that it was a different version of the video, one edited to include the ape.

If you stop to think about it you can probably come up with some examples of both of these phenomena in your own life. My recent car accident is a perfect example of inattentional blindness as I never saw the oncoming car until just before it hit me as I was busy focusing on a jeep that was making a right turn onto the same road I was trying to turn left onto. I was so focused on the Jeep that I never saw the Sebring until it hit me.

So, yes, I believe that you think you know what you saw when you show up here and try to convince me that Elvis pulled up to you on a street corner and impregnated you with a mere kiss and I'm not in any way impugning your honesty when I question you on it. **I just know that our brains experience a lot of things that aren't true as well as misses a lot of things that are true. If more people would keep that in mind, so to speak, there'd probably be less of a market for the tabloids out there.**

(THE END)

必备词汇

make sense of 感觉，感知
atheist / ˈeiθiist / 无神论者
supernatural / ˌsjuːpəˈnætʃ ərəl / 超自然的，神奇的
misinterpret / ˈmisinˈtəːprit / 曲解
optical illusion 错觉
pathetic / pəˈθetik / 可怜的，可悲的
take in 获取
inflate / inˈfleit / 吸气，膨胀
deflate / diˈfleit / 呼气，缩小
crap / kræp / 胡扯
with all the crap 糟糕的是
stimuli 刺激
reverse / riˈvəːs / 倒退，倒转
coherent perception 黏在一起的感觉
dot / dɔt / 点
break down 分解开了
ahead of time 提前
inattentional 不在意的，不注意的
subject / ˈsʌbdʒikt / 被试
substitute / ˈsʌbstitjuːt / 取代，代替
tabloid / ˈtæblɔid / 药片

重点剖析

— I think a lot of the supernatural experiences that people feel they've had are actually the result of perfectly natural phenomena which they've misinterpreted due to a lack of understanding of how their brain works. Everyone's familiar with the various optical illusions which demonstrate how easily our eyes can be fooled, but most never stop to consider that it's not our eyes that are being fooled; rather it's our brains that are being fooled. 我认为人们感到他们所经历的许多超自然的经历实际上是由于他们缺乏对自己大脑如何工作的了解而对绝妙的自然现象曲解的结果。每个人都体验过各种各样的视觉错觉，这说明我们的眼睛是可以被轻易愚弄的，但大多数人从没有停下来考虑一下，受到愚弄的不是我们的眼睛，而是我们的大脑。

— Our brains are pretty pathetic at processing all of the data they take in and so they compensate by cheating: taking shortcuts and ignoring a lot of the input. 大脑要处理获取的所有数不胜数据，它忙得“可怜”，所以它通过欺骗来补偿自己：寻找捷径、忽略许多输入的信息。

— Our brain cheats by making assumptions to fill in any gaps in data by drawing on past experience. 通过回想过去的经历，我们的大脑利用假设来填补数据中的任何空白从而欺骗我们。

— The brain is trying to do that in this illusion; it incorrectly binding color and motion so it can tell us that all the red dots are moving in the same direction throughout our "world," in this case the animation display. The illusion breaks down if you stand several feet away from the monitor, and watch the illusion (a long mouse cable or a friend is necessary to do this.) 在这个错觉中大脑正试图把颜色和运动错误地合在一起，这样它可以告诉我们，在我们的“世界”中，所有的红色点正在向同一方向移动，这样，动画就产生了。如果你站在离显示器几英尺开外，观察这个图，错觉就消失了，（这样做，需要一个长长的鼠标线或一位朋友来帮忙）。

— I just know that our brains experience a lot of things that aren true as well as misses a lot of things that are true. If more people would keep that in mind, so to speak, there'd probably be less of a market for the tabloids out there. 我刚刚知道，我们的大脑经历了许多不是真实的事情，也错过了许多真实的东西。如果有更多的人记住这一点，那么可以预言，药铺子的药可能就卖不出多少了。

(V41 真题题源)

9. Improve Athletic Performance

人类运动的体能极限

Are Olympians born, made, or both?

Coaches may argue that hard work and dedication make great athletes, but new research suggests that world-class athletes really are superhuman and born with special genes that let their bodies perform faster, longer, and better than mere mortals.

In other words, Olympians are from Mars and you're from Main Street.

"These individuals are off the chart," says Michael Meyers, PhD, director of the human performance research laboratory at West Texas A&M University and a consultant to several U.S. Olympic teams. **"They are an anomaly with some of them almost bordering on freaks of nature."**

Those genetic gifts alone might get some athletes to the elite level. But to go beyond

that and become an Olympic champion, experts say it takes rigorous training of both the body and mind.

"If we look at competition day, these athletes are bred to the highest level of performance. [Those] who can perform on that day boils down to how well trained their brain is," says Sal Arria, DC, executive director of the International Sports Sciences Association. **"If they've got great genes, but they don't have the mindset, who are you going to pick?"**

Genes Set Olympians Apart

Becoming an Olympic champion starts with genetics, say researchers.

"What we do through our training and testing is supplement what the individual has already been endowed with," says Meyers, who works with Olympic and professional teams to identify and develop talent. "We enhance what they have; you can't enhance nothing."

And what they have, according to a growing body of research, is a set of genes that predisposes them to athletic prowess.

"I think they are genetically different, but we have not been able yet to identify the genes," says Claude Bouchard, PhD, executive director of the Pennington Biomedical Research Center and director of its Human Genomics Laboratory in Baton Rouge, La. "So far we have only a very partial understanding of the genes that are involved."

In a landmark study published in 1999, Bouchard linked certain genes to maximal aerobic capacity—a key factor for endurance athletes, such as long distance runners, cyclists, and rowers. Since then, more than 100 genes have been added to his fitness and physical performance genome map.

Bouchard says most of the genes identified so far affect overall fitness, but "a couple dozen" genes are under investigation for their particular effects on individual performance traits.

One of the most studied athletic genes is the ACE (angiotensin-converting enzyme) gene, which appears in different forms in elite sprinters and long-distance runners. A variant of another gene that affects the fast-twitch muscles, known as ACTN3, has also been linked to superior performance.

Bouchard says linking specific genes to athletic traits is an extremely complex and painstaking process, and any single genetic variation may only play a minor role in affecting overall performance.

"Everything points in the direction of a multigenic system with many genes involved and many variations contributing," says Bouchard.

"It's not possible at this time to predict based on genes and DNA sequence variants who ... has the potential to reach the Olympic podium," Bouchard tells WebMD. "But research is continuing, and I'm sure that eventually it will be possible to spell out in some detail the [genetic variations] that have favorable effects."

More generally speaking, genetics also determines body size, height, body mass or muscle-to-fat ratios, and other variables of the body's physical structure.

For example, Arria says most people are born with about a 50/50 ratio of red and white muscle cells. **Red muscle cells are more efficient in extracting oxygen from blood and are critical to endurance activities, while white muscle cells are high-energy cells used to produce quick bursts of energy.**

"People with a higher proportion of white muscle cells have more explosive capabilities," Arria explains. "You're not going to find a marathon runner with a lot of white muscle cells."

Training the Mind and Body

Thanks to advances in sports science and technology, Arria says there are few hidden secrets left in training, and most coaches stick with proven training programs. At the Olympic level, those programs must not only maximize physical performance but sustain it and allow the athlete's performance to peak at the proper times.

"An Olympic athlete has to be able to perform and peak at the local, regional, and national levels and then peak again for the Olympics," says Arria, who also served as team doctor for the U.S. Track and Field team at the 1984 Olympics. "They have to be able to control their training cycle so they get the optimum performance out of their body on the day of the competition."

Genetics and training being equal, experts say it's the mind that often gives some athletes the winning edge.

Arria recalls a prime example from his days with the U.S. Olympic track team at a major international meet against the East Germans in the mid-1980s.

"World record holder Udo Beyer from East Germany was in sixth place and on his sixth and final throw. American Dave Lout had just set the American record and was in first place," says Arria. "Udo Beyer walked out, looked at Dave Lout'ss mark, looked beyond, and went back to the ring, spun, and threw that shot for a world record."

"It is the mind that controls the body to dig deeper and perform better on that day and that moment," says Arria.

"When it comes down to it, I'd say on competition day the mind is probably most powerful variable in controlling the ability to win or lose," says Arria. "because that athlete has been there before at that level and performed at that high level. But to do it on that Olympic day takes an incredible focus."

(THE END)

必备词汇

Olympian / əu'limpiən / 奥运会选手
dedication / ˌdedi'keiʃ ən / 贡献，奉献
athlete / 'æθliːt / 运动员
mortal / 'mɔːtl / 凡人
anomaly / əˈnɔməli / 异常的人或物
freak / friːk / 怪物
elite / ei'liːt / 精华，精锐
highest level of performance 最高竞技状态
boil down to 表明，意味着
perform / pə'fɔːm / 表现，表演
mindset / 'maindset / 精神状态
set apart 使分开
genetics / dʒi'netiks / 遗传学
endow with 赋予，赠予
identify / ai'dentifai / 识别，鉴别
talent / 'tælənt / 天才
enhance / in'hɑːns / 增强
predispose / 'priːdis'pəuz / 预先安排，使倾向于
prowess / 'prauis / 威力
landmark / 'lændmɑːk / 里程碑，划时代的事
genome map 基因图谱
trait / treit / 特点
sprinter / `sprintə(r) / 赛跑选手
variant / 'vɛəriənt / 变体
painstaking / 'peinsteikiŋ / 艰苦的
burst of energy 能量爆发

重点剖析

— Are Olympians born, made, or both? Coaches may argue that hard work and dedication make great athletes, but new research suggests that world-class athletes really are superhuman and born with special genes that let their bodies perform faster, longer, and better than mere mortals. In other words, Olympians are from Mars and you're from Main Street. 奥运会选手是天生的是训练出来的？还是两者兼而有之？教练们可能会争辩说辛勤的汗水和奉献精神铸就了伟大的运动员，但最新研究发现，世界级的选手确实系出超人，他们生来就有特殊的基因让身体比常人运动得更快、更久、更强。换句话说，奥运会选手来自火星，而你来自大街。

— "They are an anomaly with some of them almost bordering on freaks of nature." "他们超脱常人，有些家伙几乎可以称作大自然的怪胎。"

— Those genetic gifts alone might get some athletes to the elite level. But to go beyond that and become an Olympic champion, experts say it takes rigorous training of both the body and mind. 仅这些基因礼物就可能让一些运动员成为人上人了。但要进一步成为奥运会冠军，专家们说还需要对他们的身体和心理进行严格的训练。

— "If they've got great genes, but they don't have the mindset, who are you going to pick?" "如果他们拥有伟大的基因，但没有心理状态，你会选谁呢？"

— "What we do through our training and testing is supplement what the individual has already been endowed with," "通过我们的训练和测试所做的是为那些已经被赋予了天才的人提供补充性的帮助而已。"

— In a landmark study published in 1999, Bouchard linked certain genes to maximal aerobic capacity—a key factor for endurance athletes, such as long distance runners, cyclists, and rowers. Since then, more than 100 genes have been added to his fitness and physical performance genome map. 在他于1999年发表的一篇具有里程碑意义的研究中，Bouchard把某些基因和最大取氧能力联系了起来——这是耐力选手需要的关键的因素，如长跑选手、赛车手和划船手。自那以后，已经有100多个基因入选他的健康和身体能力基因图谱中了。

— One of the most studied athletic genes is the ACE (angiotensin-converting enzyme) gene, which appears in different forms in elite sprinters and long-distance runners. A variant of another gene that affects the fast-twitch muscles, known as ACTN3, has also been linked to superior performance. 研究得最多的运动基因之一是ACE（血管紧缩素转换酶）基因，它以不同的形式存在于顶尖赛跑选手和长跑选手的体内。另一个基因的变体，即ACTN3，影响到快速抽动肌肉，它也和优异的运动表现有关。

— "It's not possible at this time to predict based on genes and DNA sequence variants who ... has the potential to reach the Olympic podium." "目前，根据基因和DNA序列变体还不可能预测谁有潜力站在奥林匹克的领奖台上。"

— More generally speaking, genetics also determines body size, height, body mass or muscle-to-fat ratios, and other variables of the body's physical structure. 更广义地说，遗传学还决定着体型、身高、体重或者肌肉—脂肪的比例，以及身体结构的其他变量。

— Red muscle cells are more efficient in extracting oxygen from blood and are critical to endurance activities, while white muscle cells are high-energy cells used to produce quick bursts of energy. 红肌肉细胞在从血液中吸取氧气上更为有效，它对耐力运动是至关重要的，而白肌肉细胞是高能量细胞，用来制造快速能量爆发。

— Thanks to advances in sports science and technology, Arria says there are few hidden secrets left in training, and most coaches stick with proven training programs. At the Olympic level, those programs must not only maximize physical performance but sustain it and allow the athlete's performance to peak at the proper times. 由于运动科学和技术的发展，Arria说在训练中没有多少秘密可言，大多数教练员坚持按经过检验的训练计划对运动员进行训练。在奥运会级别上，这些计划必须不仅使运动员的身体状态达到最佳，而且必须保持这种状态，让选手们的状态在合适的时候达到巅峰。

— Genetics and training being equal, experts say it's the mind that often gives some athletes the winning edge. 遗传和训练是一样重要的，专家们说，通常是心理因素使运动员比其他人更胜一筹。

— "When it comes down to it, I'd say on competition day the mind is probably most powerful variable in controlling the ability to win or lose," says Arria. "Because that athlete has been there before at that level and performed at that high level. But to do it on that Olympic day takes an incredible focus." "谈到这一点，我得说在比赛那一天，心理状态可能是控制成功还是失败的最强大的变量，" Arria说。"因为运动员以前就在那个水平上了，表现水平已经很高了。但在奥运会那一天需要相当高的精神集中。"

(Newversian真题题源)

10. Treatment in Different Eras

不同年代的医疗

Medical treatments are evolved with eras, for me I personally divide the treatments in three different eras:

Era I, which can be called "mechanical medicine" and which began roughly in the 1860s, reflects the prevailing view that health and illness are totally physical in nature, and thus all therapies should be physical ones, such as surgical procedures or drugs. In Era I, the mind or consciousness is essentially equated with the functioning of the brain.

Era II began to take shape in the period following World War II. Physicians began to realize, based on scientific evidence, that disease has a "psychosomatic" aspect: that emotions and feelings can influence the body's functions. Psychological stress, for example, can contribute to high blood pressure, heart attacks, and ulcers. This was a radical advance over Era I.

The recently developing Era III goes even further by proposing that consciousness is not confined to one's individual body. Nonlocal mind—mind that is boundless and unlimited—is the hallmark of Era III. An individual's mind may affect not just his or her body, but the body of another person at a distance, even when that distant individual is unaware of the effort. You can think of Era II as illustrating the

personal effects of consciousness and Era III as illustrating the transpersonal effects of the mind.

It's important to remember that these eras are not mutually exclusive; rather they coexist, overlap, and are used together, as when drugs are used with psychotherapy, and surgery is used with prayer.

What do these eras mean for the future of medicine?

They can help us make sense of the confusion within medicine. By drawing attention to the effects of consciousness, they can help us move beyond the exclusive use of mechanical, physical measures in treating illness.

The most interesting era, in my view, is Era III. The evidence supporting Era III implies that there are no boundaries to consciousness, that it is infinite in space and time. If our minds are unbounded, then they must unite or come together at some level. This means that in some sense we are literally one. The implications of this unity are profound. If our minds are connected, then we can, and do, share any and all experiences. All the joys and sorrows of life can be mutual affairs. This means we are never alone, which relieves the twin burdens of loneliness and isolation, two major factors in illness.

The biggest payoff of Era III concerns our destiny. If our mind is nonlocal and boundless, then it is infinite in time. Therefore, the death of the body does not mean that consciousness ceases to exist; something about us endures. Era III, therefore, carries with it the promise of immortality, which is a cure for the "disease" that has caused more suffering for humans than any other: the fear of death.

How did you become interested in the effects of prayer?

I grew up in a deeply religious environment in central Texas, where people prayed all the time; but I threw religion overboard when I went off to college and fell in love with science. I had no interest in prayer again until, during my practice of internal medicine, I occasionally began to bump into patients who had horrible diseases and who received no medical treatment—yet their illnesses went away following prayer. One patient I encountered during my first year in medical practice had terminal lung cancer for which no treatment was given; members of his church prayed nonstop for him and the cancer totally disappeared. I did not take these cases seriously, however, until the mid-80s, when I discovered the existence of scientific studies, dealing with humans and animals, showing the effects of prayer. After years spent researching this evidence, I became convinced that it is one of the best-kept secrets in medicine.

Can you cite specific research that supports your theory that prayer can help people heal?

In 1998, Dr. Elisabeth Targ and her colleagues at California Pacific Medical Center in San Francisco, conducted a controlled, double-blind study of the effects of "distant healing," or prayer, on patients with advanced AIDS. Those patients receiving prayer survived in greater numbers, got sick less often, and recovered faster than those not receiving prayer. Prayer, in this study, looked like a medical breakthrough.

In 1988, Dr. Randolph Byrd conducted a similar study at San Francisco General Hospital involving patients with heart attack or severe chest pain. He found that patients receiving prayer did much better clinically than those who did not.

Currently, Dr. Mitchell Krucoff at Duke University Medical Center in Durham, North Carolina, is studying the effects of prayer on patients undergoing cardiac procedures such as catheterization and angioplasty. Patients receiving prayer have up to 100% fewer side effects from these procedures than people not prayed for.

These are impressive double-blind studies, meaning that no one knows who is receiving prayer and who isn't. This eliminates or at least reduces the placebo effect, which is the power of suggestion or positive thinking. However, the studies I find most impressive are not done on humans. For example, when bacteria are prayed for, they tend to grow faster; when seeds are prayed for, they tend to germinate quicker; when wounded mice are prayed for, they tend to heal faster. I like these studies because they can be done with great precision, and they eliminate all effects of suggestion and positive thinking, since we can be sure the effects aren't due to the placebo effect. Mice, seeds, and microbes presumably don't think positively!

The important thing is to honor the data supporting the benefits of spirituality in health, instead of continuing to ignore them. As we move forward, however, we must be very careful not to use this evidence as a pretext for pushing our private religious views onto people who are sick. I have seen a few examples of shameless evangelizing during illness, which I deplore. Above all, we must avoid making people feel as if they are spiritual failures if they get sick or don't heal, as if illness were punishment for sin.

(THE END)

必备词汇

mechanical medicine 机械式的医学
roughly / 'rʌfli / 大概
prevailing / pri'veiliŋ / 流行的，主导的
surgical / 'səːdʒikəl / 外科的
therapy / 'θerəpi / 治疗
consciousness / 'kɔnʃəsnis / 意识
psychosomatic / ˌsaikəusəu'mætik / 受心理影响的，精神心理相关的
physician / fi'ziʃən / 医生
emotions and feelings 情绪和感情
influence / 'influəns / 影响
psychological stress 心理紧张
ulcer / 'ʌlsə / 溃疡
confine to 限制在
boundless / 'baundlis / 无限的
hallmark / 'hɔːlmɑːk / 特点
unaware / ˌʌnə'wɛə / 不知道的
transpersonal / træns'pəːsənl / 超越个人的
exclusive / iks'kluːsiv / 排斥的
coexist / kəuig'zist / 共存
overlap / 'əuvəlæp / 交迭
psychotherapy / 'saikəu'θerəpi / 精神疗法，心理疗法
prayer / prɛə / 祈祷者
make sense of 了解，知道
imply / im'plai / 暗示
unbounded / ʌn'baundid / 极大的
profound / prə'faund / 深刻的，影响深远的
infinite / 'infinit / 无限的
payoff / 'peiɔːf / 结局
immortality / imɔː'tæləti / 不朽
destiny / 'destini / 命运
fall in love 爱上
internal medicine 内科
bump into 遇到
became convinced 相信
heal / hiːl / 治愈，医治
double-blind study 双盲实验
breakthrough / 'breikθruː / 突破
catheterization / -rai'zeiʃən / 导管插入
placebo effect 安慰效果
spirituality / ˌspiritju'æliti / 精神性，灵性
sin / sin / 罪过

重点剖析

— **Era I,** which can be called "mechanical medicine" and which began roughly in the 1860s, reflects the prevailing view that health and illness are totally physical in nature, and thus all therapies should be physical ones, such as surgical procedures or drugs. In Era I, the mind or consciousness is essentially equated with the functioning of the brain. 年代I，可以称为"机械式的医学"，大致开始于19世纪60年代，反映了当时的流行观点，即健康和疾病完全是生理问题，因此所有的治疗应该是身体性治疗，比如外科手术或药物。在年代I，精神或意识本质上等同于大脑的机能。

— **Era II** began to take shape in the period following World War II. Physicians began to realize, based on scientific evidence, that disease has a "psychosomatic" aspect: that emotions and feelings can influence the body's functions. Psychological stress, for example, can contribute to high blood pressure, heart attacks, and ulcers. This was a radical advance over Era I. 年代II成形于二战以后。基于科学证据，医生开始意识到，疾病有受心理影响的一面：情绪和感情可以影响到人体的机能。例如，心理紧张可以引起高血压、心脏病和溃疡。这比年代I有了实质性进步。

— The recently developing **Era III** goes even further by proposing that consciousness is not confined to one's individual body. Nonlocal mind—mind that is boundless and unlimited—is the hallmark of Era III. An individual's mind may affect not just his or her body, but the body of another person at a distance, even when that distant individual is unaware of the effort. You can think of Era II as illustrating the personal effects of consciousness and Era III as illustrating the transpersonal effects of the mind. 近年来正在发展的是年代III，它走得更远，认为意识不仅仅限制在个人的身体内部。非局部的精神——即漫无边际的心理状态——是年代III的特点。个人的心理状态可能不仅影响到他的身体，但也可能影响到身在远处的另一个人的身体，即使是远处的那个人没有意识到这种影响。你可以把年代II比作意识的个人影响，而年代III比作心理状态的超个人影响。

— It's important to remember that these eras are not mutually exclusive; rather they coexist, overlap, and are used together, as when drugs are used with psychotherapy, and surgery is used with prayer. 需要记住的是，这些观点不是互相排斥的，而是共存的、重叠的以及互相利用的，好比药物被用于精神疗法，外科手术中使用祷辞一样。

— The biggest payoff of Era III concerns our destiny. If our mind is nonlocal and boundless, then it is infinite in time. Therefore, the death of the body does not mean that consciousness ceases to exist; something about us endures. Era III, therefore, carries with it the promise of immortality, which is a cure for the "disease" that has caused more suffering for humans than any other: the fear of death. 年代III的最终结果关乎着我们的命运。如果我们的意识是非本我的、无限的，则在时间上将是无限的。所以，身体的死亡并不意味着意识停止存在了，也就是我们的某些部分是永恒的。所以，年代III承载着对不朽的承诺，而不朽是对一种疾病的根本治疗手段。这种疾病比其他任何事物都能使人类遭受痛苦，它就是对死亡的恐惧。

（V56真题题源）

11. Risk Research

冒险心理学研究

Risky business has never been more popular. Mountain climbing is among America's fastest growing sports. Extreme skiing—in which skiers descend cliff-like runs by dropping from ledge to snow-covered ledge —is drawing wider interest.

In fact, as researchers are discovering, the psychology of risk involves far more than a simple "death wish." Studies now indicate that the inclination to take high risks may be hard-wired into the brain, intimately linked to arousal and pleasure mechanisms, and may offer such a thrill that it functions like an addiction. The tendency probably affects one in five people, mostly young males, and declines with age. It may ensure our survival, even spur our evolution as individuals and as a species. Risk taking probably bestowed a crucial evolutionary advantage, inciting the fighting and foraging of the hunter-gatherer.

In mapping out the mechanisms of risk, psychologists hope to do more than explain why people climb mountains. **Risk-taking, which one researcher defines as "engaging in any activity with an uncertain outcome," arises in nearly all walks of life. Asking someone on a date, accepting a challenging work assignment, raising a sensitive issue with a spouse or a friend, confronting an abusive boss—all involve uncertain outcomes, and present some level of risk.** Understanding the psychology of risk, understanding why some individuals will take chances and others won't, could have important consequences in everything from career counseling to programs for juvenile delinquents.

Researchers don't yet know precisely how a risk taking impulse arises from within or what role is played by environmental factors, from upbringing to the culture at large. And, while some level of risk taking is dearly necessary for survival (try crossing a busy street without it), scientists are divided as to whether, in a modern society, a "high-risk gene" is still advantageous. Some scientists, like Frank Farley, Ph.D., a University of Wisconsin psychologist and past president of the American Psychological Association, see a willingness to take big risks as essential for success. The same inner force that pushed Derek Hersey, Farley argues, may also explain why some dare to run for office, launch a corporate raid, or lead a civil-rights demonstration.

Yet research has also revealed the darker side of risk taking. High-risk takers are easily bored and may suffer low job satisfaction. Their craving for stimulation can make them more likely to abuse drugs, gamble, commit crimes, and be promiscuous. As psychologist Salvadore Maddi, Ph.D., of the University of California-Davis warns, high-risk takers may "have a hard time deriving meaning and purpose from everyday life."

Indeed, this peculiar form of dissatisfaction could help explain the explosion of high-risk sports in America and other postindustrial Western nations. In unstable cultures, such as those at war or suffering poverty, people rarely seek out additional thrills. But in a rich and safety-obsessed country like America, land of guardrails, seat belts, and personal-injury lawsuits, everyday life may have become too safe, predictable, and boring for those programmed for risk-taking.

In an unsettling paradox, our culture's emphasis on security and certainty wo defining elements of a "civilized" society—may not only be fostering the current risk taking wave, but could spawn riskier activities in the future. "The safer we try to make life," cautions psychologist Michael Aptor, Ph.D, a visiting professor at Yale and author of The Dangerous Edge: The Psychology of Excitement, "the more people may take on risks."

Unique Wavelengths

It's easy to see why high-risk sports receive so much academic attention. Climbers, for example, score higher on risk-preference tests than nearly all other groups. They show a strong need for intense stimulation and seek it in environments—sheer cliffs or frozen waterfalls —that most humans seem genetically programmed to avoid.

Climbers' own explanations for why they climb illustrate the difficulty of separating genetic, environmental, and cognitive components of this or any other behavioral trait. Many say they climb for decidedly conscious reasons: to test limits, to build or maintain self-esteem, to gain self-knowledge. Some regard it as a form of meditation. "Climbing demands absolute concentration," says Barbara, a lithe, 30-ish climber from Washington State. "It's the only time I ever feel in the moment."

A Craving For Arousal

Yet as far back as the 1950s, research was hinting at alternative explanations. British psychologist Hans J. Eysenck developed a scale to measure the personality trait of extroversion, now one of the most consistent predictors of risk taking. Other studies revealed that, contrary to Freud, the brain not only craved arousal, but somehow regulated that arousal at an optimal level. Over the next three decades, researchers extended these early findings into a host of theories about risk taking.

Some scientists, like UC-Davis's Maddi and Wisconsin's Farley, concentrate on risk taking primarily as a cognitive or behavioral phenomenon. Maddi sees risk taking as an element of a larger personality dimension he calls "hardiness," which measures individuals' sense of control over their environment and their willingness to seek out challenges. Farley regards risk-taking more as a whole personality type. **Where other researchers speak of Type A and B personalities, Farley adds Type T, for thrill seeking. He breaks Type-T behavior into four categories: T-mental and T-physical, to distinguish between intellectual and physical risk taking; and T-negative and T-positive, to distinguish between productive and destructive risk taking.**

A second line of research focuses on risks biological roots. A pioneer in these studies is psychologist Marvin Zuckerman at the University of Delaware. He produced a detailed profile of the high-sensation seeking (HSS) personality.

Wired For Thrills

Researchers have long known of physiological differences between high- and low-sensation seekers. According to Zuckerman, the cortical system of a high can handle higher levels of stimulation without overloading and switching to the fight-or-flight response. Psychologist Randy Larsen, Ph.D., at the University of Michigan, has even shown that high-sensation seekers not only tolerate high stimulus but crave it as well.

Larsen calls high-sensation seekers "reducers": Their brains automatically dampen the level of incoming stimuli, leaving them with a kind of excitement deficit. (Low-sensation seekers, by contrast, tend to "augment" stimuli, and thus desire less excitement.) Why are some brains wired for excitement? **Since 1974, researchers have known that the enzyme monoamine oxidase (MAO) plays a central role in regulating arousal, inhibition, and pleasure. They also found that low levels of MAO correlate with high levels of certain behaviors, including criminality, social activity, and drug abuse.** When Zuckerman began testing HSS individuals, they, too, showed unusually low MAO levels.

Psychologist Aptor suggests that the willingness to take risks, even if expressed by only certain individuals, would have produced benefits for an entire group. Upon entering a new territory, a tribe would quickly need to assess the environment's safety in terms of "which water holes are safe to drink from, which caves are empty of dangerous animals." Some risk takers would surely die. But, Aptor points out, "it's better for one person to eat a poisonous fruit than for everybody."

(THE END)

必备词汇

extreme / iks'triːm / 极端的
descend / di'send / 下来，下降
risk / risk / 冒险，风险
inclination / ˌinkli'neiʃən / 倾向，爱好
intimately 密切地
arousal / ə'rauzə / 激励，刺激
mechanism / 'mekənizəm / 机制
thrill / θril / 非常兴奋，振颤
addiction / ə'dikʃən / 沉溺，上瘾
spur / spəː / 刺激，鼓舞
forage / 'fɔridʒ / 袭击，破坏
confront / kən'frʌnt / 对抗，使面对
outcome / 'autkʌm / 成果，结果
delinquent / di'liŋkwənt / 过失，犯错误
impulse / 'impʌls / 刺激，推动力
upbring / 'ʌpbriŋiŋ / 抚育，教养
craving / 'kreiviŋ / 渴望
gamble / 'gæmbl / 赌博
peculiar / pi'kjuːljə / 特殊的
cortical / 'kɔːtikəl / 脑皮层的
correlate with 和……关联
enzyme monoamine oxidase (MAO) 一元胺氧化酶

重点剖析

— In fact, as researchers are discovering, the psychology of risk involves far more than a simple "death wish." Studies now indicate that the inclination to take high risks may be hard-wired into the brain, intimately linked to arousal and pleasure mechanisms, and may offer such a thrill that it functions like an addiction. The tendency probably affects one in five people, mostly young males, and declines with age. It may ensure our survival, even spur our evolution as individuals and as a species. Risk taking probably bestowed a crucial evolutionary advantage, inciting the fighting and foraging of the hunter-gatherer. 实际上，如研究人员发现的那样，冒险心理涉及的东西远远不止是“遗嘱”那样简单。目前的研究表明，对高度冒险的爱好可能已经深深地扎根在大脑里了，它和刺激和快感机制有密切关系，它可以使人获得一种像上了瘾似的兴奋。这一倾向在每5人中的一人身上存在，且大多数是年轻的男性，并随着年龄增长而呈下降趋势。它可以确保我们的生存，甚至激发个人和物种的进化。冒险可能赋予了重要的进化优势，煽动起（原始社会中）以狩猎为生的人之间的争斗和袭击。

— Risk-taking, which one researcher defines as “engaging in any activity with an uncertain outcome,” arises in nearly all walks of life. Asking someone on a date, accepting a challenging work assignment, raising a sensitive issue with a spouse or a friend, confronting an abusive boss—all involve uncertain outcomes, and present some level of risk. 一名研究人员将冒险一词定义为：“从事具有不确定结果的活动”，几乎在生活的各个层面都会存在。请求某人约会、接受一份挑战性的工作、向配偶或朋友提出一个敏感的话题、面对一位残暴的老板——这些都涉及到不确定的结果，具有某种程度的冒险性。

— Researchers don’t yet know precisely how a risk taking impulse arises from within or what role is played by environmental factors, from upbringing to the culture at large. 研究人员还没有确定冒险刺激是如何从内心出现的，也不知道环境因素如成长环境和文化等在其中起到了什么作用。

— Yet research has also revealed the darker side of risk taking. High-risk takers are easily bored and may suffer low job satisfaction. Their craving for stimulation can make them more likely to abuse drugs, gamble, commit crimes, and be promiscuous. 然而，研究也发现了冒险的更为黑暗的一面。高度的冒险者很容易会变得无聊，可能对工作不满意。他们对刺激的渴望会使他们更有可能滥用毒品、参与赌博、自杀、男女滥交。

— Climbers’ own explanations for why they climb illustrate the difficulty of separating genetic, environmental, and cognitive components of this or any other behavioral trait. 登山者自己对他们为什么要登山的解释表明，要把冒险行为特征或任何其他行为特征的基因、环境和认知成分分清楚是多么的难。

— Where other researchers speak of Type A and B personalities, Farley adds Type T, for thrill seeking. He breaks Type-T behavior into four categories: T-mental and T-physical, to distinguish between intellectual and physical risk taking; and T-negative and T-positive, to distinguish between productive and destructive risk taking. 其他研究者倡导A型和B型个性，Farley也把T型作为冒险的特点。他把T型行为分为四类：T-mental和T-physical，分别为智力和体力冒险；T-negative和T-positive，分别为破坏性和生产性冒险。

— Since 1974, researchers have known that the enzyme monoamine oxidase (MAO) plays a central role in regulating arousal, inhibition, and pleasure. They also found that low levels of MAO correlate with high levels of certain behaviors, including criminality, social activity, and drug abuse. 自1974年以来，研究人员已经了解到一元胺氧化酶（MAO）在调节刺激、压抑的情绪和快乐感觉方面扮演着关键的角色。他们还发现低水平MAO和某些行为的高水平有关联，这些行为包括犯罪、社交活动和毒品滥用。

（V14真题题源）

12. Sick Building Syndrome: Causes and Effects

工作场所综合征

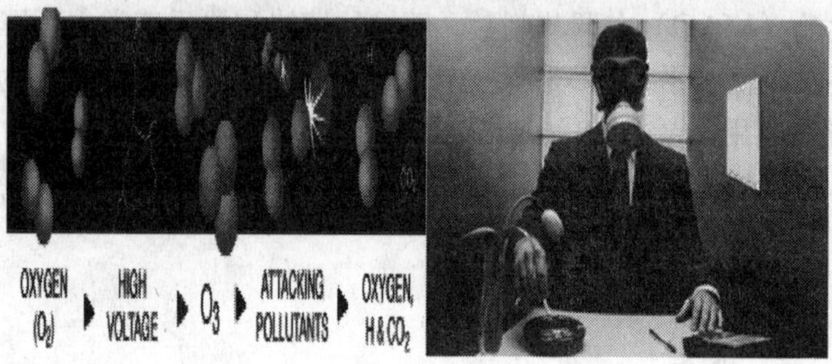

Historical Background

Indoor air pollution is a health threat common to buildings, especially modern ones, in many countries. Numerous studies by international health and environmental scientists have documented the widespread nature of the problem. The World Health Organisation estimated in 1989 that 30 percent of all new or refurbished buildings have indoor air pollution.

Between 1989 and 1992 the Harris Research Centre conducted polls of office worker attitudes in the U.K., Singapore, Germany, France, Italy, Belgium, South America, Australia and across several states of the USA. **Of those questioned, sixty-eight percent thought their work rate would improve in a cleaner, fresher environment. Thirty-one percent admitted to taking two or more days off work each year because of symptoms they blamed on office air quality and seventy-two percent claimed the air in which they worked was often stuffy or stale.**

A Florida woman in June 1987 won a workers' compensation case claiming that she was exposed to pathogenic moulds that caused her to become hypersensitive. The woman's physician stated that her illness was directly attributable to exposure to contaminants inside her building and that she was no longer able to work there. The woman is now receiving medical and compensatory benefits and will continue to do so indefinitely.

To indicate the potential scale of the problem

- A four year study of approximately 400,000 recruits at four U.S. Army training cen tres found that trainees housed in modern, energy efficient barracks were about fifty percent more likely to contract a respiratory infection than were trainees in older, less air tight buildings. The study conducted at the Walter Reed Army Institute, was published in the Journal of the American Medical Association (1988).
- Respiratory tract infections annually account for $15 billion of direct medical care costs, approximately $150 million in indirect costs such as lost income from work through absenteeism in the United States alone, according to a review by Garibaldi and Dixon published in the American Journal of Medicine (1985).

Whether the driving force is the threat of litigation or the push to improve productivity and reduce operating costs, it is hardly surprising to see an increasing focus on indoor air pollution and the study of sick buildings.

Symptoms And Effects

Today the term "Sick Building Syndrome" has become interchangeable with "tight building syndrome". **This terminology applies to any building in which more than twenty percent of the employees experience symptoms such as headaches, fatigue, or eye, nose or throat irritation that cease once the employee leaves the building.** This definition does not fit the classical symptoms of Legionnaires' disease since, with this disease, many of the symptoms become more severe over time. The distinction is due to the presence of an infection that can be determined by medical diagnosis and laboratory tests. Thus, when true infections are identified due to bacteria, fungi, or viruses, they are classified as a "Building Related Illness". In these cases, the percentage of occupants affected is highly variable. Only two employees need to contract the infection before that building is suspect.

In the case of so-called sick buildings, the problems lies in the internal environment. **In the experience of Healthy Buildings International (HBI) most cases of sick building syndrome are due to indoor pollutants in the air, however, comfort conditions are important since complaints due to cold, excess heat, or draughts are common. Humidity can be part of the problem, as can lighting, noise, vibration, radiation, odour perception and other factors, such as overcrowding, office layout and personal**

conflicts. These variables can be compounded by the employee's anxiety about other problems in the workplace.

There is also a complication in the way different people tolerate different conditions. For example, individuals have different metabolism for temperature, causing varying rates of internal heat output and, of course, people dress differently. Also, some people work near windows and are exposed to more draughts and radiant heat.

Similarly, if we consider odour perception, there are major differences in people's ability to identify or tolerate odours in an environment. Invariably, the odour perception of most people diminishes with time. Thus, a visitor may react adversely to an environment that seems fine to long term occupants.

Considering all these variables, it is impossible to satisfy everyone. In fact, in attempting to optimise any internal environment, the conditions necessary to satisfy the maximum percentage of occupants will still result in at least five percent thereof being dissatisfied. So while it is virtually impossible to satisfy one hundred percent of a building's occupants, it is possible to alleviate the problem to the satisfaction of the vast majority of employees by correctly identifying the cause of the problem instead of focusing on the symptoms.

Causes Of Indoor Pollution

One difficulty in effectively studying indoor air quality is that several diverse areas of expertise are needed, including chemistry, microbiology and ventilation engineering. HBI integrated these skills in forming unique diagnostic teams to study internal air quality.

In reviewing buildings studies worldwide, HBI scientists have found that sixty-three percent of the problems with contaminated air are due to ignorance of correct operating practices and/or inadequate maintenance, rather than any fundamental building design problems.

While it is true that pollutants in buildings emanate from the outdoors and indoors—carpets, furniture, people, equipment, ventilation systems and staff activities such as cleaning, smoking and food preparation — correctly designed and operated ventilation systems are built to handle these challenges. Unfortunately, because some building operators or maintenance employees are apathetic or ignorant of the ventilation system, the problem of poor indoor air quality standards persists.

In 1987, the United States National Institute for Occupational Safety and Health

(NIOSH) studied 446 buildings following staff complaints of upper respiratory illness and poor air quality. The study concluded that more than half of the problems were due to inadequate ventilation.

At HBI, the findings have been similar. After inspecting more than 1136 major buildings totalling more than 15.7 million square metres of property, the three most common causes of "sick buildings" were:

1. Poor Ventilation: fifty percent of the buildings had inadequate fresh air and an alarming eighteen percent were operating with no fresh air whatsoever.
2. Inadequate Filtration: fifty-six percent of the buildings had inefficient filters, forty-one percent were basically low-grade filter pads, scarcely better than butterfly nets, and fifteen percent were of reasonable quality but poorly installed.
3. Lack of hygiene: forty-two percent of the ventilation systems were dirty including nine percent with grossly contaminated ductwork. Such contaminated systems make perfect breeding grounds for bacteria, moulds and fungi.

In fact, only thirty-eight percent of the buildings studied were well ventilated with efficiently filtered air handling units and clean, well maintained ventilation systems. Significantly, there were no complaints of poor air quality by employees in these buildings.

(THE END)

必备词汇

indoor air pollution 室内环境污染
refurbished 装修过的
World Health Organisation 世界卫生组织
poll 民意测验
symptom / 'simptəm / 症状，征兆
blame / bleim / 谴责，责怪
stuffy/ 'stʌfi / 污浊的
stale / steil / 不新鲜的
pathogenic / ˌpæθə'dʒenik / 致病的，发病的
mould / məuld / 霉菌
hypersensitive / ˌhaipə(ː)'sensitiv / 过敏
attributable to 可归与……的
contaminant 污染物
indefinitely 不确定地
contract / 'kɔntrækt / 感染
respiratory infection 呼吸感染
respiratory tract 呼吸道
absenteeism / æbsən'tiːiz(ə)m / 矿工
sick building syndrome 病态建筑综合征
interchangeable / intə'tʃeindʒəb(ə)l / 可互换的
tight building syndrome 密闭建筑综合征
fatigue / fə'tiːg / 疲劳
irritation / ˌiri'teiʃən / 过敏

complaint / kəm'pleint / 抱怨，投诉
draught / drɑːft / 干燥，干旱
humidity/ hjuː'miditi / 湿度
odour / 'əudə / 气味，臭味
complication / ˌkɔmpli'keiʃ(ə)n / 复杂性
invariably/ in'veəriəb(ə)li / 不变地，总是
expertise / ˌekspə'tiːz / 专业，专门技术
microbiology / maikrəubai'ɔlədʒi / 微生物学
ventilation engineering 通风工程
emanate / 'eməneit / 散发，发出
apathetic / ˌæpə'θetik / 无动于衷的，缺乏兴趣的
persist / pə(ː)'sist / 持续

— Of those questioned, sixty-eight percent thought their work rate would improve in a cleaner, fresher environment. Thirty-one percent admitted to taking two or more days off work each year because of symptoms they blamed on office air quality and seventy-two percent claimed the air in which they worked was often stuffy or stale. 在被调查人员中，有68%的人认为他们的工作速度在更为清洁、更为新鲜的环境中时会提高。31%的人承认由于他们讨厌办公空气质量而一年中要请假两天以上，72%的人声称他们工作地方的空气常常污浊或不新鲜。

— A Florida woman in June 1987 won a workers' compensation case claiming that she was exposed to pathogenic moulds that caused her to become hypersensitive. The woman's physician stated that her illness was directly attributable to exposure to contaminants inside her building and that she was no longer able to work there. 佛罗里达的一名妇女于1987年赢得了一场工人赔偿官司，声称由于暴露在致病的霉菌下她患上了过敏症。这名妇女的医生声明，她的疾病是直接暴露在她建筑物内的污染物有关的，并说她不能再在那里工作了。

— Whether the driving force is the threat of litigation or the push to improve productivity and reduce operating costs, it is hardly surprising to see an increasing focus on indoor air pollution and the study of sick buildings. 无论其中的推动力是诉讼威胁或是提高劳动力和压缩运营费用的压力，可以几乎不稀奇地说，人们越来越关注室内空气污染并注重研究病态建筑。

— This terminology applies to any building in which more than twenty percent of the employees experience symptoms such as headaches, fatigue, or eye, nose or throat irritation that cease once the employee leaves the building. 如果一个建筑物里的有超过20%的员工患有头痛、疲劳、咽、鼻或喉过敏等症状并且在离开该建筑物后，症状消失，那么这一术语适用于该建筑。

— In the experience of Healthy Buildings International (HBI) most cases of sick building syndrome are due to indoor pollutants in the air, however, comfort conditions are important since complaints due to cold, excess heat, or draughts are common. Humidity can be part of the problem, as can lighting, noise, vibration, radiation, odour perception and other factors, such as overcrowding, office layout and personal conflicts. These variables can be compounded by the employee's anxiety about other problems in the workplace. 按照健康建筑国际中心（HBI）的经验，大多数病态建筑综合症的情况是因为室内存在污染物的缘故。舒适条件是很重要的，因为对寒冷、过热或干燥的投诉很普遍。湿度也是问题的一个方面，还有光照、噪声、振动、辐射、气味感觉以及其他因素如过度拥挤、办公室的布局和个人冲突。这些变量可以和员工由于工作场所中存在的其他问题而产生的焦虑感交织在一起。

— There is also a complication in the way different people tolerate different conditions. For example, individuals have different metabolism for temperature, causing varying rates of internal heat output and, of course, people dress differently. Also, some people work near windows and are exposed to more draughts and radiant heat. 还有一个复杂的问题是不同的人要忍受不同工作条件。例如，个人在不同温度有不同的新陈代谢，引起不同的内热散发速度，当然，人们穿着也会不同。此外，有些在靠窗户工作的人也暴露在更多的干燥和辐射热量下。

— Considering all these variables, it is impossible to satisfy everyone. In fact, in attempting to optimise any internal environment, the conditions necessary to satisfy the maximum percentage of occupants will still result in at least five percent thereof being dissatisfied. 考虑到所有这些变量，让每个人都满意是不可能的。事实上，在试图优化任何内部环境时，满足最大多数居住者的条件仍旧使至少5%的人感到不满意。

— In reviewing buildings studies worldwide, HBI scientists have found that sixty-three percent of the problems with contaminated air are due to ignorance of correct operating practices and/or inadequate maintenance, rather than any fundamental building design problems. 在审查全世界范围内的建筑物时，HBI的科学家已经发现，其中63%的与污染空气有关的问题是因为忽视了正确的操作和维护，而不是基本的建筑设计问题。

— In 1987, the United States National Institute for Occupational Safety and Health (NIOSH) studied 446 buildings following staff complaints of upper respiratory illness and poor air quality. The study concluded that more than half of the problems were due to inadequate ventilation. 1987年，在员工投诉上呼吸道疾病和糟糕的空气质量后，美国国家职业安全和健康学会（NIOSH）研究了446座建筑物。研究的结论是有一多半问题是和通风不良有关。

— In fact, only thirty-eight percent of the buildings studied were well ventilated with efficiently filtered air handling units and clean, well maintained ventilation systems. Significantly, there were no complaints of poor air quality by employees in these buildings. 事实上，这些被研究的建筑物中只有38%用有效过滤的空气处理设备和干净、维护良好的系统进行通风的。值得注意的是，这些建筑物中居住的员工没有对劣质空气质量的投诉过。

(V22真题题源)

13. Smoking in the Workplace

工作场所吸烟

There are three main problem areas associated with smoking in the workplace: the harm passive smoking causes to non-smoking employees and customers; absenteeism and loss of smoking staff due to ill health or even death; lost productivity and other additional costs. These are considered below.

Harm to non-smokers

The authoritative report of the government's Scientific Committee on Tobacco and Health (SCOTH) demonstrates that passive smoking is a cause of heart disease and increases the risk of lung cancer by 20-30 percent. Exposure to passive smoking can increase a non-smoker's risk of having a stroke by up to 82 percent. In 1993 the US Environmental Protection Agency classified tobacco smoke as a Class A carcinogen. (This puts tobacco smoke in the same category as asbestos and arsenic.) The government's advisory committee on tobacco estimates that there are several hundred lung cancer deaths each year resulting from passive smoking in the UK, while more tentative estimates suggest several thousand deaths a year from all passive smoking-related disease. Breakdown products of tobacco smoke have been found in the human foetus. Children are particularly susceptible to the effects of passive smoking and are more likely to suffer from a variety of respiratory complaints. **Research funded by the National Asthma Campaign has shown that babies whose mothers continue to smoke during pregnancy have almost a 50 per cent increased risk of being wheezy or having breathing problems.**

For most people, passive smoking is an irritation and cause of discomfort or minor conditions but people with asthma are particularly vulnerable to attacks brought on by exposure to smoke.

Passive smoking has been found to be an independent risk factor for a number of conditions and diseases in adults. These include:

Heart disease
Lung cancer
Stroke
Nasal cancer
Asthma exacerbation
Reduced Fertility
Decreased lung function

There are other diseases for which the evidence is less conclusive, identified by the California Environmental Protection Agency and listed in its 1999 Report.

Fatal diseases

According to a British Medical Journal study, a passive smoker typically takes in up to 1% of the smoke that an active smoker inhales. If the risk to health was 1% that of active smoking, this would still be very high compared to other hazards in the workplace - simply because the risks of active smoking are so great. **A regular smoker has a one-in-two chance of dying prematurely as a result of smoking. This breaches the common regulatory practice of reducing the risk of deaths in the workplace to below 1 in 10,000.**

Lung cancer

The SCOTH report concluded that passive smoking is a cause of lung cancer in adult non-smokers. This should be regarded as an authoritative scientific view and ASH's legal advice suggests it would be regarded as authoritative in law — that is, employers can no longer claim the science is uncertain or that they had no knowledge of the problem.

The British Medical Journal found that:

"The excess risk of lung cancer was 24% (95% confidence interval 13% to 36%) in non-smokers who lived with a smoker (P<0.001). Adjustment for the effects of bias (positive and negative) and dietary confounding had little overall effect; the adjusted excess risk was 26% (7% to 47%). The dose-response relation of the risk of lung cancer with both the number of cigarettes smoked by the spouse and the duration of exposure was significant. The excess risk derived by linear extrapolation from that in smokers was 19%, similar to the direct estimate of 26%.

The study of 37 other studies on this issue concluded that there was, "compelling confirmation that breathing other people's tobacco smoke is a cause of lung cancer."

In 1998, a study commissioned by the World Health Organisation (WHO) showed a probable link between environmental tobacco smoke (ETS) exposure and lung cancer in non-smokers. **The WHO study is mentioned here because the tobacco industry and a newspaper has claimed, wrongly, that the study shows that" passive smoking doesn't cause cancer. "In fact, the study showed a 16%—17% increase in lung cancer risk, but because of the sample size it was not possible to conclude that this study in isolation proved the link with 95% confidence—the confidence was 80%.** However, this finding, when taken with other studies and other types of evidence, strengthens the scientific consensus that passive smoking can cause lung cancer in non-smokers. It certainly does not support the tobacco industry argument that there is no significant risk.

Heart disease

For lung cancer, the risk to non-smokers is approximately in line with exposure. However, the risks for heart disease appear to be sharply non-linear: Passive smokers may face 25% of the risk faced by active smokers, though they take in only 1% of the smoke. According to a study published in the British Medical Journal, a passive smoker may have as much as half the heart disease risk faced by a 20-a-day smoker. Given that some 26,500 active smokers die from heart disease each year as a result of smoking, the effect on non-smokers could be very large. A 1994 study of Chinese female workers found that exposure to passive smoking at work increased the chances of coronary heart disease and concluded that urgent public health measures were needed to reduce smoking and to protect non-smokers from passive smoking. It is thought that a small exposure to ETS causes the blood to thicken-a phenomenon known as 'platelet aggregation'. This thickening does not increase linearly as smoke exposure increases—if it did, a smoker's blood would solidify! Thus, for low levels of smoke, a passive smoker faces a high proportion of the heart disease risk faced by an active smoker.

A Japanese study published in the Journal of the America Medical Association in 2001 revealed that just 30 minutes of passive smoking can impair the coronary blood supply of non-smokers to the same extent as a smoker. The study found that the lining of the coronary arteries was damaged by tobacco smoke, reducing their blood carrying capacity. The heart and circulation system are very sensitive to small doses of tobacco smoke.

Absenteeism amongst smokers

Another study in Scotland estimated that absenteeism due to smoking cost employers more than ￡33 million during 1995. A business may also lose highly-valued or vital staff due to illness or death through smoking. Half of all teenagers who currently smoke will die from diseases caused by tobacco if they continue to smoke. Twenty-five per cent of them will die before the age of 70, losing, on average, 23 years of life. Before death, there may be a long period of incapacitation in which the smoker is unable to work and the general quality of a smoker's life will be poorer.

Restricting smoking in the workplace does not necessarily turn smokers into non-smokers, but it does increase the likelihood that smokers will try to quit, and that they will succeed. A study of Australia Telecom found that after a no-smoking policy was brought in on average smokers smoked 3-4 cigarettes less each day and enjoyed a higher quit rate than the local community. Given that 71% of smokers say they would like to give up, a non-smoking atmosphere could help smokers to reduce consumption or quit-especially if the employer introduces a cessation programme with the aim of increasing staff welfare and productivity.

(THE END)

passive smoking 被动吸烟
absenteeism / æbsən'tiːiz(ə)m / 旷工
stroke / strəuk / 中风
heart disease 心脏病
lung cancer 肺癌
tobacco / tə'bækəu / 烟草
carcinogen / kɑː'sinədʒən / 致癌物质
asbestos / æz'bestɔs / 石棉
arsenic / 'ɑːsənik / 砷，砒霜
foetus / 'fiːtəs / 胎儿

susceptible / sə'septəbl / 易受影响的
respiratory complaints 呼吸病
pregnancy / 'pregnənsi / 怀孕
wheezy / '(h)wi:zi / 气喘的
irritation / ˌiri'teiʃ ən / 愤怒
discomfort / dis'kʌmfət / 不适
vulnerable / 'vʌlnərəb(ə)l / 易受攻击的
nasal cancer 鼻癌
asthma exacerbation 哮喘加剧
reduced fertility 怀胎率下降
decreased lung function 肺功能减弱
inhale / in'heil / 吸入
active smoking 主动吸烟
incapacitation 无能力
give up 放弃，戒掉

重点剖析

— There are three main problem areas associated with smoking in the workplace: the harm passive smoking causes to non-smoking employees and customers; absenteeism and loss of smoking staff due to ill health or even death; lost productivity and other additional costs. 在工作场所吸烟和三大问题有关：被动吸烟给不吸烟的员工和客户造成伤害；由于健康差或甚至死亡使吸烟的员工旷工或永远无法工作；降低劳动效率以及产生其他额外费用。

— Research funded by the National Asthma Campaign has shown that babies whose mothers continue to smoke during pregnancy have almost a 50 per cent increased risk of being wheezy or having breathing problems. 国家哮喘运动中心资助的研究表明，在怀孕期间，仍旧吸烟的母亲的婴儿患气喘或呼吸疾病的几率几乎增加了50%。

— For most people, passive smoking is an irritation and cause of discomfort or minor conditions but people with asthma are particularly vulnerable to attacks brought on by exposure to smoke. 对大多数人来说，被动吸烟只是让人愤怒和不适或是个小问题，但患有哮喘的人们特别易在吸烟环境中受到危害。

— A regular smoker has a one in two chance of dying prematurely as a result of smoking. This breaches the common regulatory practice of reducing the risk of deaths in the workplace to below 1 in 10,000. 经常吸烟的人，两人中有一人有可能由于吸烟而早逝。这违反了要把工作场所死亡的危险降低到1万人中有1人以下的一般法规规定。

— The WHO study is mentioned here because the tobacco industry and a newspaper has claimed, wrongly, that the study shows that "passive smoking doesn't cause cancer." In fact, the study showed a 16%—17% increase in lung cancer risk, but because of the sample size it was not possible to conclude that this study in isolation proved the link with 95% confidence — the confidence was 80%. 之所以提到世界卫生组织（WHO）的研究，是因为烟草业和报刊错误地认为该研究表明“被动吸烟不会引致癌症”。实际上，此项研究显示患上肺癌的危险性增加了16%~17%，但因为样本数量有限，此项研究的信度没有达到.95—信度系数只有.80。

— For lung cancer, the risk to non-smokers is approximately in line with exposure. However, the risks for heart disease appear to be sharply non-linear: Passive smokers may face 25% of the risk faced by active smokers, though they take in only 1% of the smoke. 对于肺癌来说，不吸烟者的危险与暴露在吸烟环境是基本成线性的，但是患上心脏病的危险却似乎是非线性的：被动吸烟者可能面临的危险是主动吸烟者的25%，虽然他们只吸入了香烟的1%。

— A Japanese study published in the Journal of the America Medical Association in 2001 revealed that just 30 minutes of passive smoking can impair the coronary blood supply of non-smokers to the same extent as a smoker. The study found that the lining of the coronary arteries was damaged by tobacco smoke, reducing their blood carrying capacity. The heart and circulation system are very sensitive to small doses of tobacco smoke. 2001年在《美国医疗协会》杂志上发表的日本的一项调查显示，仅仅是30分钟的被动吸烟就可以削弱不吸烟者冠状血液的供应，这和吸烟者的损害程度是一样的。该研究发现，冠状动脉的内层受到吸烟的损害，降低了它们血液输送的能力。心脏和循环系统对小剂量的烟雾特别敏感。

— Restricting smoking in the workplace does not necessarily turn smokers into non-smokers, but it does increase the likelihood that smokers will try to quit, and that they will succeed. 在工作场所限制吸烟并不是强迫吸烟者转变成不吸烟者，但这确实增加了吸烟者试图戒掉并且戒烟成功的可能性。

(V25真题题源)

14. A Weighty Issue and Sports

运动与英国青少年健康

It's easy to be complacent about weight and long-term health issues, especially when you're young, carefree and only living for tomorrow, but recent statistics provide a harsh wake-up call for teens and children.

According to a report produced by the British Medical Association (BMA), the state of adolescent health in the UK is in a poor condition. **A key problem is obesity, which is thought to be caused by a poor diet with too many high-fat, high-calorie foods, along with a lack of exercise. In fact, the report claims that excess body weight is "now the most common childhood disorder in Europe", and a staggering one in five youngsters aged 13 to 16 are overweight and nearly one in five 15-year-olds are obese.**

The figures are worrying as being obese can cause both immediate and future serious health problems. These include the risk of high blood pressure, heart disease and type 2 diabetes. It's also the "most important dietary factor in cancer", said a spokesperson for the British Nutrition Foundation (BNF), and can cause complications during and after pregnancy.

Type 2 diabetes used to only affect middle-aged people, but in recent years cases have been detected in teens as young as 13-years-old for the first time. This, in itself, is believed to be another direct factor linked to the rising levels of obesity.

Health implications

Neville Rigby, from the International Obesity Task Force, expressed concern at the levels of teen obesity. "It's very worrying because of the high risk that people who are obese in their teenage years will continue to be in adulthood", he said. Putting things into perspective, he added, **"Children affected by obesity are likely to have a shorter lifespan than their parents."**

As well as physical illness and disease, being obese or overweight can cause a range of psychological problems too. The BMA report highlighted that it can significantly affect well-being, "with many adolescents developing a negative self image and experiencing low self-esteem." It can also lead to eating diseases, bullying, depression, and feelings of loneliness and nervousness.

This is something that the charity Weight Concern is keen to emphasise. "Obesity can have detrimental effects on children's psychological well-being," said a spokesperson. **"Many overweight children report social difficulties, which in turn may contribute to anxiety and depression, and obese children are often subject to teasing and bullying. All this can have devastating effects on their self-esteem."**

Weight distribution

Doctors use a measurement system called the body mass index (BMI) to assess whether people are a healthy weight, overweight or obese. It's worked out by dividing a person's weight in kilograms by their height in metres squared. For example, if I am 1.7 metres tall and weigh 68 kilos, my BMI would be 23.5 (68 divided by 1.7 × 1.7), which falls into the desirable or healthy range. According to the BMI chart, adults (over 18s) are overweight if they have a BMI of between 25 and 30, and they're obese if it's 30 or over.

Body Mass Index (BMI) guide for people aged 18 and over

BMI (kg/m^2)	
Less than 20	Underweight
Over 20 to 25	Desirable or healthy range
Over 25 to 30	Overweight
Over 30 to 35	Obese (class I)
Over 35 to 40	Obese (class II)
Over 40	Severely obese (class III)

A similar method is used for children, but instead it has a sliding scale linked to age.

As well as BMI levels, the areas where the fat is deposited in the body is important, too, explained a spokesperson for the BNF. 'People who have extra fat around their middle, a body we call apple shaped, are at a greater risk of some diseases than those who have most of the extra weight around their hips and thighs, or are pear shaped.s

For those wanting to measure their waist circumference, increased risk for the over 18s occurs in men whose waist circumference is 94cm/37 inches or over, and in women whose waists are 80cm/32 inches or more. The risk is significantly increased at 102cm/40 inches for men and 88cm/35 inches for women.

Prevention and treatment

When it comes to preventing and treating excess weight and obesity, experts believe a healthy balanced diet and regular exercise are crucial. The key to maintaining a good weight is to balance your energy intake and output, as weight is gained if you regularly eat more than you burn off.

Obese children may require a specially developed programme, said Weight Concern, which is likely to focus on healthy eating, exercise and social support. In the case of children, it's beneficial for the whole family to adopt healthier behaviours and it's important not to single out a child.

Likewise, the Royal College of Paediatrics suggests parents should be actively involved in helping children manage their weight, and says obesity problems should be dealt with slowly, by making gradual changes to eating habits and physical activity.

Losing weight can be tough, but although crash diets sometimes sound appealing, the Food Standards Agency stress that they don't work. Instead, their top tips for losing weight include eating the recommended five portions of fruit and vegetables each day, cutting down on sugary and fatty foods, opting for lower-fat versions of dairy products and increasing your intake of starchy foods.

Increasingly inactive lifestyles and couch-potato tendencies, for example watching television and playing computer games, are thought to be contributors to obesity, so being more active is very helpful. The minimum recommended level of activity is at least 30 minutes of moderate-intensity activity, five days a week. Moderate intensity means a state in which your breathing and heart rate are faster than normal.

Siobhan Weir, physical activity programme manager at the Health Protection Agency said, "Getting people to take some moderate activity as opposed to being sedentary is likely to have the greatest beneficial effect on their health."

A good form of exercise for those who have been leading fairly inactive lives-and one that's free-is walking, she says. **"Research shows that walking a mile briskly uses the same energy as running a mile and regular physical activity can reduce weight by as mush as one stone in three months. To really reap the benefits, aim to walk briskly so that you are feeling warmer and slightly out of breath."**

If walking isn't for you, there's a whole range of other activities available, from team sports such as football, hockey or basketball, classes such as aerobics or sessions at the gym, to alternatives such as martial arts, yoga or tai chi. The key is to find something you enjoy and stick to it.

It's easy to put off healthy eating habits and exercise, but the sooner we start, the better the outcome for our health. By starting at a young age, the chances are good habits will continue into the future, too.

(THE END)

必备词汇

complacent / kəm'pleisnt / 自满的，得意的
carefree / 'keəfriː / 无忧无虑的
harsh / hɑːʃ / 刺耳的，尖锐的
adolescent / ˌædəu'lesnt / 青少年
obesity / əu'bisiti / 肥胖
complication / ˌkɔmpli'keiʃ(ə)n / 并发症
highlight / 'hailait / 强调，突出
well-being 健康
self-esteem 自信
depression / di'preʃən / 消沉
nervousness 神经过敏
charity / 'tʃæriti / 慈善团体
detrimental / ˌdetri'mentl / 有害的
tough / tʌf / 困难的
sedentary / 'sedəntəri / 坐久的
stick to 坚持

重点剖析

— A key problem is obesity, which is thought to be caused by a poor diet with too many high-fat, high-calorie foods, along with a lack of exercise. In fact, the report claims that excess body weight is 'now the most common childhood disorder in Europe,' and a staggering one in five youngsters aged 13 to 16 are overweight and nearly one in five 15-year-olds are obese. 一个突出的问题是肥胖，报告认为这是由质量差的饮食引起的，这些饮食中含有太多的高脂肪和高热量，而且这些人也缺乏锻炼。实际上报告认为，体重过度是“目前欧洲最普通的儿童紊乱症”，令人惊讶的是，在五名13~16岁的青少年中就有一名体重超标，几乎每5个15岁的青少年中就有一人是肥胖的。

— The figures are worrying as being obese can cause both immediate and future serious health problems. These include the risk of high blood pressure, heart disease and type 2 diabetes. 数字是令人担忧的，因为肥胖可以很快就要或在将来引起严重的健康问题。其中包括高血压、心脏病和乙型糖尿病。

— Type 2 diabetes used to only affect middle-aged people, but in recent years cases have been detected in teens as young as 13-years-old for the first time. This, in itself, is believed to be another direct factor linked to the rising levels of obesity. 乙型糖尿病过去只影响中年人，但近年来，有病例显示，有个13岁的少年首次被诊断出患有该病。这本身被认为是和肥胖等级日益增高有关的另一个直接因素。

— 'Children affected by obesity are likely to have a shorter lifespan than their parents.' "受肥胖影响的孩子可能比他们的父母的寿命要短。"

— 'Many overweight children report social difficulties, which in turn may contribute to anxiety and depression, and obese children are often subject to teasing and bullying. All this can have devastating effects on their self-esteem.' "许多肥胖的孩子说他们遇到了社交困难，这进而可能引起焦虑和抑郁，肥胖的孩子经常受到嘲弄，遭到欺负。所有这些对他们的自信造成消极影响。"

— When it comes to preventing and treating excess weight and obesity, experts believe a healthy balanced diet and regular exercise are crucial. The key to maintaining a good weight is to balance your energy intake and output, as weight is gained if you regularly eat more than you burn off. 谈到预防和治疗体重过度和肥胖问题时，专家相信健康平衡的饮食结构和经常进行锻炼是很重要的。保持良好的体重的关键是平衡你的能量摄入和消耗，因为如果你经常吃得多而消耗得少，体重就增加了。

— Increasingly inactive lifestyles and couch-potato tendencies, for example watching television and playing computer games, are thought to be contributors to obesity, so being more active is very helpful. 渐渐地，人们认为不经常活动的生活方式和懒懒散散的倾向如看电视打电脑游戏等是引起肥胖的因素，所以更积极地活动是很有益的。

— 'Research shows that walking a mile briskly uses the same energy as running a mile and regular physical activity can reduce weight by as mush as one stone in three months. To really reap the benefits, aim to walk briskly so that you are feeling warmer and slightly out of breath.' "研究表明：精神抖擞地步行一英里消耗的能量和跑一英里消耗的能量是一样的，经常进行身体锻炼在三个月内体重的降低量相当于一块大石头的重量。要真正得到这个益处，需要你精神饱满地去步行，走到你感到身体热起来，并有轻微的喘息。"

（V42真题题源）

15. Voltage and Human Psychology

电压对人体的心理实验

This year, Stanley Milgram published an article, which revealed the "bad" side of human nature, and explained the conditions under which ordinary people are willing to cause pain to their fellow human beings for the sake of following orders. Milgram's study also helps us to explain how obedience to authority on a societal level can result in traumatic historical events such as holocausts and mass murders that reoccur in many parts of the world in the name of ethnic cleansing and other "reasons".

During the process of early socialization, children in most societies are extensively trained to obey authority. In many cases, this training ensures that children are kept away from dangerous situations and that they are more controlled and co-operative with caregivers. As Bandura notes, obedience is rewarded and lack of compliance is punished since early socialization. A certain degree of obedience does serve a purpose in society and is necessary for a democratic order, especially if the laws that govern that society are fair and well regarded by most citizens. **However, we must understand the power of authority and recognize its limitations so that we can raise legitimate questions to move society forward.**

In Milgram's experiment, conducted in a lab in Yale University, subjects were "naive" participants who were told that the study they had responded to was related to learning and memory. There was always a "confederate" who was an actor while the subjects were "naive" since they were unaware of the real purpose of the study. The process was rigged so that the confederate would always end up as the learner and the subject was the one who must teach and administer shock of increased intensity each time the learner made an error. **Shock intensity started at "slight shock" rising gradually by 15 volts to "Moderate", "Strong", "Danger: Severe Shock" and finally to "XXX".** The subject watched the learner (actor) being strapped into a chair where the shock would be felt. Moreover, the subject was also given a sample shock of low voltage to further authenticate the experiment. The subject was told that although painful the shocks would not harm the learner.

The role of the experimenter was played by a 31 year old high school teacher who appeared stern and authoritative. Forty men of different professions ranging from skilled and unskilled blue collar, white collar workers and professionals were selected for the experiment. They were each paid $4.50 for their participation but were also told that the payment was simply for coming to the laboratory and the money was theirs irrespective of what occurred after they arrived.

Prior to the study, 12 senior psychology majors were asked to predict the outcome of hypothetical subjects. The university students thought that a maximum of 3% would go the "XXX" (450 volts). Milgram's colleagues predicted that most subjects would stop at "Very Strong Shock" (195-240 volts).

The results, however, showed that 26 out of 40 subjects (65%) went to "XXX" (450 volts). Of the remaining 14 subjects, 5 of them terminated the experiment at "Intense Shock" (300 volts), 8 stopped at "Extreme Intensity Shock" (315 to 360 volts), and 1 stopped at "Danger: Severe Shock" (375 volts).

When the subjects protested that they might be hurting the learner, the experimenter asked them to continue with statements that were called "prods" numbered 1,2,3, and 4 so as to standardize the experiment. Prod 1 was "please continue" or "please go on"; Prod 2 was "the experiment requires that you continue"; Prod 3 was "It is absolutely essential that you continue" and Prod 4 "you have no other choice, you must go on". After Prod 4 the experiment was terminated. With the "prods" the experimenter asserted authority over the subject.

Under pressure, subjects were observed to "sweat, tremble, stutter, bite their lips, groan and did fingernails into their flesh" and "nervous laughing fits". **One person was observed to have full blown uncontrollable seizures as a reaction to stress at which point the experiment was terminated. Of the 26 that went to the end, there were sighs of relief, rubbing of fingers over eyes or fumbling for cigarettes.** Some subjects had remained uncanningly calm throughout the experiment and showed minimal signs of tension.

Two unexpected results emerged from the experiment. One finding relates to the sheer strength of obedience which took precedence over the fundamental moral learning of the subjects about not hurting another human being. It is clear that the subjects were against what they believe yet they continued to do so under perceived authority. The second finding rests on the results that despite incredible tension subjects did not simply terminate the experiment.

Milgram manipulated psychological distance in later studies based on the same premise. When the victim's cries could be heard through an open door, more subjects were likely to discontinue the experiment compared to the original results. Rather than being out of sight the subject was seated next to the learner (confederate) and was asked to physically press the victim's hand upon the shock electrode and required to hold it down while the victim was shocked. **In this situation, disobedience was at 70%. If the urging of the experimenter was given through a telephone (in the original experiment, the experimenter was physically present), the subjects were less likely to be obedient. Hence, psychological distance or the degree to which the victim is dehumanized had varied results on the outcome.**

One of Milgram's subjects explained: "You really begin to forget that there is a guy out there, even though you can hear him. For a long time I just concentrated on pressing the switches and reading the words". The dehumanization of the victim by use of language is a common theme of war. War terminology in the World War II included such terms as "final solution" (the mass murder of six million people) and "special treatment" (death by gassing). The Gulf war in 1991 included such terms as "smart bombs" (good targets that still kill people) and "new world order". The televised version displayed an inanimate computer game and this distanced our minds from the people that died. The war in Afghanistan dehumanized human casualties with terms such as "price of war" or "collateral damage" (loss of human life whether or not the bombs reached their target).

"Deindividuation" is a psychological phenomenon that plays a role in instances of war and ethnic cleansing. When a Nazi soldier acted on his orders he did so as the faceless emissary of the government. His uniform contributed to anonymity and he was deindividuated. He did not feel responsible for his actions. In the Argentina of the 1970s, 30,000 people were kidnapped, tortured and "disappeared" by the military and the paramilitary, and in the trial that took place in the early 1980s the main argument advanced by the task forces was that they were obeying orders from their authorities, and that such principle was above their own moral considerations. Most of them were pardoned based on that principle, which was called "obediencia debida" (due obedience).

Similarly, in Milgram's experiment some subjects felt that they were acting as agents of the experimenter, and therefore the pain caused to the learner was the responsibility of the experimenter and not theirs.

Blaming the victims is another way of alleviating the responsibility of the agent. When the British forced a number of civilians to walk by a Nazi camp, one of the citizens was heard to have said "what terrible criminals these prisoners must have been to get such punishment".

Cognitive theories suggest that such extreme attitudes toward obedience do not come about quickly. The process is gradual and occurs in small steps, very much like the Milgram experiment where the voltage of shock was increased in small intervals. This is true of draftees who undergo basic training at first and are gradually taught the rules of obedience. Not following orders is a strongly punishable act. Instant obedience is doctrined into soldiers who will at the end of training follow commands to kill in an instant. At the onset of training, if the soldier was asked to point a rifle at a human, they would likely refuse.

Publication of Milgram's findings caused an uproar in the scientific community. Some of those who protested argued that Milgram must have used "flawed" subjects. Milgram's used of deception was highly criticized on ethical grounds, as it was argued that his methods might have been "personally damaging" to the subjects. At the end of the experiment the subjects were informed of the real purpose of the study and sufficient sensitivity was exercised toward them to the satisfaction of the researcher. There appeared to be no irreparable damage. The American Psychological Association banned the "unwarranted use of deception" in similar research.

In conclusion, obedience is a highly desirable trait in human social interaction and this has a large impact on the order in society. However, Milgram's experiment makes one aware of the need to be critical of obedience so that we keep our actions in balance. It demonstrates that group pressure and conformity can also have detrimental effects in causing racial stereotyping or the dehumanization of victims in instances of war or criminal activity. It opens our eyes to the limitations of obedience and creates an awareness that sometimes resistance to conformity in society is needed to bring about change. In the final analysis, experiments such as these demonstrate the need for critical thinking and for strong human values, which raises the need to question conformity and to bring forth new ideas that can contribute to a better understanding of our society and our fellow human-beings. As C. P Snow once noted, **"When you think of the long and gloomy history of man, you will find more hideous crimes have been committed in the name of obedience than have been committed in the name of rebellion".**

(THE END)

必备词汇

obedience / əˈbiːdjəns, -diəns / 服从

authority / ɔːˈθɔriti / 权威，权力

holocausts / ˌhɔləˈ seljuləus / 大屠杀

ethnic cleansing 种族清洗

caregivers 照看人，养护人

regard / riˈgɑːd / 尊重，重视

confederate / kənˈfedərit / 同伙，合作者

subject / ˈsʌbdʒikt / 受试者

psychology majors 专修心理学的学生

premise / ˈpremis / 前提

discontinue / ˌdiskənˈtinju(ː) / 终止，放弃

electrode / iˈlektrəud / 电极

disobedience / ˌdisəˈbiːdjəns / 不服从

alleviate / əˈliːvieit / 减轻

cognitive theories 认知理论

draftees 应征入伍者

uproar / ˈʌprɔː / 轰动

deception /diˈsepʃən / 欺骗

trait / treit / 特性

detrimental / ˌdetriˈmentl / 有害的

hideous crimes 骇人听闻的罪行

重点剖析

— This year, Stanley Milgram published an article, which revealed the "bad" side of human nature, and explained the conditions under which ordinary people are willing to cause pain to their fellow human beings for the sake of following orders. Stanley Milgram 今年发表的一篇论文揭示了人性"坏"的一面，解释了普通人在什么情况下愿意忍受痛苦来听从命令。

— However, we must understand the power of authority and recognize its limitations so that we can raise legitimate questions to move society forward. 但是，我们必须要明白权力的局限性，以便能提出合理的问题，而推动社会的进步。

— Shock intensity started at "slight shock" rising gradually by 15 volts to "Moderate", "Strong", "Danger: Severe Shock" and finally to "XXX". 电击强度逐渐从 15 伏增加到"强烈"、"危险：严重电击"，最后达到"XXX"。

— The results, however, showed that 26 out of 40 subjects (65%) went to "XXX" (450 volts). Of the remaining 14 subjects, 5 of them terminated the experiment at "Intense Shock" (300 volts), 8 stopped at "Extreme Intensity Shock" (315 to 360 volts), and 1 stopped at "Danger: Severe Shock" (375 volts). 然而，结果却表明，40名受试者中，有26名（占65%）承受了"XXX"（450V）的电击，有5人在"严重电击"（300V）时终止了试验，8人在"极强度电击"（315~360V）时退出试验，1人在"危险：严重电击"（375V）时终止了试验。

— One person was observed to have full blown uncontrollable seizures as a reaction to stress at which point the experiment was terminated. Of the 26 that went to the end, there were sighs of relief, rubbing of fingers over eyes or fumbling for cigarettes. 观察到有一人由于紧张过度而无法控制地乱抓东西，这时试验就停止了。进行完试验的26人中，有人发出痛苦过后的嘘声，有人用手指揉搓眼睛，有人到处摸索着找香烟。

— In this situation, disobedience was at 70%. If the urging of the experimenter was given through a telephone (in the original experiment, the experimenter was physically present), the subjects were less likely to be obedient. Hence, psychological distance or the degree to which the victim is dehumanized had varied results on the outcome. 在这种情况下，不服从的比例是70%。如果实验者通过电话来催促（在起初的试验中，实验者是亲自在场的），受试者就不太可能服从命令。所以，心理上的距离或受害人受到不人道对待的程度会对结果产生影响。

— When you think of the long and gloomy history of man, you will find more hideous crimes have been committed in the name of obedience than have been committed in the name of rebellion. 当你回想漫长的人类历史的时候，你会发现，以服从命令为由而犯下的骇人听闻的罪行要比以反抗的名义而犯下的罪行要多得多。

第三章 雅思考试常见问题

什么是 IELTS 雅思

IELTS 雅思是 International English Testing System (国际英语语言测试体系)的简称，它是为准备进入以英语为主导教学语言的国家所属高等教育机构就读进修而设的语言测试制度，也用于测试准备到以英语为母语国家(主要指英联邦国家)定居人士的英语水平。此考试由剑桥大学地方考试委员会(The University of Cambridge Local Examinations Syndicate-UCLES)、英国文化委员会(The British Council)和澳大利亚高校国际开发署(IDP Education Australia)共同管理。

它是一种国际认可的英语熟练程度测试考试，主要测试四个方面：听力、阅读、写作及口语。英国、澳大利亚、新西兰、北美的许多大学以及用英语讲授某些特殊课程的众多非英语国家的大学都选择雅思作为英语水平考试。

另外，许多大型培训计划的国际组织也常参考这一考试来决定培训事宜。

其考试结构以“专业”和“普通”兼备的形式，即能按某一项工作或活动的标准对考生进行测试，同时又能考查他们的总体语言水平。

在各个考试点可免费索取手册，该手册详细介绍考试情况和报告考试成绩的方式。

考试收费目前是每人 1450 元人民币。

考试由哪几部分组成

所有的申请人都要参加听、说、读、写四个方面的考试，他们所参加的听、说考试的模式都是一样的，读和写考试的模式会因申请人报考类别的不同而有所不同。

雅思考试是如何分类的

海外留学的人应该选择学术类，这种模式可评估申请人是否准备以在校生或研究生的水平去留学或接受培训。

准备移民或接受培训工作的人，以及希望完成再教育的人应该选择培训类，这种模式并不是为测试学术所需的正规语言技巧的各个方面而设计的。

应该参加学术类(A类)还是普通培训类(G类)考试，哪一类更难

学术类 IELTS 考试适用于以英语为工具去海外留学的考生，专门测试考生是否具备在英语环境中完成至少 1 年的本科或硕士课程的学习或培训能力。

培训类IELTS考试适用于以英语为工具到国外接受短期培训或到英语国家工作、或移民国外并被要求提交IELTS成绩以证明英语语言能力、或希望到国外完成中学教育的考生。培训类考试不适用于那些想去学习1年或1年以上课程并需要测试全面语言水平的考生。

如果考生暂时无法决定是申请留学还是移民，可参加学术类的考试，学术类的成绩移民局也可以接受。

哪一种更难？两种模式的目的不同，所测试的技能也不同，通常情况下，考生感觉学术类较难。

报考雅思需要申请人具备什么英语水平

没有固定的标准，经过多年的英语学习并具备一定语言基础的人会轻松一些，但总的来说雅思不适合16岁以下的人报考。

雅思考试的用处是什么

雅思可用于出国留学或移民，也可用于前往澳大利亚或英国从事某些职业工作。

哪些国家和机构承认雅思成绩

留学：英国、澳大利亚、加拿大、美国(至少300个美国机构已经承认了雅思的考试成绩)、新西兰、欧洲。

移民：澳大利亚、新西兰、加拿大。

雅思和托福哪一种更难

在中国，英语教学注重语法和词汇，并把托福测试经验当作参考，事实上在写作和口语方面没有足够的训练。根据两种测试的特点来看，学员们甚至不用掌握足够的实践技巧就可以获得很高的托福学分，所以一些有很好托福成绩的学员并不能自如地运用英语交流。相反，如果学员频繁地使用英语并且达到了一定的熟练程度，而且也了解雅思的形式，他们就会得到很好的成绩。

如何选择考试时间和地点，每年会举行多少次考试

现在在105个国家中有226个考点都可以报考。在中国一些大的考点，如北京、上海、广州、深圳、沈阳，每月都有2～3次考试，而且为了满足报考的需要还会相应增加考试。

在其他考试中心，通常每1～2个月进行一次。请与最近的考试中心联系以获取准确的考试日期。

您可以在英国文化委员会授权的任何一个考试中心报考，成绩均被认可。报名时请携带考试报名费、身份证及近照三张。考试当日，您必须使用同一张身份证件参加考试。如果有变化，请务必提前通知考试中心或英国使馆文化处，否则您会被禁止参

加考试。

如何选择报名时间，我是否可以用外省的身份证登记报考，报名后考生是否会得到准考证

一般情况下，您必须提前至少2周报考。有些考试中心随时接受报名，但有些考试中心如北京会提前公布报名日期，则需要您提前2个月开始报名。

只要身份证有效就可以，没有别的限制。

考生报名考试时，考试中心会发给考生准考证，通知其考试的具体要求和详情。

英国文化委员会或考试中心是否接受邮寄的报考申请表

接受，但是申请人必须亲自填表，并提供相关的文件。

注：北京考点不接受邮寄报名。

雅思的及格分数是多少，满分是多少

雅思考试的评分没有固定的及格分数线，这取决于申请人的英语水平是否达到了留学、培训在语言上的要求。大学通常要求6分或6分以上，满分为9分。

考号是什么

在考试当天进场时，您的身份证件背后贴的标签上的四位数字的号码就是您的考号。

考生在考试时可以带什么入场

只能带您的身份证件、木杆铅笔、一个转笔刀和一块橡皮。您不能携带移动电话入场，如果发现将以作弊处理，您将会被要求退场并没有成绩。当您报名时，您会收到一份中英文的考生须知，您务必认真阅读并签字接受这些规定。如果您在考试中违反了规定，您必须退场，并且不会收到考试成绩。

考生是否可以在一天内完成全部的考试

口试的时间有可能在周六下午或周日，所以您应做好准备需要两天完成考试。近来由于考生人数的增加，在一些考试中心有可能将口试安排在周一。对来自外地的考生，考试中心会尽量避免但不排除将口试安排在周一。

在听力和口试中可能会听到什么地方的口音

因为雅思考试是国际英语语言测试考试，所以在两类考试中会包含各式口音的英语，原因在于不同的英语国家，您能听到的口音也各有不同。

听力磁带中是否录有必要的停顿和说明

是的。听力磁带长约40分钟，在考试时磁带会提示先让考生阅读第一部分的问题，

然后开始听第一部分的内容并答题，第二、三和四部分也是一样。所有的听力题目历时30分钟，最后10分钟留给考生将答案写到答题纸上。

在开始播放听力磁带后，考生是否可以要求停止播放

不可以。磁带开始播放后，考生可以先听到考试说明及一个例题，这些可以帮助考生习惯磁带中的声音，考官可以将音量调节到适合大家的最舒适的程度，所以在考试前一定要试好耳机。

在阅读考试中，会遇到有许多生词的科普性文章吗？在阅读考试结束后，是否还有额外的10分钟可以用来写答案

所有的阅读材料的信息都很常见，如果出现一些专业词汇的话，会给出注脚或注解的。

阅读考试没有额外时间，您必须在阅读考试结束前将所有答案写到答题纸上，阅读部分的考试时间只有1个小时。

如果我把阅读和听力部分的答案写反了，应该怎么办

请立即通知考场内考官。

在阅读考试期间，我是否可以修改听力部分的答案

不可以，这是作弊行为，因为听力考试已经结束。

我是否可以用钢笔答题

不可以，您必须使用木杆铅笔。

我是否可以在答卷上做标注

可以，但考官只会对答题纸上答案评分，不会考虑标注的内容。

在写作的作文纸上，如果我把第一题错写在第二题的位置怎么办

请立即通知考场内的考官。

什么是口试

口试是由一位经认证的考官经过面对面的测试评估考生的语言水平，口试的过程会被录制在磁带上。

在口试中考生应该带什么

考生需要携带与笔试相同的证明资料，因为我们仍需要与报名表中的资料核对。在考生进入口试教室之前，考场管理人员和口试考官都会检查这些文件。

成绩表包括什么内容

成绩表上会列明考试的分数，还有一些申请人的详细资料，如国籍、母语、出生日期、身份证号码及以前是否参加过雅思考试。

考试成绩代表什么

雅思考试的成绩分为四个单项成绩 (听力、阅读、写作和口语) 和一个总平均分，所有的部分都是9分制，满分为9分。

申请人什么时候能得到考试结果

最快在考试结束两星期之内能够知道，考生将在考试结束后1个月内收到成绩单，英国文化委员会将在考试后10个工作日将成绩单寄往各考试中心。

考试中心能把雅思成绩直接寄往接收的学校或其他机构吗，如何确认是否已经寄送

可以。在3个月内免费为考生向海外院校及其他国家的使馆寄送5份成绩单。如果你需要在此基础上额外寄送，你需每份另外支付60元。但是，我们不能把额外的成绩单直接寄给您本人。

如果申请人丢失了成绩表或需要一份复印件该怎么办

申请人考试后的2年之内，可以向报名考试的机构申请成绩表的复印件，考试机构会收取少量的费用。

申请人能够消分数吗

不能，但是他们有权要求不把分数公布出去 (注: 不适用驻中国香港的加拿大总领馆)。

如果申请人因不可抗力因素无法参加考试,应该怎么办

考试中心为申请人提供一次更改考试时间的机会，同时申请人需提供有关资料说明原因。

多长时间内申请者可以再参加考试

申请者在3个月之内不可以在任何考点重新报名。

考官判卷是否客观

拥有相应资历的考官都是根据标准的判分制度进行阅卷，考官为此接受认真的培训，并定期接受检查。

分数出来后能否查阅自己的试卷

不能。

如果申请人对他们的成绩有疑问的话，能要求重新评分吗

可以，考生需要向英国使馆文化教育处另外付690元，并附上本人雅思成绩单的原件和务必用英文书写的重新判卷申请信。请自己保留一份成绩单的复印件。申请重新判卷必须在参加考试后6周内以书面的形式提出，逾期不予受理。之后，所有的考卷包括口试记录将会被寄往英国文化委员会英国总部，整个过程至少历时2个月，如果重判的结果比原判的成绩高，英国使馆文化教育处将退还给考生等值于40英镑的费用(即540元人民币)。

我可以变更或取消考试吗

可以。对于在考试前14个工作日以上收到的退考申请，我们可以返还考生500元人民币。但如果在考前14个工作日之内接到的申请，我们将不退款。请注意工作日指的是周一至周五的工作时间。具体手续请与英国使馆文化教育处(北京市朝阳区东三环北路8号亮马河办公楼1座4层)联系。

申请人想尽快拿到测试成绩单可以吗

不可以，快速评分服务已经被取消。

英国使馆提供的材料适用于哪一种模式

《如何准备雅思考试》更适用于学术类的，而《雅思模拟样题》则适用于两种模式。

有以前的雅思考试卷样本出售吗

没有，但是模拟样题就与考卷很相似。

何处负责收有关雅思考试的投诉和建议

各考试中心和英国使馆文化教育处负责受理考生的各种投诉和建议。

附录 雅思题源目标英文网站

英国《经济学家》 **http://www.economist.com**
美联社 **http://wire.ap.org/GoToAP.cgi**
英国 BBC **http://news.bbc.co.uk**
《纽约时报》 **http://www.nytimes.com**
普利策新闻奖 1995～2001 年全部获奖作品 **http://www.pulitzer.org**
美国全国广播公司 **http://www.msnbc.com/news**
《华尔街日报》评论 **http://www.opinionjournal.com**
香港《南华早报》 **http://china.scmp.com/index.html**

［新闻收藏夹］

CNN 可以直接访问的地址 **http://asia.cnn.com**（亚洲版）
CNN 可以通过代理服务器访问的地址 **http://207.25.71.5**（国际版）
BBC 可以通过代理服务器访问的地址 **http://212.58.240.36**
《华盛顿邮报》社论版可以通过代理服务器访问的地址 **http://64.215.175.141/wp-dyn/opinion**

［英美外电新闻］

《泰晤士报》 **http://www.thetimes.co.uk**
《基督教科学箴言报》 **http://www.csmonitor.com**
《今日美国》 **http://usatoday.com**
美国广播公司 **http://abcnews.go.com**
英国《观察家》 **http://www.observer.co.uk**
英国《每日电讯》 **http://www.dailytelegraph.co.uk**

［英美周刊杂志］

《每周标准》 **http://www.weeklystandard.com**
《外交事务杂志》 **http://www.foreignaffairs.orghttp:/...eignaffairs.org**
《沙龙》 **http://www.salon.com**
《美国观察者》 **http://www.gilder.com/amspec/index.html]　http://www.gilder.com amspec/index.html]　http://www.gilder.com/amspec/index.html**

《新共和》 **http://www.tnr.com**
《国家评论》 **http://www.nationalreview.com**
《国家杂志》 **http://nationaljournal.com/about/njweekly/stories**
《纽约客》 **http://www.newyorker.com**
《纽约书评》 **http://www.nybooks.com**
《外交政策》 **http://www.foreignpolicy.com**
《大西洋月刊》 **The Atlantic Onlinehttp://www.theatlantic.com**
《外交政策聚焦》 **http://www.foreignpolicy-infocus.org**
《民族》 **The Nationhttp://www.thenation.com**
《进步》 **Homepage of The Progressive magazinehttp://www.progressive.org**
《洋葱》 **http://www.theonion.com**（有趣新闻站点）

［时事资料］

安全政策研究中心 **http://www.centerforsecuritypolicy.org**
美国国务院各国背 **http://www.state.gov/r/pa/bgn**
世界各国地图 **http://www.lib.utexas.edu/maps/index.html**
卫星照片 **http://www.spaceimaging.com**
网上各国政府资料 **http://www.gksoft.com/govt/en**
中国外交部各国背景 **http://www.fmprc.gov.cn/chn/c242.html**

［英美常用经济网站］

英国《金融时报》 **http://news.ft.com/home/rw**
《商业周刊》 **http://news.ft.com/home/rw**
《财富》 **http://www.fortune.com/fortune**
《远东经济评论》 **http://www.feer.com**
《福布斯》 **http://www.forbes.com**
哥伦比亚广播公司《市场观察》 **http://cbs.marketwatch.com/news/default.asp?siteid=mktw**
《街》 **http://www.thestreet.com**

［非英美周刊杂志和资料站点］

德国《镜报》 **http://www.spiegel.de/spiegel**（点击 English Texts）
教廷《罗马观察家》 **http://www.vatican.va/news_services..._eng/index.html**
捷克《布拉格邮报》 **http://www.praguepost.cz**
《俄罗斯周刊》 **http://www.russiajournal.com**
英国《简氏防务周刊》 **http://www.janes.com**（出色的军事杂志）

埃及《中东时报》http://www.metimes.com
《巴勒斯坦时报月刊》http://www.ptimes.com
巴勒斯坦《耶路撒冷时报》http://www.jerusalem-times.net
埃及《Al-Ahram 周刊》http://www.ahram.org.eg/weekly
阿富汗研究 http://www.institute-for-afghan-studies.org
中东新 http://www.middleeastwire.com
以色列 DEBKA 档案 http://www.debka.com（一个情报站点）
保加利亚《首都周刊》http://www-us.capital.bg/old/weekly/index.html
皇帝的新装 http://www.emperors-clothes.com
全球主义者 http://www.theglobalist.com
台湾《东森新闻报》http://www.ettoday.com

［非英美外电新闻］

《东盟新闻》http://www.aseanreview.com
菲律宾《星报》http://www.philstar.com/htmtest/index.htm
菲律宾《每日调查》http://www.inq7.net
印尼《雅加达邮报》http://www.thejakartapost.com/headlines.asp
新加坡《海峡时报》http://straitstimes.asia1.com.sg/home
巴基斯坦《黎明报》http://www.dawn.com
《印度时报》http://www.timesofindia.com
尼泊尔新闻 http://www.nepalnews.com.np
德国《法兰克福汇报》http://www.faz.com/IN/INtemplates/eFAZ/default.asp
俄罗斯《莫斯科时报》http://www.moscowtimes.ru
保加利亚《新闻报》http://news.bg/en
保加利亚《索菲亚回声报》http://www.sofiaecho.com
《爱尔兰时报》http://www.ireland.com
以色列《哈阿雷兹》http://www.haaretzdaily.com
伊拉克新闻 http://www.uruklink.net/iraqnews/eindex.htm
《约旦时报》http://www.jordantimes.com
阿联酋《Khaleej 时报》http://www.khaleejtimes.com
古巴《格拉玛》http://www.granma.cu/ingles/index.html
阿根廷《布宜诺斯艾利斯先驱报》http://www.buenosairesherald.com
泛非洲在线 http://allafrica.com
联合国新闻中心 http://www.un.org/News
http://hnbc.hpe.sh.cn/01/01A/04/UVWX.HTM 可以在线阅读英文小说
《时代周刊》www.time.com
《国家地理》http://www.nationalgeographic.com
《新闻周刊》http://www.msnbc.com/news/NW-front_Front.asp